CAN ANYONE
HEAR ME?

CAN ANYONE HEAR ME?

TESTING TIMES WITH
TEST MATCH SPECIAL
ON TOUR

PETER BAXTER

CORINTHIAN BOOKS

Published in the UK in 2012 by
Corinthian Books, an imprint of
Icon Books Ltd, Omnibus Business Centre,
39–41 North Road, London N7 9DP
email: info@iconbooks.co.uk
www.iconbooks.co.uk

Sold in the UK, Europe, South Africa and Asia
by Faber & Faber Ltd, Bloomsbury House,
74–77 Great Russell Street, London WC1B 3DA or their agents

Distributed in the UK, Europe, South Africa and Asia
by TBS Ltd, TBS Distribution Centre, Colchester Road
Frating Green, Colchester CO7 7DW

Published in Australia in 2012
by Allen & Unwin Pty Ltd,
PO Box 8500, 83 Alexander Street,
Crows Nest, NSW 2065

ISBN: 978-190685-043-2

Typeset in Century Old Style by Marie Doherty

Printed and bound in the UK by
CPI Group (UK) Ltd, Croydon,CR0 4YY

For Claire and Jamie –
With apologies from such an absentee father

Contents

Contents

Introduction

On Christmas Day 1972 England won a Test match in Delhi. I was staying with my in-laws and trying to find out what had happened in the match. It was not always easy to do so in the days before the internet and rolling news networks.

There was no *Test Match Special* on that series. In fact, since the retirement from the BBC staff in September that year of Brian Johnston, there was no BBC cricket correspondent at all at the time. The reports on the tour were done – on a rather hit-or-miss basis – by Crawford White of the *Daily Express*, when he could find a phone. Communications from India were not that good in those days.

I had then been at the BBC for seven years and in my frustration I vowed – I suppose rather arrogantly – that if I were ever to become the cricket producer I would make sure that this situation never arose again. I certainly didn't imagine that in three months time I would, indeed, be asked to be cricket producer.

My predecessor, Michael Tuke-Hastings – who had been doing the job since before the concept of continuous commentary on a combination of radio networks under the title *Test Match Special* – had grown bored with cricket. So, in early 1973, the head of Radio Outside Broadcasts, Robert Hudson, took the bold step of inviting this 26-year-old to take over.

A producer's job can encompass many things. In television,

with more elements (and more people) involved in broadcasting a programme, the duties are, of necessity, more cut and dried. In radio, and particularly in the world of outside broadcasts, anything it takes to get that programme on the air is your responsibility.

A great deal of this is inevitably more administrative than creative. You are the BBC point-of-contact with the relevant sporting body and the ground authority. When I started, negotiating the broadcasting rights was part of the job. These days the rights have become such a huge business that the producer will be only marginally involved.

Commentators have to be selected and briefed, commentary boxes have to be checked, renovated or sometimes built, and all the technical arrangements must be made with the engineering side. Billings have to be written, the fine details of planning and presentation have to be worked out with the host network, and listener correspondence has to be dealt with. In my first couple of seasons in the job, I was very much a one-man band, laboriously typing out all the commentators' contracts myself.

Apart from the Test matches and international cricket, there is the coverage of the county game to be dealt with too. Matches have to be selected. In the seventies we would probably have had commentators at three championship games on a Saturday afternoon so engineers, scorers and broadcast lines had to be arranged for each of those. At least technical arrangements have become much simpler in that area, with the advent of the more flexible dial-up ISDN lines.

At a Test match itself I used to say that the job simply requires getting on and off the air on time and making sure the needle on the meter registering the outgoing sound keeps ticking in between. There is a little more to it than that.

Commentary rotas have to be drawn up, which sometimes involves negotiation with those who have other duties to fulfil. Intervals have to be filled with interesting and appropriate subject matter. Frequently decisions have to be made about what to do in the event of bad weather. Sometimes a quiet word may need to be had with a commentator about his reluctance to give the score or recap often enough. When it is all ticking over nicely, you might be able to find a spot to settle at the back of the box to deal with the administrative details of the next Test match.

Just after I was appointed cricket producer, there were considerable changes to the way sport was covered on BBC Radio. The amalgamation of Sports News with the Outside Broadcasts department transformed several job descriptions. Presenters who might have relied on other people's scripts were now expected to write their own. In other cases the use of a script at all was a new approach – the old-school outside broadcasters scorned reading a report. Much more emphasis was placed on interviews and frequently it was reckoned to be part of a producer's duty to do these himself. Everyone was expected to be capable of doing any part of the job.

By the next winter after my appointment, the BBC also had its second cricket correspondent – Christopher Martin-Jenkins – and at the start of 1974 he went off to the West Indies to cover England's tour there. We took little commentary from that, though when it became apparent that Mike Denness's team were going to win in Trinidad to square the series, I did persuade Radio 2, the vehicle for sports broadcasting in those days, to carry the local commentary that included CMJ.

Up to that time the only guaranteed commentaries from overseas tours were from Australia, usually just for the last session of play and accompanied by all the whistles, bangs and general mush of the old Commonwealth Pacific cable (COMPAC). Many people of my generation remember listening under the bedclothes to just such an imperfect broadcast in the early morning, or shivering by an old-fashioned radio, waiting for the valves to warm up.

Until Sky took up the mantle in the nineties, television coverage from overseas was a rarity. BBC television did broadcast the 1987 World Cup in India and Pakistan, and mounted highlights programmes from Australia, though they were often broadcast so late at night that the next day's play would already be underway. The editing by Channel Nine for an Australian audience was frequently none too sympathetic to an English point of view, either.

Meanwhile, with a new young cricket correspondent and increased radio sports coverage, I was making a priority of improving our reporting from England's overseas tours. When we did take commentary, it was by arrangement with our opposite numbers in each country, who would include our man in their team on a reciprocal basis.

That mould was broken in India. New Zealand went there in late 1976 and with them went the New Zealand commentator, Alan Richards. Included in the All India Radio commentary team, he commented on some of the more outrageous umpiring decisions that went against his countrymen. An edict went out from All India Radio that never again would they include a visiting overseas commentator in their team.

England arrived in India hot on New Zealand's heels accompanied by Christopher Martin-Jenkins, for his first tour of the sub-continent. Tony Greig's team won in Delhi and then in Calcutta and when it became apparent that they might seal the series in Madras, my suggestion of carrying commentary was approved.

With the All India Radio ban on visiting commentators, CMJ had to raise a commentary team in very quick order, fortunately finding Henry Blofeld, who was there for the *Guardian* and Robin Marlar of the *Sunday Times*. And so *Test Match Special* came live from India for the first time.

That seemed to spark an increase in the amount of commentary we took from overseas – still usually on the basis of joining the local broadcaster.

Don Mosey and Henry Blofeld mounted a *Test Match Special* from Pakistan in 1977. That was another place in which Alan Richards' presence had fostered reservations about shared commentary. On that occasion, Radio New Zealand had been carrying the local output and Alan had done the second 20-minute description of the opening day of the first Test. He finished, as he had been instructed by his hosts, by handing on to the next commentator, who thanked him in English and then launched into 20 minutes of commentary in Urdu. Back in Wellington all became pandemonium as they wondered what on earth had happened to their broadcast.

It was more BBC politics than practicality which drove the decision to send a producer on an England cricket tour for the first time in 1981. In fact, my brief then was more to do the news reporting, 'Oh, and you can also produce *Test Match Special*.' Up to that point my touring involvement had been all the logistical support – booking lines and any commentators that might be needed and liaising with my opposite numbers in the various countries, many of whom became friends long before I met them. Then there were the overnight or early morning vigils in studios in Broadcasting House, anxiously waiting for lines to appear and filling in when they didn't. Going on a full tour myself would be a very different story.

The working relationship of a producer and his

correspondent is probably never closer than on tour, even when the producer is thousands of miles away in a London studio. In the last fifteen years of my BBC career the cricket correspondent I travelled the world with was Jonathan Agnew, who always took to the touring life and could usually be relied on to uncover the quirky side of things. Before him it was Christopher Martin-Jenkins, whose career as BBC correspondent had started pretty much in parallel with mine as producer.

Christopher had revolutionised cricket reporting with concise, thoughtful summing up – a fact which might amuse his more recent colleagues who were more used to a cavalier relationship with the clock. At the time of writing, he is fighting a battle against a serious illness, in the course of which, the absence from the *Test Match Special* box of his companionship, the detailed, easy commentary style and, yes, the idiosyncrasies, has been felt by all.

When I first went on tour – to India – I decided to keep a daily diary of my experiences. That became a habit over the next quarter of a century as I visited all the Test-playing countries and battled to get *Test Match Special* on the air from them. In this book I have used selected extracts from these rather battered notebooks, which still bear the scars of their travels, to give a taste of life on an overseas tour.

Freed from most of the office work, I was able to concentrate more on the cricket. Production really did become a matter of getting the programme on the air by hook or by crook. In 25 years, I only had the luxury of an engineer travelling with us on two occasions, so my rudimentary technical abilities were hastily learned and often severely tested. As if that wasn't enough, any of the other radio disciplines might be required at any time. Reporting and interviewing were expected. When there were not enough ball-by-ball commentators available, that had to be done. Sometimes a scorer might fall by the wayside, so I might have to take up the pencil myself. And in many places the role of diplomat and negotiator was required.

Looking through these diaries years afterwards, I find incidents which I had misplaced in my memory and some which I had totally forgotten – though there are others which are all too painfully clear in their detail! I can see how my major preoccupation was always with sorting out the tortuous problems of communication.

It is difficult nowadays to remember life before mobile phones. We take it for granted that we can get in touch with anyone, whenever we need to. That was far from the case in 1981. Recent technical advances have improved not only the ability to get through, but also the sound quality when we do. In those days we put up with extraordinarily scratchy broadcasting lines, which would probably not be allowed on the air now.

Thus the rather anguished title of this book – *Can Anyone Hear Me?*

Peter Baxter, 2012

1. The Mysterious East

A track wound between some large bushes. Brightly coloured shamiana canopies stretched over bamboo poles appeared through the undergrowth. And between them I could make out figures clothed in white. Thus, in an unlikely clearing in the grounds of a maharaja's palace, I caught my first glimpse of an England cricket team playing abroad.

It was November 1981 and my predominant emotion was one of relief as I came down the track in the grounds of Baroda's Motibaug Palace, 36 frustrating hours after my arrival in India. What I found was a scene almost reminiscent of Arundel. For the previous day and a half I had felt fairly isolated, so to be suddenly surrounded by the familiar faces of the travelling press corps was a wonderful moment.

I had landed at Bombay at two in the morning the previous day. It was a great cultural shock, one that even my previous experiences of such places as Singapore, South Arabia and Kenya had not fully prepared me for.

Everywhere there was a babble of noise and more people than you could imagine. Hands grabbed for my luggage to get me to a taxi – I supposed – and eventually I found myself in the back of a grubby, antique vehicle. Knowing that my flight on to Baroda was not scheduled till the middle of the afternoon, I found a none-too-flashy hotel near the airport.

After a reasonable sleep, I made my way to the domestic

terminal to check that all was well with my flight, only to be told that it had left at seven o'clock in the morning. 'The change was well publicised,' I was told.

'Not in Hertfordshire,' I informed the lady at the desk. She agreed to book me on the next morning's flight.

I checked back into my hotel (where travellers experiencing such problems seemed to come as no surprise) for an extra night. After trying unsuccessfully to raise my colleague Don Mosey, already in Baroda, on the phone, I sent him a telex message to explain my delayed arrival, though the hotel operator helping me held out little hope. 'The lines are unclear,' was his technical explanation. (When I did eventually catch up with Don, he showed me a completely incomprehensible message he had been delivered, which certainly fulfilled the description 'unclear', though it had at least given him a clue that I might have arrived in the country.)

Saturday 21 November 1981

Six a.m. found me at the airport, confronting an enquiry desk, where I was told that there was a two-and-a-half hour delay to my flight to Baroda. Would I ever get there?

More doubts were raised when I was informed that my reservation was only on a standby basis. I was 29th on the waiting list and it was not promised to be a very large aircraft.

Fortunately my determination to get on that flight got me to the front of the rowdy crowd around the check-in counter as a very softly-spoken Indian Airlines official read swiftly down the list, and at my name I gave a loud 'Yes!' and thrust my case onto the scales.

It was the first time the BBC had sent a producer on a cricket tour, but it was not principally production that had been the instigator of my being dispatched to India.

The decision to send me had come after what had been a momentous year for cricket. Probably until England's Ashes victory in 2005, 1981 was the pre-eminent year for cricket gaining the attention of the wider public. It had started with Ian Botham in command in the Caribbean, where his tour was blighted by a succession of troubles. Two players had to return home early with medical problems and the replacement for one of them was to cause a Test match to be cancelled.

When Bob Willis pulled out after the first Test, the Surrey bowler, Robin Jackman, was sent out to take his place. These were the days of South Africa's sporting isolation over the evils of apartheid and Jackman, with a South African wife, spent most of his English winters in that country. He had warned the Test and County Cricket Board of this situation when he was put on the reserve list for the tour and had been told that it was not a problem. But, as he headed for Guyana to join the team, politicians in the region started to stir the pot.

Don Mosey, the often irascible 'Cock of the North' (as he liked to describe his position as North of England outside broadcasts producer in the BBC's Manchester office) had been the BBC's man on the tour. He was not officially the cricket correspondent, but, since Christopher Martin-Jenkins had left to edit the *Cricketer* magazine, he had fulfilled much of that role.

A Yorkshireman, Don had come to the BBC in the sixties from being the northern cricket correspondent of the *Daily Mail*. He had been on the staff for ten years when he at last got the chance to join the commentary team on *Test Match Special*. His bombast meant that on the whole his London-based colleagues would avoid trespassing on 'his patch' as much as possible, a state of affairs which suited Don, who professed a disdain of 'southern softies' in general and, as I was to find to my cost, public school educated ones in particular. A journalist of the old school, he relished the English language, a trait that was to manifest itself when I got him to do close-of-play summaries, which he accomplished brilliantly. For all his grumbling, he also relished touring.

When the Guyanese government refused to allow Jackman to play in their country in 1981 because of those South African connections, and with England stating their position as 'accept the team as a whole or we don't take part', Mosey found himself in the most difficult part of the Caribbean for communications, making his coverage of the unfolding news story difficult.

That eased with the move to Barbados, after the Jackman furore had caused cancellation of the second Test, but then came another incident – the sudden death of the team's coach, Ken Barrington, in the middle of a Test match. At the same time, rumours abounded about the captain, Botham's, extracurricular activities.

In London the BBC radio newsroom were not overjoyed with Don's coverage. Some of the problems, like the difficulties of getting through to London from Guyana, were of course not his fault. But in the case of Barrington's death, they felt that he should have tipped them off as a warning, even with an embargo, instead of waiting until he was sure the family had been told before he made contact. That approach meant that he was not the first to tell them. When they rang him up to let him know the rumour of the death and he said casually that he already knew, they were not pleased.

The West Indies tour was followed by a sensational Ashes series in England, when Mike Brearley was recalled to the colours to inspire England and their hero, Botham, to snatch victory from the jaws of defeat.

With cricket such hot news, when the head of Radio Sport announced that Mosey would be our man covering the winter's tour of India, the news department expressed their concern and began to consider sending a reporter of their own.

It was the sports editor, Iain Thomas, who came up with a solution. Peter Baxter could go to India to take the news reports off Don's hands and also relieve Don of the worry of getting *Test Match Special* on the air. The newsroom were happy with that and Don only heard the latter part of the arrangement and probably reckoned he'd been given a bag-carrier. He was content at least for me to do all the player interviews, though he sneered at the modern thirst for them. The only exception to this was Geoffrey Boycott, whom Don insisted on interviewing himself, claiming that Boycott would only talk to him.

There had to be some matrimonial consultation before I accepted the invitation to tour, but in early November 1981 I embarked on an Air India jumbo to Bombay. Sitting next to a charming Indian doctor from New York, I received a few tips about India during the journey, one of the most useful of which was that women would always be more helpful than men if you had a problem there.

Communications were my major concern, but in those darker days there was less pressure of expectation. Within the next ten years, television, with its own satellite technology bringing perfect sound and vision, would change that. Back in 1981 there were places where getting through at all was regarded as achievement enough.

We relied a lot on hotel telephones and the hotel operators themselves quite clearly never expected to get through to London, which in those days, outside the big centres, might as well have been on the Moon. The print press wrote their stories on portable typewriters and then had them telexed to their newspapers from camp telegraph offices at the cricket grounds or the central telegraph office in any town.

On a few occasions, Mosey and I tried splitting forces, with him trying to get through from the ground, while I did the same from the hotel. Indeed, after that first game in Baroda, while he waited with the press bus for the last of the journalists to file their copy before moving on to Ahmedabad, our next port of call, I was allowed to hitch a ride on the team coach to get there more quickly and try my luck in getting through from the new hotel.

It will sound remarkable to today's touring cricket press that I could do that, but we lived much more in each other's pockets then, particularly in touring the sub-continent, and that sharing of the team bus was not a unique experience on that tour. Team and press luggage was moved from place to place as one consignment. Of course both parties, particularly the press, were much smaller in number than they were to become 20 years later. After the Test matches started, we picked up a three-man BBC television news crew, one of whom was permanently shuttling backwards and forwards to either Bombay or Delhi, the only places from which they could send their stories.

Anyway, the team's generosity on this occasion brought me no luck and even on the morning of the one-day international in Ahmedabad – my first *TMS* production abroad – the prospect for communications looked bleak. Although I had found the commentary box on my visit to the ground the day before, it had been utterly barren. As we were dependant on All India Radio for all our technical support, I made contact with them and was told that no equipment would be arriving until the morning.

To my relief, when I turned up the next day, the box was unrecognisable. Radio engineers bustled about, setting up equipment and, for all that it looked past its best, this was an encouraging sign. I found a telephone in the telegraph office that was set up for the benefit of the press and sent a telex to the BBC sports room to give them the number as a safety measure. (I later discovered that the message actually never got there.)

Mosey arrived from the hotel and Tony Lewis from the airport, having flown into Bombay overnight, so our commentary team was assembling as planned. Gradually, however, my confidence in the communications started to wane. The game started and still we had made no contact with London. I called out in vain, with the antique headphones pressed to my ears, straining for a response. At long last I heard it: a faint and distant voice calling out, 'Hello, hello.'

This was a breakthrough. I called back, excitedly, 'Hello Bombay! Can you put me through to London, please?'

The faint voice persisted, 'Hello, hello.'

'Come on, Bombay,' I said, 'We should have been on the air an hour ago.'

The voice failed to acknowledge me, though continued to call out, to my increasing frustration.

Now Tony Lewis made his first contribution to the tour, tapping me on the shoulder to indicate the turbaned engineer sitting immediately behind me and calling out, 'Hello, hello.'

The message was conveyed to me that we had no line

bookings. As I had all the paperwork, I knew this was wrong, but this was the word from the Overseas Communications Service in Bombay. Over subsequent tours of the sub-continent I became used to this as a standard delaying tactic to put the annoying Englishman on the back foot.

Wednesday 25 November 1981

Play was well under way and we still had no contact with the outside world, when Tony gave me some excellent advice. He muttered that Henry Blofeld had found that a well-timed outburst of indignation and even rage was sometimes quite effective in these parts.

Amazingly, it worked. Within seconds of demanding angrily to speak to the man in charge of communications in Bombay, I was actually speaking to London, where Christopher Martin-Jenkins had been filling time manfully, with readings from a series of telexed scores from the BBC's man in Delhi, Mark Tully.

As regards the advice about the flash of temper, it's worth noting that while such tactics are occasionally effective in India, they are thoroughly counter-productive in other places, notably the Caribbean.

England's win by five wickets in that first one-day international in 1981 was to be their last in India on that tour. Again it is a measure of the way things have changed that I interviewed the captain, Keith Fletcher, in the dressing room after the game. It was the only remotely peaceful place on the ground. While such an entry was always strictly on the captain's invitation, it became quite normal on that and my next tour of India.

As dusk fell on Ahmedabad that November evening in 1981, with a rabble at his dressing room door, Keith Fletcher was a fairly contented man. That would change over the following weeks, but just then we could look forward to the comforts of the Taj Mahal Hotel in Bombay, to which we were all bound that night, there to prepare for the first Test Match.

As a result of my experience in Ahmedabad, my most urgent mission when we arrived in Bombay was to visit the Overseas Communications Service and go through all our line bookings for the tour with them. These were, after all, the people who had claimed that we had no bookings. Disarmingly, they produced all the paperwork we had exchanged via British Telecom. It seemed they were just reluctant to believe it until they had actually seen someone from the BBC. It certainly taught me a valuable lesson for all future tours: to start with this kind of personal contact. While I cannot claim that everything always worked like clockwork thereafter, it did help immeasurably.

In fact, generally on all my early tours, the first thing to do on arrival anywhere was to make contact with the people who were going to help us get on the air. The problem in some places was identifying the crucial person who was actually going to make it work. In India I would go to the local All India Radio station, there to be introduced to the station manager and his chief engineer, sometimes together, but more usually separately in their offices, in which I would be given a mandatory refreshment – tea in the northern half of the country and coffee in the south, but always syrupy sweet.

After visiting the OCS in Bombay, I went to the All India Radio station, not far from the Test match ground, the Wankhede Stadium.

Thursday 26 November 1981

I found myself ushered into the local commentators' pre-Test meeting. We sat around the station controller's office, sipping impossibly sweet tea, until the controller called us to silence.

'Gentlemen, we must not be biased,' was his only pronouncement. We all nodded sagely at this great wisdom and the meeting broke up.

I did manage to get a meeting with the chief engineer and some of his staff, but the BBC requirements seemed to baffle them. In particular the need for a telephone for reports at the same time as the commentary was going out was hard to grasp.

I was reminded of the advice I had received on the flight out, that in India women are much more helpful than men, when I met our allocated engineer, a lady called Veena. She seemed to understand immediately what we needed and took me back to the ground to show me where everything would be tomorrow.

The cricket on this tour was fairly dire, though on the first day Ian Botham enlivened proceedings by scything through the Indian batting.

Friday 27 November 1981

Our glassed-in commentary box gave us little of the noise and atmosphere of the occasion, but with tiered rows of chairs in the back of the box, we found we were acquiring a crowd of our own.

'It's filling up nicely,' was Tony Lewis' comment, as he drew my attention to the massed ranks.

I thought I ought to make enquiries as to who these people were. The first I asked announced herself as the wife of the Director General of All India Radio. I withdrew.

India won that low-scoring first Test by 138 runs, thanks to the spin bowling of Dilip Doshi in the first innings and the seam and swing of Kapil Dev and Madan Lal in the second. In a six-Test series, this was to be the only positive result.

The Test match ended a day and a half early. This had one benefit, in that the BBC, worried about the quality of the microphones we had been furnished with by AIR, had despatched a pair of their own to me. Little did we know when the arrangement was being made, what a rigmarole would ensue.

To start with, I had to meet our local shipping agent at the hotel on the rest day, an occasion which gained me a nickname that has stuck for a generation.

Monday 30 November 1981

I agreed to meet the agent in the hotel foyer and, while I waited for him, a porter came past carrying a board with the name 'Mr Bartex' on it. Michael Carey of the Daily Telegraph was keeping me company and, with an eye for a crossword clue, pointed out that this was an anagram of 'Baxter'. And sure enough, it turned out that it was me he was paging on behalf of the shipping agent.

The shipping agent is at his wits end. He asked me to supply him with a letter for the customs, to reassure them that the microphones will be re-exported after use, which I did. But later in the day he reported that his efforts had not been successful and they remain in their custody. Things were more confused by the customs' apparent belief that, like All India Radio, the BBC is a government ministry. It looks as if I shall have to go and see them as soon as the Test Match ends.

And so it turned out.

Wednesday 2 December 1981

I took a taxi to the shipping agent's small office near the airport. The man himself was fulsome in his apologies for the red tape over which he had no control. He took me to the cargo terminal. I picked up the tone of the place from the sight of a pig leaving the building as I arrived.

We entered an office where four rows of seats were fully occupied in front of a man at a desk. We went to the front immediately and the nearest members of the crowd, who might have thought they were at the head of the queue, were ushered away with the peremptory order, 'Wait half an hour.'

My friend the agent (who never did reveal his name) showed him the shipping order.

'Passport,' he snapped.

I showed it.

'Has he a TBRE?'

My friend looked at me enquiringly – and rather pointlessly, because he had asked me the same question several times earlier and I still had no idea what a TBRE was.

Not for the first time I asked, 'What is a TBRE?'

'Downstairs,' was all the answer I got.

In another office on the floor below we were issued with a form and I sat in the corridor to fill it in with the agent's help. He took it away with the instruction, 'Wait five minutes.'

As good as his word, he was back half an hour later, brandishing a wodge of paper. 'We go to customs hall.'

To get into that we had to call at another office, where the passport and the wodge had to be examined. The paper was thrust back into my hand with the explanation, 'TBRE!'

Two yards further on, a man in khaki uniform wanted to see it all again. And then we were in the bonded warehouse. There was an ominous line of eight desks, each manned by an official in white uniform. Happily, we by-passed the first seven desks. The man at the eighth predictably started with, 'Passport.' Then, 'TBRE.'

'Can you tell me what it stands for, please?'

'Tourist Baggage for Re-Export.'

He stamped the paperwork noisily, but that was not the end of it. We did have to visit each of the other seven desks after all, where the same procedure was gone through. By now, to slow the whole business down, we had to talk cricket at each desk, too.

At the end of the line I was suddenly presented with the package. To my dismay, I had to go back to desk number one to open it. Two microphones of a type I wasn't familiar with lay inside, with accompanying attachments.

'What is this?' said the customs officer, pointing at something that looked like a large screw.

'God knows,' said I, though I did better with the next piece he chose. 'Ah, that's a windshield.'

The manifest had to be signed and then taken for further stamps all the way down the line of desks again, though the atmosphere was much more friendly. After all, I was becoming an old friend and it appeared that all these people had nothing else on today apart from stamping my paperwork. 'What do you think of Kapil Dev?' was the most frequently asked question.

'We still have the register to sign,' said my friend, when we seemed to have finished. Even that took four desks to complete.

As we emerged after over three hours in the building, he asked, 'Why did you ask for them to be sent?'

'I didn't.'

And with that I was just in time to join my colleagues arriving at the airport for our evening flight to Hyderabad.

In my early days on these tours, the concept of back-to-back Test matches had not yet surfaced, so between Tests we would usually be in smaller cities for matches against regional teams, which would take place in some interesting venues. The early call on the All India Radio station would be quite a revelation.

In Hyderabad on this 1981–82 tour, I found the AIR station was in the splendidly appointed former guest house of the Nizam, the erstwhile princely ruler, immediately across the road from another of his old palaces, which now housed the local government offices. Several years of broadcasters' occupation had taken some of the lustre off the guest house, but you could get some idea of its previous glory.

Here I met what we believed to be the world's first female cricket commentator. She was Chandra Nayudu, daughter of India's first cricket captain, C. K. Nayudu. She was elegant and softly spoken and contemplating the start of what was only her fourth commentary in five years.

The next day I found myself invited to sit alongside her in the AIR commentary box to help her with the names of the England fielders.

Much later in the tour, we were in Indore in the centre of India, where the local AIR station was more prosaic than the Nizam's guest house. I found that I was expected there.

Thursday 21 January 1982

The radio station was a bungalow on the outskirts of the town and at its gates I found the entire staff drawn up for my inspection. I had to pass down the line like visiting royalty inspecting a guard of honour.

Friday 22 January 1982

Our day at the Nehru Stadium was enlivened by the quickest century I have ever seen. Ian Botham had made it pretty clear to the press the previous evening that he reckoned playing in these provincial matches (this one was against Central Zone) was a waste of time and warned that he intended to alleviate his boredom with some fireworks. He reached three figures from 48 balls and his whole innings of 122 occupied only 55 balls. It contained seven sixes and quite a few of his sixteen fours fell only just short of the boundary rope.

I now had a good story to report at the close of play and so I made my way up to the AIR commentary box on the floor above the press box. For half an hour we tried unsuccessfully to raise London. After that time the engineers suggested that we would be better off trying from their studios at the radio station.

Arriving at the AIR bungalow I was proudly told, 'We have allocated you our best studio. This is our music studio.' However, when I saw this jewel in their crown it became apparent that I would not have any two-way communication from the studio itself, but only from the control room telephone before I went in. The first part of the line to London had just been established, that being the rather shaky microwave link to Delhi. The operator there enjoyed an over-indulgence of their habitual 'hello, hello' routine and then, when I was at last speaking to London, interrupted several times with the command, 'Speak to London,' until he received a good blast of Anglo Saxon from me, which hugely amused the engineers at my end and shut him up for good. After this I was taken into the pride of AIR Indore – the Music Studio.

I was shown into a large, square, heavily carpeted room. It had not a stick of furniture in it, save for a microphone on a short stand in the middle of the floor. The intention was that I should sit on the floor – presumably cross-legged, as if playing the sitar – to deliver my reports. I described the scene to the London studio, before embarking on my accounts of Botham's remarkable innings.

As soon as we arrived in Jammu, up in India's north-west, close to the border with Pakistan, I went with a party of journalists to locate the central telegraph office in the town.

Tuesday 15 December 1981

The CTO was a remarkably small office with bat-wing doors like a Wild West saloon. Even the browbeating given to the staff by the Press Association's man looked unlikely to bear much fruit.

Wednesday 16 December 1981

At the huge, wide-open concrete saucer of the Maulana Azad Stadium, things looked a little more promising. In the open compound of the stand set aside for the press there were a couple of telephones. The newspaper correspondents were less impressed. There were telex operators, but no telex machines. The press's tour leader is Peter Smith.

'We were promised three machines,' he complained.

'Oh sir, there are three machines. One telex three kilometres away and two men with bicycles.'

I may have chuckled at that, but I was in just as bad a position. Those telephones flattered to deceive and we two from the BBC went for four days without ever making contact with London. It was only later that I discovered that London had been kept up-to-date by reports from the celebrated Delhi correspondent, Mark Tully. One writer's copy did get through – to a clothing factory in Lancashire, where it was discovered when the staff returned after the weekend.

I did have one moment of excitement when the press box

phone rang on the second afternoon. The operator handed me the receiver and a faint voice asked me to record a report. I did so rapidly, terrified of losing the line, but when I asked to speak to the editor afterwards, the voice at the other end told me I was getting faint in a way that made me suspicious. I looked round the press box and saw the *Daily Mirror*'s seat empty. Sure enough within a minute, emerging from the pavilion on the far side of the ground and whistling in triumph, came their correspondent, Peter Laker. In fairness, he had done pretty well to get a call through over even that short distance.

Following that match, an all-day coach journey in convoy with the players' bus and police vehicles took us to Jullunder in the Punjab for the second one-day international. Even with a police escort and the supposed high status of a visiting national cricket team, negotiating the dues to be paid at the state border we had to cross caused a major hold-up.

Jullunder raised further transport-related problems. These started early on the morning of the match, as I set off for the ground, which I had not had the chance to inspect the day before.

Sunday 20 December 1981

In the rather foggy dawn I left the hotel on, in the absence of any taxis, the back of a cycle rickshaw propelled – slowly – by an emaciated old chap. 'To the cricket stadium, please,' I placed my request.

Half an hour later I was a little surprised, therefore, when we arrived at the bus station. Thankfully a women waiting there spoke good enough English to understand me and translated my desired destination to the rider.

Unfortunately it became apparent that the bus station is on the opposite side of town from the Bishen Bedi Stadium, just recently renamed from having been known as Burlton Park.

I was beginning to feel concerned about my frail driver, as well as feeling that I wouldn't mind a go on the pedals to warm myself up on that distinctly chilly morning. We did cause considerable amusement, though, for the occupants of the England team bus as it overtook us en route for the ground. At least it was an indication that we were now on the right road.

At the ground I found our commentary position on an open concrete platform, which looked to be half constructed (or half demolished – it was difficult to tell which). At least if the chilly mist lifted we would have a good view. Its main drawback was that a ten-foot ladder was required to get to it and there was no such piece of equipment in sight.

After a long wait, a bamboo ladder was requisitioned from the builders (or demolition workers) and I was able to gain access to the commentary point with the AIR engineers who were to look after us. They were puzzled that I was asking for headphones, as they insisted that we would not be able to hear anything from London. The fact that we might need to hear from London to get on the air in the first place did not seem to have occurred to them.

While they wrestled with that conundrum, I went to book my telephone calls for Radio 2 on a phone kindly lent by the local television service and situated just below their platform, which was next to ours and sharing the service of the bamboo ladder. Though the calls all came through on time, the summoning of the ladder wallah every time I needed to get down to the phone provided some delay.

The return circuit from London did appear – to the astonishment of our engineers – and we were able to have a rare conversation with the studio, as well as hear the cue to get on the air.

Each new location on the tour brought with it tales of doom and gloom from those members of the press party who had been there before, usually concerning the hotel. In Jullunder it was the wholly inappropriately named Skylark Hotel, where I shared a large and very shabby room with the correspondent of the *Evening Standard*, the late John Thicknesse, who was to become, over several tours, my most regular room-mate, whenever it was required. On this occasion I can remember drifting off to sleep after our arrival to the sound of the card school he had set up with Mike Gatting and others.

Our time in Jullunder had come after Jammu, where the winter chill necessitated electric fires in the rooms. You had to ask for these at reception, after which one would be obligingly provided in your room by the evening. However, there were not enough to go round, so the next day you would find that your fire had been removed to the room of someone else who had asked.

Later on, the Hotel Suhag in Indore was plagued by power cuts, frequent enough to make the use of the lift something of a lottery and by the end of our time there we were all resisting the blandishments of the hotel staff as they beckoned us towards it.

The third one-day international was staged in the eastern city of Cuttack, which apparently had no suitable hotel accommodation. So we all stayed an hour's drive away in Bhubaneswar, where we had to be spread over a selection of hotels. It was here in Cuttack that the Indian batsmen easily disposed of a fairly average target to secure the one-day series two-one.

Wednesday 27 January 1982

After the press party had got through the problems of repeated power cuts in the telex office, our return journey to Bhubaneswar was enlivened when our police escort decided on a short cut through the back streets of Cuttack. The small jeep leading us shot below a very low railway bridge, which our bus was quite clearly never going to get under. This fact only dawned on our driver at a frighteningly late stage in our rapid progress towards it – and a long time after his passengers were aware of the danger. The failed short cut added about three-quarters of an hour to the trip.

Arriving back in the bigger centres for Test matches was always something of a relief, both on the comfort front and because of the chance to unpack completely. This has become more of a problem in recent years for those involved in one-day series, when the routine of travelling, sorting out the logistics and then covering the game before moving on again leaves little time for settling in and often stretches laundry arrangements.

Bangalore's West End Hotel is spread through delightful gardens, in which my ground floor room was to prove handy for Tony Lewis, whose hotel had run out of hot water. He was able to climb over my balcony railing of a morning to come for a shower. He repaid me with dinner at his hotel.

'You must come and hear the world's worst saxophonist,' was his invitation. This judgement turned out to be completely accurate.

In Bangalore the frustration of the England team started to surface on-field, as India determined to sit on their one Test lead through the last five matches. England might be able to make 400 in a first innings, but, with no minimum number of overs to be bowled in those days, India were going to make sure it took them a very long time to get there. Dilip Doshi, bowling off about three paces, could nonetheless take eight minutes to deliver an over. The captain, Sunil Gavaskar, would often stroll from first slip before each ball to consult with his bowler and adjust the field.

The umpiring occasionally raised eyebrows, too – there were no neutral country umpires then. On the second day, after being given out caught behind, the England captain, Keith Fletcher, tapped a bail off with his bat. In the commentary box at the time, our view had been obstructed by the wicket-keeper, but back at the hotel in the evening I found it was all the talk of the press. The BBC news cameraman showed me a replay on his camera, which left me still wondering if it was an act of dissent or disappointment. I put a call in to the BBC in London to record a new piece, as I was sure that this was going to be the headline story in most of the papers – and so it proved.

The third Test in Delhi followed the same sort of pattern – a large England first innings followed by a similar Indian reply occupying most of the five days. But in Calcutta for the fourth Test, the frustration was slightly different. In a comparatively low scoring game, England came out on the fifth morning with a chance of bowling India out to win the match.

Wednesday 6 January 1982

We have all become well aware that Calcutta is one of the world's most polluted cities. All the residents seem to cough as a matter of course and most of us have picked up sore throats in our week here. In the morning it is quite normal to find smog settled over the city. On the rest day it was well past midday before the sun pierced the gloom, so the England camp was always afraid of this halting their progress. In the event, this morning's mist was comparatively light and the Sun was able to cast shadows.

However, Sunil Gavaskar, as captain of India, is a powerful figure and again he convinced the umpires that the light was completely unplayable, although we did have the farce, after his initial appeal, of one ball being bowled, which was perfectly middled, before the umpires decided to come off for bad light for an hour and a quarter.

The England players registered their own protest at the decision by staying on the outfield to sunbathe ostentatiously, before they were summoned in by a more diplomatically-minded manager.

Whether England could have won if they had had a full day's play is of course uncertain, but the delay had also taken any chance of an Indian victory out of the equation.

Calcutta also saw the end of the Test career of Geoffrey Boycott. In Derek Underwood's words at the time, it was the end of an era.

At the third Test in Delhi, Boycott had become the highest scoring Test batsman in history at that time. With a four through mid-wicket on the first day he had overtaken

Gary Sobers' total of 8,032. On the second day – Christmas Eve, incidentally – he went on to an inevitable century.

I made no diary entry about the fact that Boycott declared himself unfit to field for the last day of the Calcutta Test match. And I did not know until much later that, to the fury of many of his team-mates, he went off to play golf during this period of injury. I can forgive myself a little for the omission, when I see that Wisden's account of the match also makes no mention of this, though, perhaps significantly, it notes that Boycott began his innings 'with unfamiliar levity'.

Generally, knowing what I later knew, I see that I missed a few clues along the way, which will become clear. The day after the Test, having agreed with Don Mosey that we would each take an up-country match off during the tour, I was setting off with my wife for a three-day break in Kathmandu. The team and press had left early in the morning by train for Jamshedpur, where England were to play a game against the East Zone.

Before we left for the airport, I was aware of the captain, Keith Fletcher, and the manager, Raman Subba Row (neither of whom had accompanied the team to Jamshedpur) in earnest conversation. The subject of their discussion became apparent three days later when we returned to Calcutta shortly before the bulk of the press arrived. I got a shock when the first of them turned up.

Sunday 10 January 1982

A reference was made to 'the Boycott story'. Gradually I discovered that I had missed the biggest news story of the tour. At about the time we were landing in Kathmandu on Thursday, Geoff Boycott had been leaving India for England.

I gathered that the official version was that it was 'by mutual agreement' with the tour management, though his decision to play golf when he had declared himself unfit to field appeared to have been the final decider.

I felt bad about having been away when this story broke, particularly when I was regaled with tales of the press – Don amongst them – trying to file pieces late into the night in the central telegraph office in Jamshedpur, with rats running round their feet. In reality, of course, I knew that there was nothing extra I could have done.

The real reasons for Boycott's departure were to emerge at the end of the tour, but for now it just seemed sad that so many of the team appeared glad to see him go.

My wife, Sue, had joined us on the tour just in time for Christmas in Delhi, which fell on the rest day of the third Test match. This was the first of my eleven Christmases on tour. For three others I managed to slip back home just in time.

Coming from an army family, Christmas in a warmer climate was not a completely novel experience for me, but I never got entirely used to the slightly bleak feeling of celebrating the day in a foreign hotel. There was usually a relaxed air about the press party, with no papers on Christmas Day or Boxing Day. There were also few BBC outlets, as most of the programmes – at least until the arrival of Radio 5 Live – were recorded.

Friday 25 December 1981

The day started with a call from Frank Keating of the Guardian to join him for buck's fizz in his room. Most of the press were there and we moved on in due time to the traditional press drinks party for the team. That broke up when the players went to change into fancy dress for their lunch. The theme had been set as 'my hero' and we had glimpses of Geoff Boycott in a commissionaire's uniform as Ranjitsinjhi, Keith Fletcher and Graham Dilley as two of the cast from 'It Ain't Half Hot, Mum' and Raman Subba Row (the manager) as Kermit the Frog, which has become the team's nickname for Mr Wankhede, the President of the Indian Cricket Board.

We in the press party were joined for our Christmas lunch by two team wives – Anne Subba Row and Dawn Underwood, who were excluded from the team-only lunch.

After the festive meal, Sue and I slipped away for a guided sight-seeing tour of Delhi. It may be the only time I shall spend Christmas Day visiting a Hindu temple and a Muslim mausoleum – Humayun's tomb.

Saturday 26 December 1981

Back to work after the holiday. Our Indian colleagues were most felicitous with their wishes for a happy Christmas, although I got a bit bogged down explaining a few times what Boxing Day meant.

On the whole the hotels we were installed in for Test matches were clean and comfortable and sometimes more than that, but our time in India ended in Kanpur, which was something of an unpleasant exception.

Thursday 28 January 1982

In the early evening we landed at Lucknow, from where we were expecting a two-hour bus ride to Kanpur. Press and players were crammed together on one bus, with the Indian team following behind in another. First we were held up by a succession of road works and then because a public bus overtaking the convoy scraped along the Indian team coach. Our police escort gave chase, stopped the bus and dragged the driver from his cab by the hair, to subject him to a sustained beating with their batons. One of his passengers then had to be recruited to drive the bus before we could all move on towards the fairly modest charm of the Meghdoot Hotel in Kanpur.

Friday 29 January 1982

Well before dawn I was woken by a bellowing, rumbling, shouting cacophony, which, when I peered out of the ill-fitting and now rattling windows, turned out to be a herd of buffalo being steered along the main road into town. At breakfast I discovered that my colleagues billeted on the other side of the hotel had a different wake-up call to deal with, as a minaret immediately outside their windows delivered the sound of a muezzin calling the faithful to prayer at 5 a.m.

The AIR station director here told me that our match previews would have to be delivered from their studios in Lucknow, as they had limited facilities in Kanpur itself, but remembering the previous evening's tortuous journey, I suggested that, instead of going there, we might get the commentary box at the ground up and running on the eve of the Test match – a totally revolutionary idea for them.

The camp telegraph office at the ground – Green Park – constructed out of the usual gaily coloured shamiana canopies, was very helpful and welcoming, at least until I discovered on the first morning of the match that they had registered all the bookings I had placed for telephone reports for Radio 2 as fixed-time telex messages, which were not a great deal of use for radio. So, we missed the first two, but thankfully all went well after that.

They had further problems on the third morning, when it rained …

Monday 1 February 1982

The coloured shamiana over the telegraph office had – as anyone could have predicted – provided limited protection from the elements. As the operators were uncovering their telex machines ready for business, the pools of water overhead started to break through. The result of each deluge hitting a machine was an explosion of sparks, so that soon the tent sounded like the battlefield at the Somme.

That Test match, in common with the previous four, was drawn. The combination of the bad weather and a shirt-front of a pitch meant that we did not even get to the end of the second innings, though at the death we were treated to the lob bowling of David Gower gathering his one and only Test wicket. It was not a bad one, either – Kapil Dev, who was very annoyed with himself for getting caught at square leg for 116.

That first tour was a lengthy affair for me. It was made easier by having my wife join me for almost four weeks of it. However, there was still more than a month to go when she left. After six largely unexciting Test matches, the tour moved on to Sri Lanka, which, after three months in India, seemed refreshingly sophisticated.

At that time it was extremely difficult to import anything into India which might put jobs at risk, so foreign-made cars were almost never seen there. This was the first striking difference when we arrived on her smaller neighbouring island. Our short tour in 1982, centred as it was on the inaugural Sri Lankan Test match, was confined to Colombo and Kandy and in those relatively cosmopolitan places, accustomed to foreign visitors, I found making myself understood very much easier.

After a gruelling three months in India there was a holiday feel about much of our time here, which may have been responsible for England finding themselves in danger of losing the inaugural Test match.

Saturday 6 February 1982

By a quirk of timing, our flight from Madras landed in Colombo five minutes after a flight from Gatwick, which disgorged several players' and journalists' wives. The tearful reunions on the tarmac between the two aircraft would have done justice to any film script.

For the first time for three months, the press and the players are in different hotels, a mile apart along the sea front and Galle Face Green, which I look out on from my room. This afternoon it was covered with people flying kites.

Sunday 7 February 1982

I took the opportunity to visit what will, in a few days' time, become the world's 53rd Test ground, the Colombo Oval, otherwise given the catchy title of the P. Saravanamuttu Stadium. It is still under construction in some places, which worryingly include the press and commentary boxes. I am dubious about whether it can be ready for a Test match in ten days' time, but a representative of the club there told me that if I had seen it ten days ago I would understand what can be achieved. We shall see.

The following morning we took the train up to Kandy for a warm-up game.

Monday 8 February 1982

For my afternoon inspection of the ground it was a delight to be able to walk through the streets from the Queens Hotel to find the narrow lane that led up to the Asgiriya Buddhist temple and the cricket ground.

If I was surprised yesterday by the apparent disarray at the Colombo Oval, I was flabbergasted by any notion that this ground could stage a first-class match within a year, let alone tomorrow. The pavilion was barely half completed and what I eventually discovered to be the media stand was not as advanced as that.

As it is a terrace on a hillside, the whole ground has been lowered by ten feet or so, to enlarge the playing area. As a result, the outfield is so bare in places and littered with builders' rubble, that I could not imagine either side fancying fielding on it. If this is intended to become Sri Lanka's second Test Match ground, as is the plan, there seems to be a great deal of work ahead.

A little more than a year later the Asgiriya Stadium in Kandy did indeed stage its first Test match. And somehow things did work for us during the match we were about to witness between England and a Sri Lanka Board President's XI, though there was a surprise at the breakfast table on the first morning.

Tuesday 9 February 1982

Our plan had been for Don to cover the first day of the match and me the second, to allow us each the chance of sightseeing. A front page piece in the local paper this morning, though, announced that the SLBC would be 'joined by guest commentators, Don Mosey and Peter Baxter'.

Don was irritated, not so much by the fact that no one had asked us as by the description of me as a commentator. At any rate it looked as if I would not be having my day off, at least until I had found out what this was all about.

It turned out that they expected us to be available to them throughout the day and as I knew we would be needing their good will and assistance later I thought it would be as well to do our best for them. As the first drinks interval of the day approached, I was asked to take a seat in their box. A microphone was put in front of me and I was left to talk solo through the drinks break. At the close of play I was asked to do a three-minute recorded summary of the day's play.

In those days we were less familiar with Sri Lankan names

and I can remember that being a major concern, as this daily summary became a regular assignment for me throughout our time in the country.

Recorded in my notebook, but not in my diary, is the remarkable dismissal of an eighteen-year-old left-handed batsman called Arjuna Ranatunga, who cut a ball from John Emburey hard onto the buttocks of David Gower, taking evasive action at silly point. From that posterior it lobbed to the wicket-keeper, Jack Richards. Despite its slightly comical end, it had been an impressive first sight of a youngster who would go on to captain Sri Lanka to the winning of the World Cup.

Two very tight one-day internationals at the Sinhalese Sports Club, now the premier Test ground in Colombo, which finished one apiece, preceded the inaugural Test.

The day before the Test match a combined party of players and press were invited to lunch on the *Queen Elizabeth II*, as the liner was currently visiting Colombo. It was a great experience, one which I was lucky enough to repeat twenty years later in the same port, when a great friend of Jonathan Agnew was the ship's doctor.

On this occasion in 1982, during our tour of the ship, I was standing behind John and Susie Emburey as they looked at a huge map of the world mounted on a bulkhead. I overheard Susie pointing out that it was not very far as the crow flies from Colombo to Johannesburg. John hastily shut her up and I was such a useless journalistic sleuth that I registered nothing odd.

Ten days later, when we were all back home, this remark as well as other little straws in the wind during the tour came back to me, as an England rebel tour set off for the currently isolated South Africa.

Ian Botham's agent had visited him in Bangalore and it now turned out that this had involved earnest discussion on an offer made to him to join the rebels. He turned it down, but Geoff Boycott had been a prime mover and that had inevitably contributed to his withdrawal from the full tour in Calcutta.

I was not alone among journalists kicking themselves for an inability to put the clues of what had been organised under our noses together. Five of the players whom we had accompanied round India had joined the rebel tour and most of the others had been approached.

As well as John Emburey, Graham Gooch, John Lever and Derek Underwood, of those who had just toured India, joined Boycott in South Africa. All were subjected to a three-year ban from international cricket, which ended the Test careers of all but Gooch and Emburey.

We departed Colombo after four months on tour, with the feeling that we had been living this itinerant life for ever. I certainly joined in the general relief that it was over and the joy at returning home. But the germ of the thrill of touring had taken hold. Sometimes the heart would sink a little at setting off and it would always leap at returning. But in the touring itself and, for my part, in simply making it work and covering the cricket without so much of the tedious administrative work of the office, I was to discover a seductive enjoyment over the next quarter of a century.

The Cricket Highlights (i)

Colombo 1982

The date 17 February 1982 is a hugely important one in Sri Lankan cricket history – and probably, knowing the passions of that beautiful island, in the country's history. It is the day they became a Test nation.

England had come on from a long tour of India, which included six Test matches. They had lost the first and then endured five draws. Lovely as Sri Lanka is, most in the party just wanted to be heading home. But we had to be aware that this was a big moment for Sri Lanka.

Wednesday 17 February 1982

There was a huge buzz of excitement at the Colombo Oval when I got there, well ahead of the press party. And why not on the day of Sri Lanka's entry to Test cricket?

The Sri Lankan Air Force band played and the President met the two teams on the outfield. It was an interesting choice of music as he did so: John Lennon's 'Imagine', followed by the Monty Python theme tune.

On their day of celebration, Sri Lanka won the toss and, after a shaky start, gloried in a brilliant innings of 54 from a left-handed schoolboy, Arjuna Ranatunga, who we'd seen in the warm-up match in Kandy. Madugalle, who'd made a hundred there, was 64 not out at the close. Unfortunately our day was rather marred by considerable trouble with the broadcast lines.

After being 183 for eight at the end of the first day, Sri Lanka lasted only another 45 minutes on the following morning, with Ranjan Madugalle adding only one more, before he became Underwood's fifth victim. But some lively tail-end batting had taken them to 218.

England had lost three wickets before lunch, all of them to the medium paced Asantha de Mel, with 44 on the board, but David Gower and Keith Fletcher stopped the rot in the afternoon, adding 80 for the fourth wicket. 186 for five at the close of the second day was disappointing, but should be the basis for a substantial lead, particularly with Gower still there on 79.

In the event, after the rest day, Gower only added another ten and England's lead was kept to just five, as the spin-bowling de Silvas got to work. Somachandra, the leg spinner, took three, including Gower caught behind, and Ajith, the slow left-armer, took two.

When Sri Lanka had reached 101 for one at tea on the third day, alarm bells were ringing in the England camp. With the prospect of batting fourth against three wily spinners, a wretched end to a disappointing tour seemed very much on the cards. They managed to capture two more before the close, but the Sri Lankan lead was now 147, with seven wickets in hand and two days to go. The chance of glory on their first Test outing was starting to seem more likely than not. Word reached the press box at the start of the fourth day that the England vice captain, Bob Willis, had addressed the team in fairly straight terms about their predicament.

Half an hour into the fourth day, Duleep Mendis launched Derek Underwood over long on for six. It might have been a portent of things to come – but it wasn't. Over the next eleven overs, John Emburey bowled probably the spell of his life. In it he took five for five and Sri Lanka lost their last seven wickets while adding eight runs. Emburey finished with six for 33 and Underwood took the last wicket, his eighth of the match and the 297th of his Test career. We thought it possible that he might not get the chance to get to 300, but we did not know then that it would be a prohibited tour to South Africa that was about to end his Test career.

England now had just over five sessions to score 171 to

win. It could still have been a trial against the spinners, but Chris Tavaré was the rock around whom Gooch and Gower played. He was third out for 85 and in the last session of the fourth day, Gower made it clear that he had no intention of dragging the match into a fifth day. England had survived their scare and they won by seven wickets.

2. The Lands Down Under

Friday 5 November 1982

Colder than I expected and puddles on the ground, but at
5 a.m. in Perth, I was not going to pass a conclusive verdict
on Australia as my German-born taxi driver delivered me
to my hotel and a welcome bed after a 21-hour journey via
Bombay (with smells evocative of last winter's tour) and
Kuala Lumpur.

That was my first reaction to Australia.

Four months earlier, I had thought that I probably would
not be making this first tour Down Under, when I expressed
reluctance to go along with my boss's plan to repeat the combination of Mosey and Baxter from the previous winter in
India. I really didn't think I could face another lengthy spell
of dealing with the obstinate Yorkshireman. But, to my considerable surprise, they did decide to send me, with the brief
to raise a *TMS* commentary team there, a solution for which
Don Mosey never forgave me.

I see from my diary that on that first day in Perth I had
to handle a contract crisis with the Australian Cricket Board,
as the rights were still being negotiated only a week before
the start of the first Test. I also met the colourful character
in charge of ABC Radio Sport in Western Australia, George

Grjlusic, who Henry Blofeld told me later in the day he always called 'Grillers'. The stories from and about George are legion throughout the ABC. I can remember standing with him at the back of the ABC box in Perth as he chain smoked beside the 'no smoking' sign and said, disarmingly, 'Have I told you about my colonic irrigation?'

I was reluctant to say 'No', for fear of what might follow.

I do remember surprisingly clearly that my first day in Australia ended in splendid style with dinner with Henry Blofeld and the *Times* correspondent, John Woodcock, at the wonderful old colonial Weld Club, where they were staying.

In those days the Western Australian Cricket Association ground, happily always known as 'the WACA', was a small affair with not much more seating than a county ground. My first experience of a match in Australia was to see England sneaking home by one wicket against a full strength Western Australian side, Dennis Lillee and all. The ABC commentary box was a new structure on stilts behind the sight screen at the Swan River end, where subsequently the large Lillee-Marsh stand would be built. Then the only permanent building on the ground was the stand at the Gloucester Park racecourse end.

On the second day of the Perth Test match there was no doubt about the incident to be discussed.

Saturday 13 November 1982

As England passed 400 in the late afternoon (an event certainly not predicted by Australians), a group of about twenty waving a large Union Flag ran onto the field.

The Australian players' habit in recent years has been to give chase in such circumstances and Terry Alderman did just that to one invader who had cuffed him on the back of the head. He tackled his quarry round the legs, but as he fell he dislocated his shoulder badly and was carried off in agony. The invaders were removed by the police and it subsequently turned out that they were Western Australian residents, although 'Pom' supporters.

The affair cast a gloom over the day and was the main topic of all our reports and interviews.

The match itself, after both sides had passed 400 and Derek Randall had made a second innings century, was drawn.

By the time I next saw Perth, in 1990, the big new stand at the Swan River end was built, with our commentary position on the high camera gantry. There were massive concrete floodlight pylons and the grassy banks had acquired a more formalised appearance, raised on either side of the ground between the banks of seating.

Perth's time difference with the UK – eight hours in a British winter – generally makes life easier when it comes to making contact with home. The office is fully manned in London before you reach the close of play, although the start of the day's cricket comes at three in the morning. For the locals the time difference within their own country – three hours from coast to coast – creates its own problems. In offices on the east coast, people will reach for the phone to ring Western Australia first thing, before remembering that dawn has not yet broken on the far seaboard.

During an Australian summer places like Sydney and Melbourne are eleven hours ahead of GMT, which make for some awkwardness. Although I did work with an editor who used the rule of thumb that everywhere in the world was eight hours away (occasionally that worked), things seem to have become worse with the new breed of producers and editors that swept in with the creation of Radio 5 Live. Early on in the 2002 tour, one of these bright young editors expressed astonishment that I was living Australian hours, instead, presumably, of staying up all night for three months and never seeing a ball bowled in the cricket.

These editors can be slow to understand the advantage that this difference gives broadcasters over newspapers. When readers in Britain are seeing a preview of a match at their breakfast tables, the first day's play has already happened. Team management do their best to help – for instance by releasing team news early.

On my first visit to Sydney, the team for England's game against New South Wales was announced 36 hours before the game, to help the newspapers. But I had it too, so that was the report I sent over for the morning sports bulletins. The following evening I sent over something else, including an interview with Bob Willis, the captain.

As I was preparing for bed, the sports room in London rang. 'All the papers have gone on the team for tomorrow's game,' I was told.

'That's what I did yesterday,' I said.

'Well, that's what we want.'

I said that the script was still there in the wastepaper basket and if they really wanted it, I would do it again. That was what the minion on the phone had been told by the editor to demand, so I fished it out and delivered it again. The editor in question was not with us for long.

My first sight of Sydney had been from an aeroplane window as we descended over the harbour, flying in from Perth. It was a classic view, with the harbour bridge and opera house sitting there in all their glory, startlingly like a tourist poster. On my first two tours to Australia, the press contingent stayed in the notorious King's Cross area, which was certainly an eye-opener, with its opportunities for distraction of almost any nature. Another first-time visitor with the press party was convinced by his mischievous colleagues that if he got up early he could go down to see the harbour bridge open to let large ships in and out. The bridge doesn't open, of course. Whether the poor fellow discovered this in time to avoid getting up at the crack of dawn on a fool's errand, I don't know.

There was one other iconic Sydney landmark to visit, during a comparatively low-key tour match at the SCG.

Saturday 20 November 1982

During the day I fulfilled a lifetime ambition to go and sit on the famous Sydney Hill, under the old scoreboard (now a protected building). I took my tape recorder to try to record some of the typical Hillites' abrasive comments and I sat with some of them to talk about the game in general and about the match at hand. It was a very enjoyable hour and I was provided with a beer, but I found them so civilised and friendly that the idea had largely lost its point as far as being an example of the bawdiness of the Hill went.

Taxi drivers, however, were more likely to express a pithy view and I see that that evening one of them asked, 'Haven't you Poms got the bloke who bats for five days and doesn't score a run?' He obviously was not aware that outside Tests Chris Tavaré had been hitting sixes.

The Sydney Cricket Ground Trust used to operate a policy, not unlike that of the MCC at Lord's, by which they did not accept the Australian Cricket Board's passes for the media. For the fifth Test at the start of 1983, I had put in my requests well in advance for what was a rather augmented commentary team. Brian Johnston had just arrived, as had Trevor Bailey and I had been using Mike Denness as well.

Friday 31 December 1982

The man behind the desk was not impressed as I tried to pick up my passes. 'You should have one for Trevor Bailey,' I tried.

He looked blank.

'The great old England all-rounder?' I suggested, feeling that he was of a vintage to remember.

Nothing.

'Mike Denness?' I said. 'England captain here eight years ago? We lost,' I added, thinking that might help.

Still nothing.

I was desperate. 'Brian Johnston,' I offered. 'Music hall entertainer.'

The Sun came out. 'Aw, she'll be right,' he said and all the passes I had ordered were forthcoming.

It was a good day for Johnners, as my diary entry from earlier that same day recalls.

Friday 31 December 1982

The best thing to wake up to on the last day of 1982 was the news that BJ had received an OBE in the New Year's

Honours. He had arrived in Sydney two days before, so I was able to ring my congratulations.

The next morning, my phone rang. 'The thing to do on New Year's Day is to go to Bondi Beach!' declared the unmistakable voice of Johnners. And he was round within the hour, piloting a borrowed Mini and sporting a remarkable Hawaiian shirt.

Two days later, the second day of the Sydney Test, Brian had something more to celebrate. A phone call via our studio in London told me that he had just become a grandfather for the first time. His daughter, Clare, had given birth to Nicholas. Champagne was immediately sent for.

This first tour of Australia was the first time we had mounted our own separate commentary there. As a result there was a certain amount of bemusement from local ABC people and from the ground authorities themselves.

In Brisbane, the secretary of the Queensland Cricket Association said he had heard nothing of us coming at all. It was a combination of help from ABC Television and a photograph I remembered of CMJ and Blowers reporting during an Australia v West Indies match a few years before that helped me identify a position on camera scaffolding above the press box. It was a slightly ramshackle set-up, but I became rather fond of it over several tours.

In those days the Gabba in Brisbane was a bit of a hotch-potch, with a dog track running round the ground, which players had to cross on a little bridge to take the field. But it did have character. There was a grassy hill below the old scoreboard, beyond which could be seen the bright orange flowers of the poinciana trees around the practice area.

Christopher Martin-Jenkins, arriving at the Gabba one Test match morning, thought he had better check that he had got the identification of the trees correct.

'Are they poincianas?' he asked the taxi driver.

He apparently had not picked an expert on botany. 'They're buggered-if-I-know trees,' was the answer.

When they started the redevelopment of the Gabba, driven not by cricket, but by the expansion of Australian Football League (AFL) – never really a Queensland game originally – we found ourselves in a sealed-in box at the top of a towering stand. From there in 1998, Jeff Thomson said that he could see the storm that eventually saved England in that Test coming 'over Boggo Road Gaol'. Now the skyline is all but invisible, with the towering stands forming a complete circle. The old scoreboard that told you everything – once you could work it out – has been replaced by a giant screen which frequently, thanks to replays and advertisements, shows no score at all for up to four minutes. That is a nightmare for someone doing a live radio report.

While I think I preferred the old *al fresco* scaffolding commentary position at the Gabba, I am not sure that it would have been ideal for all today's demands. My diary from 1982 has several references to being in a stiff breeze. Our Australian engineer rigged up a tarpaulin behind us against the traditional evening thunderstorms and it would billow alarmingly in the prevailing wind from the east.

Saturday 27 November 1982

The telephone installed for my frequent reports for Radios 2 and 4 was handily placed by the television cameras on the gantry next to our commentary position. But in the teeth of the gale, hanging onto notes, stopwatch and phone – which had to be pressed against my ear to hear the hand-over from London – proved to be difficult.

It was in Brisbane in 1994 that I first became aware of the Barmy Army. Indeed it may well have been their first ever campaign, though the seeds were sown by the supporters who followed the England team during the World Cup in Australia and New Zealand in 1992.

I remember thinking that some Australians and certainly some Australian stadium stewards, who are not celebrated for their sense of humour and tolerance, might lose patience with the Barmies. But that has not proved the case. Their eccentric charm – usually cheering England on in the face of inevitable defeat – seems to have endeared them to natives of other cricketing countries.

Generally I have always enjoyed the company of the journalists I have shared so many tours with, but the Gabba did witness the start of one spat that lasted a few weeks. In 1990 Mike Gatting was under suspension, following his 'rebel' tour of South Africa. However, he was in Brisbane to see the first Test. After being fairly evenly poised, that game ended in a rush with Australia winning by ten wickets on the third day. So there were days spare for extra practice.

Tuesday 27 November 1990

Much in evidence was Mike Gatting, limbering up to help in the practice session. But after a bit questions were asked by some of our number of the manager, Peter Lush, about the wisdom of using Gatt while he was banned from international cricket. Gatt himself left, ostensibly for a lunch appointment, though we inevitably reckoned it to be more to do with the fuss.

The following day, by which time we had moved on to Adelaide, the story – in the absence of any other – was still rumbling on. As we talked it over in the bar in the evening, one tabloid writer rounded on me for refusing to share his pretended moral outrage. He became even more incensed when I suggested that when Mike Gatting had appeared, it had inevitably become a story either way. 'England reject Gatting's help' or 'England use rebel Gatting'. While his colleague fulminated, quietly and with a chuckle, the man from the *Sun* said to me, 'You're quite right.'

The Gabba now is a soulless bowl. Somehow the Melbourne Cricket Ground gets away with being that because of its awe-inspiring size. My first sight of the world's largest cricket arena was from my hotel window at the Hilton, a short walk away across Yarra Park. In 1982 that first experience of the MCG was for England's game with Victoria. The most notable thing about that match was that it was the first time a giant replay screen had been used for cricket. It was evidently a novelty for me.

Saturday 4 December 1982

For most of the time, the screen was acting as a scoreboard, but from time to time it showed television shots of the play, with replays of fine strokes, near misses and wickets. LBWs were noticeably not shown, to avoid too much pressure on the umpires. Picking up the flight of the ball on the screen was anyway virtually impossible, but this is the first time the screen has been used for cricket.

This was something of a dress rehearsal for the Boxing Day Test match. It was a novelty for the players, too, of course, and I do remember on the second day that Vic Marks took a sharp catch at square leg and turned to watch the replay on the big screen, only to find at the vital moment two enormous hands coming over his eyes to block his vision. Ian Botham had crept up behind him.

On Boxing Day I see I made another comment on the screen.

Sunday 26 December 1982

We gradually got used to the fact that every event produced a double reaction from the crowd – first to the happening itself, then, a few seconds later, to the replay. Also the trick for commentators and reporters was to make a very quick note of the score at the fall of a wicket, before the scoreboard was wiped for the replay.

That latter comment was particularly pertinent for me, doing the telephone reports for Radios 2 and 4. I had a position for the Test match on a bench in front of the enclosure in the stand which was our commentary position and with the crowd noise and public address often deafening under the roof it was next to impossible to hear the cue from London. Our ABC engineer, seeing the problem, came up with a big leather equipment case into which I could thrust my head to cut out most of the noise. The obvious drawback was that in the dark inside it I could see neither play, nor scoreboard, nor notebook, so, as I made my opening remarks, I had to be getting my head out again pretty quickly.

I remember on the last morning of that 1982 Test finding

every splinter in that old bench, as I shuffled around anxiously, witnessing the tensest of finishes. It had been my first experience of the Melbourne Boxing Day Test.

Sunday 26 December 1982

Outside the huge MCG stands the queues had formed, even when I arrived two hours before the start. Later in the morning they got so long that some of the commentary team – along with many others – had difficulty getting in. The crowd was given as seventy thousand, amazingly still fifty thousand below capacity for football, but still an incredible sight.

There was a neatness about proceedings over the first three days. Each day contained one completed innings. England were put in and bowled out for 284 on the first day.

After Norman Cowans had shocked Australians by removing John Dyson and Greg Chappell with successive balls, a couple of decent partnerships saw Australia take a first innings lead on the second day. But it was a slender one – just three runs.

England fared only a little better on the third day. Again their innings occupied just the full day, making 294, with Graeme Fowler, the top scorer with 65, having his toe broken by a Thomson yorker along the way.

The fourth day, like the previous three, started with a fresh innings. Australia set off to make 292 to win.

Wednesday 29 December 1982

With the match so delicately poised, we decided to take *Test Match Special* through the night, when we had previously

only been doing the last two hours. The greatest fillip was
given to night-owls in England by Norman Cowans, snapping
up the first two wickets – Wessells and Chappell.

Cowans ended the day with six wickets, having all but bowled
England to victory. When Jeff Thomson, the number eleven,
came out to join Allan Border, who had been in poor form in
the series thus far, Australia still needed 74 to win.

England pushed the field back for Border, despite that
form, and concentrated on attacking Thomson – without success on the fourth evening. We would have to come back on
the fifth morning, with Australia's last pair now needing 37.

It could have ended with one ball, but ten thousand took
advantage of free admission to see a possible miracle on the
fifth day.

Thursday 30 December 1982

Far from being one ball, the action went on for an hour
and a half, as Border and Thomson played with complete
confidence. Dropping the field back to try to give Thomson
the strike was not working, particularly when they
managed to take twos. At last a sharp piece of fielding by the
substitute, Ian Gould, kept Thomson at the business end for
the start of a Botham over. But only four were needed to win.

As the ball left the edge of Thomson's bat, I thought for a
split second it was going through the slips for four. Tavaré
dropped the chance, but Geoff Miller, running behind him,
took the catch. England had won by three runs.

One of the Australian journalists drawled that it had, 'Ruined
a good finish.'

Years later Allan Border told me that the start of that over was the first time he had allowed himself to believe that they might win.

The old ABC commentary box was a really tiny hut amongst the seats, a little behind our position in the top tier of the members' stand. Its roof was deliberately low, to avoid impairing the view of too many behind it. I can remember Alan McGilvray emerging at a crouch, desperate for a cigarette after a commentary stint. In the years before I first went there, he would probably have been accompanied by the delightful Lindsay Hassett, the former Australian captain who was an ABC summariser for many years. He was always anxious to get his pipe re-lit, or, as Alan always used to say, 'I think he only smokes matches.'

That members' stand is no more, as the MCG – 'the Mighty G' to many Australians and in particular, Victorians – has become one huge continuous circle of stands, principally, of course, with football in mind. Generally I like more character about any cricket ground, but in the case of the MCG, that is its character – just its sheer vastness.

The Boxing Day Test match having become a tradition, touring Christmases in Australia are always in Melbourne. It may be the height of summer there, but it is extraordinary how many of the Christmases I remember there have been cold. Boxing Day 1998 was a case in point, when not a ball was bowled and I saw spectators in thick British warm overcoats. Melbourne's locals have learned a thing or two.

In 2006, we arrived in the city to find it shrouded in smoke from bush fires burning in the surrounding country after a prolonged drought. Nevertheless, on Christmas Day my hotel window was rattled by hail, and snow was reported in the nearby hills.

My first Christmas there, however, was warm enough for our festivities to be held round the hotel pool after the management had informed us that all their restaurants would be closed for the day. 'People usually go home for Christmas,' I was told rather aggressively by a receptionist, who evidently wished we would do just that.

Thereafter the press had an ongoing agreement with an excellent French restaurant in the city to open just for us on Christmas Day every four years when we were there. Increasingly over the years players and press have come to have their families with them over this period. That can make it a hard day for those who do not.

On a couple of tours I have taken the opportunity to move on from Melbourne to Adelaide by road. More often, though, I have arrived by air, coming in on the final approach, which takes you right over the Adelaide Oval. When I first saw its distinctive long, narrow shape from the air in 1982, it was almost exactly in the condition it had been 50 years earlier, when the Bodyline series erupted at the height of its controversial progress. The only permanent buildings were the long, red-roofed stand stretching down the western side of the ground and the elaborate old scoreboard on its grassy bank in front of St Peter's Cathedral.

The ABC and BBC radio boxes were temporary cabins on scaffolding at the Cathedral end, with the Channel Nine television boxes similarly perched on the turf 'hill' at the Torrens River end. It was there that I had to go every day of the 1982 Test to negotiate with the celebrated producer David Hill for the release of Fred Trueman to come to our end of the ground to join the *Test Match Special* team for a bit. Hill was quite grumpy about it, clearly despising radio and any organisation as 'establishment' as the BBC.

By the next time I toured Australia a new stand had been built at the Torrens River end, inevitably called the Bradman stand. That housed all the media, which is good for the press, who used to be on open desks in the stand at square leg.

More than any of the other Test grounds, the authorities here have always been keen to preserve the traditional look of the elegant ground. But considerations other than cricket have had to be taken into account. Two stands appeared opposite the main one and in front of the Vic Richardson gates in time for the 2003 Rugby World Cup and when the BBC asked me to conduct a facilities reconnaissance before the 2010-11 Ashes series, I found that even the famous sweep of the red-roofed George Giffen Stand was no more. Not that its much larger replacement was not elegant in itself. Again, the driving force was not cricket, but AFL.

Back in 1982 I see I was quite enthusiastic about our *TMS* cabin.

Wednesday 8 December 1982

The box itself is easily the best placed of the tour so far, between ABC Radio and Television positions, in a purpose-built hut on scaffolding behind the sight screen. There is only one problem. Without leaning out of the window, you can't see the scoreboard.

This problem had clearly been noticed, as it was resolved by the installation of a closed circuit camera trained on the board, with a monitor provided in each box.

Saturday 11 December 1982

The spectators were entertained during the day by one splendid public address announcement, asking the owner of a particular car to go to the car park. 'He's left the hand brake off and the attendant can only hold it so long.'

In those days we still had rest days in Test matches. In Adelaide the tradition was for the players, press and an assortment of others associated with the match to enjoy the hospitality of Wyndham Hill-Smith's Yalumba vineyards in the Barossa Valley. The teams would fraternise, which meant the unfortunate intrusion of photographers and television cameras, looking for the candid shot, but otherwise my one experience of this was thoroughly enjoyable. The food – and of course the wine – were wonderful and it was extraordinary to find myself in a group of people including Don Bradman himself. He started an enthusiastic conversation with Fred Trueman, who was a big hero worshipper of the truly great players.

Bradman somehow seemed to be able to keep away from the television cameras that hunted down the players at these sorts of gatherings. Most of the radio and television coverage in Australia is locally based, so I remember that in each post- or pre-match scrum Greg Chappell, the Australian captain, looking round for a familiar face, would light on me – the man from the BBC – as the one constant factor among the radio reporters on the tour. Eight years later I was to find myself commentating alongside him for ABC radio.

These media scrums also made me realise the necessity for an identifying microphone collar, which the BBC did not use at that stage. I pressed to have one made up for my next tour. Nowadays you see them in every press conference and interview situation. Though the BBC are always keen to brand them for a particular network, when for overseas use at least, you just want a big 'BBC' on show.

The 1982 Adelaide Test was infamous for England's

decision to put Australia in – and to lose by an innings. That left me with the afternoon of the fifth day completely clear and my wife Sue and I decided to walk along the Torrens River to the zoo. We had a very enjoyable late afternoon strolling round its peaceful surroundings. Suspiciously peaceful, in fact. As we made our way to the exit at about 6 o'clock we found out why – it had been closed for an hour. Luckily a keeper who was cleaning out a nearby cage was able to let us out.

Not all memories of Adelaide are as peaceful. In January 1999 England met Sri Lanka in the triangular series of one-day internationals. Muttiah Muralitharan's relationship with Australia had always been a little strained over the question of his bowling action. He had been no-balled for throwing by the Australian umpire, Ross Emerson, three years before and in the run-up to this particular match there were rumours that something similar might be in the air, with Emerson standing again.

Saturday 23 January 1999

It turned out to be an extraordinary day. In the eighteenth over – Muralitharan's second – he was called for throwing by the umpire, Ross Emerson, from square leg.

A huge row blew up on the field. Ranatunga was there, prodding the umpire in the chest and then leading his team to the pavilion rails, where he was given a mobile phone and apparently called Colombo for instructions.

The match referee, Peter van der Merwe, got involved and after a quarter of an hour we got going again. Murali finished his over and changed ends, having another row with Emerson, as he got him to stand right up to the stumps.

Later we found that the floodlights in one of the four pylons
had failed. (I heard after the game that the Sri Lankans
claimed that this was a plot and said they wouldn't carry on,
but the umpires and referee rated the light good enough.)

The rest of the game became a very bad-tempered affair. The
umpires made mistakes and there was acrimony on the field,
with Alec Stewart overheard by the pitch microphones telling
Ranatunga that he was a disgrace as an international captain.
Stewart later described it as the least enjoyable day's cricket
he had ever had. It could not have helped that Sri Lanka won
by one wicket with two balls to spare.

I had another problem, in that I was putting the final
touches to a book on cricket's World Cups, with the seventh
tournament due in England that year. I had included interviews with all the winning captains except the most recent
– Arjuna Ranatunga. In the past I had always found him very
approachable for interview, but on this tour he was proving
more elusive and I had rather earmarked our time in Adelaide,
while three one-day games were played, as my best chance to
pin him down. Now I felt I had no chance at all.

Australia played Sri Lanka the day after that acrimonious
game. ICC hearings and legal consultations were in the air
and even on the Monday when I rang Arjuna at his hotel I
was sure he would be reluctant to speak. In fact he agreed to
do it immediately and I got just the piece I needed, though
when I broached the question of a comment on the events of
Saturday evening (having made sure of my bit for the book)
all I got was a smile and a shake of the head.

The hearing with the match referee over Ranatunga's conduct was three days later in Perth on the eve of England's
next meeting with Sri Lanka. My abiding memory is of a

very sad Peter van der Merwe regretting bitterly that the game had come to this, with lawyers far too heavily involved. They had tied his hands over the extent of the penalties he could impose, so that a six-match ban had to be a suspended sentence.

Many Englishmen who were in Adelaide at the beginning of December in 2006 will carry the mental scars of what they witnessed there. It was the second Test of what was an unhappy winter for England, who were defending the Ashes they had won back at long last in 2005. Australia had already won the first Test in Brisbane by a crushing 277 runs.

After that, to make 266 for three on the first day in Adelaide was something of a relief. Paul Collingwood was 98 not out overnight and the next day he went on to a double hundred, putting on 310 for the fourth wicket with Kevin Pietersen, who made 158. This was heady stuff for beleaguered Poms, as England declared on the second evening at 551 for six and even snatched a wicket before the close.

It took Australia until late on the fourth day to get to their eventual reply of 513, with centuries from Ponting and Clarke.

Monday 4 December 2006

Barring something extraordinary, the Test is heading for a draw.

Tuesday 5 December 2006

The extraordinary thing happened. England collapsed and in between the wickets they became completely strokeless, so that when they were all out at tea, Australia turned it into a cakewalk and won with three overs to spare.

It was a shattering finish, which has left us all feeling
numb.

Shane Warne had been at the heart of it. Perhaps he was lucky
to be given Strauss's wicket to start him off, when England
were looking secure enough at 69 for one, but he also bowled
Pietersen round his legs and ran out Bell. He seemed to be
willing Australia to victory. England were dismissed for 129,
having lost nine wickets for 70 in the day.

Australia needed 168 to win from 36 overs and despite losing four wickets, the force was very much with them. They
went on, of course, to take the series five-nil.

I did not cross the Tasman Sea to New Zealand until the
1992 World Cup and only ever covered one Test tour there
– that in 2002. Starting that tour in Christchurch, I stayed in
an hotel right by the cathedral, the shattered tower of which
would become a symbol of the devastating earthquake of
2011. I watched the live television pictures of that destruction
from Australia in horror.

Many of the principal New Zealand grounds are also rugby
stadiums, which makes them not always ideal cricket venues,
not least because of the reliance on drop-in pitches. The character of these changes during the course of a game in a very
different way from conventional pitches.

Lancaster Park in Christchurch (officially known as Jade
Stadium in 2002) was a case in point. The Super Rugby tournament of teams from New Zealand, Australia and South
Africa was growing in strength and popularity at that stage
and we were approaching the start of that season when we
were there, so all the gearing up at the ground was for their
home team, the Crusaders.

Our commentary on the first one-day international was

abruptly interrupted. A mechanical digger had apparently severed a cable in Sacramento, California. Astonishingly, this put us off the air in Christchurch, New Zealand.

When this sort of thing happens, we make do with some commentary on the telephone while we assess the scale of the problem. These days our portable satellite dish – a wonderful technological breakthrough – then comes into play. On this occasion, so confident was I of the excellent technical service that we had so far enjoyed, that I had left the equipment back in the hotel. That meant a hasty dash was needed, followed by the dismantling of a louvred window that faced in the right direction to find the satellite, which is stationed more or less over the Equator. From the South Island of New Zealand, that means you are pointing your dish at a comparatively shallow angle and buildings or tall trees can offer an obstruction. However, on this occasion, with miles of the outside broadcast producer's best friend, gaffer tape, holding the dish precariously out of the window, we got the commentary back on the air in decent quality.

For the Test Match there, the new drop-in pitch provided a steady clatter of wickets for the first two innings, with a century from Nasser Hussain separating the sides. Then, from the middle of the third day, the pitch seemed to flatten out dramatically and from 106 for five, we saw Andrew Flintoff making a rapid first Test hundred and Graham Thorpe racing to 200 in 231 balls. For only a matter of hours it was the third fastest double hundred in Test history.

Then, on the fourth day, needing 550 to win and despite losing their sixth wicket when they were still 300 adrift, New Zealand gave England quite a scare. Nathan Astle made the fastest ever Test double century. It took him only 153 balls and his second hundred came in 39 balls. He made his last 88 runs batting with the number eleven, an injured Chris Cairns.

England did win and the margin of 98 sounds comfortable enough, but the abiding memory was of England's fast bowlers craning their necks as successive deliveries were smacked out of the ground by Astle in his 222.

Over the last ten years or so, one-day internationals in Wellington have been played at the Westpac Stadium, known to one and all, because of its shape, as the Cake Tin. It is a multi-purpose stadium, principally – this being New Zealand – used for rugby. And it feels even less like a cricket ground than the other similar grounds.

My only experience of cricket in this stadium was a rain-affected one-day international in which England's demise was dramatic enough to attract the local headline, which is so beloved in the Antipodes, 'THESE PATHETIC POMS'. In the interval the crowd were invited to contribute to the sound effects for the second 'Lord of the Rings' film, which was being made at the time. By stamping their feet and beating their chests, they became the Orc Army. I was trying to conduct the *Test Match Special* interval programme at the time and had to explain to listeners what was going on, but I think of that evening whenever I see the orcs marching on Helm's Deep in *The Two Towers*.

By contrast, Wellington's Test ground, the Basin Reserve, is very much a cricket ground. It does, however, have the dubious distinction of being a traffic roundabout. The Test match there in 2002 was blighted by the news that arrived with us during the third morning, that Ben Hollioake, who had been part of the touring team for the one-day internationals at the start of the tour and in India before that, had been killed in a car crash in Western Australia overnight. Such a sudden loss seemed to knock the stuffing out of England even more than the southerly gale, which can be the curse of Wellington.

That tour ended with a Test in Auckland at Eden Park, another ground famed for rugby, having staged two world cup finals, in 1987 and 2011, both won by New Zealand. As a result the ground has a special place in New Zealanders' hearts.

It is not a great cricket ground, though. To play cricket, the pitch – another drop-in these days – is orientated on a diagonal corner-to-corner line. That can mean, for instance, that fine leg is practically in the batsman's back pocket, while the square leg boundary is in a far-distant corner. That seems to create more of a problem with field settings in one-day cricket.

The most bizarre thing I saw there, though, was the cold and rain-interrupted third Test of the 2002 tour. On the fourth day, New Zealand were batting with a first innings lead of forty under their belts. With playing hours extended to make up for lost time, the floodlights came on during a gloomy afternoon and, probably sensing the fielders' desire not to continue, the batsmen turned down offers of bad light from the umpires and continued to build their lead past 300.

It was apparent that fielders simply could not see the red ball against the dark stands, but play continued into the evening in a way that was subsequently ruled out by the guidelines for Test umpires.

That lead enabled New Zealand to give themselves a day to bowl England out and they managed it before the tea interval.

These days, tours of Australia have lost something, with the paucity of up-country games, when everyone could see a bit more of the nation than the increasingly sophisticated major cities. Touring teams are less likely now to hear the cheerfully partisan public address announcement once delivered, 'From the Piggeries End it's gonna be Stormy Gale. And let's hope he puts the wind up the Poms.'

At least most major tours do start with a festival game at Lilac Hill in a Perth suburb, the home of the Midland Guildford club, where sponsors' tents round the boundary make for an apparently relaxed atmosphere, belying the determination of whatever scratch XI has been put together to embarrass the Poms. The first of these fixtures came on the 1990–91 England tour, two days after a rather calamitous start at another Perth club.

That was a delightful ground in an affluent suburb – the Melvista Oval. Mobile phones were still not part of our kit then, so the lack of any telephone on the ground had the potential to be slightly problematic. Things became a bit more urgent, though, when Graham Gooch, the captain on that tour, injured his hand, going for a return catch off his own bowling and had to go off to hospital for an X-ray.

Tuesday 23 October 1990

There was talk of a phone box nearby, but I could find no sign of it. I asked a gardener who was trimming some bushes. 'People round here have phones in their houses,' he informed me curtly.

There was a golf course bordering the cricket ground and so I tried that and found a payphone in the upstairs bar. A ladies' medal tournament was in full swing, but they seemed happy for me to use their phone and as the Gooch injury scare became the lead item in all the morning sports bulletins, we got to know each other very well.

Though Gooch returned to the ground later and the story was rather played down, his wound became infected and he was out of action for a month.

There was another up-country match before we encountered a major ground on that tour, with England taking on a Western Australian Country XI in Geraldton, about 250 miles north of Perth, where a penetrating gale seemed to blow constantly. One rather novel feature of an otherwise undistinguished place and its cricket ground, Wonthella Park, was the vertical ladder out of the gents' loo that took me up to the ABC broadcasting point.

That 1990 tour was probably the last one with a full five weeks' run-up to the first Test. After leaving Perth, we went to Port Pirie, about 135 miles north of Adelaide, for which journey we crammed four of us and our luggage into a car, stopping en route at a lonely pub called the Dublin Hotel to watch the Melbourne Cup, the race that brings the whole of Australia to a standstill. In an otherwise seemingly deserted cluster of houses the pub was packed with drinkers, all slightly surprised to find four English journalists coming in out of the dust and heat.

While we were taking the low road, the team had an alarmingly bumpy flight through an electrical storm in a small aircraft. They arrived at the civic dinner (a grand name for generous helpings of beef stroganoff on paper plates) to which we had all been summoned, very late and looking rather shaken.

On the same tour England had a couple of games against the Australian Cricket Academy at a school ground in Adelaide, in preparation for the one-day series.

Tuesday 29 November 1990

St Peter's College ground turned out to be more like an English public school idyll than anything actually in England. There were beautiful trees and a small stand at midwicket where the press gathered, the headmaster's house bordered the ground and there was a comparatively ancient chapel across an adjacent lawn.

I found a phone in the tuck shop for early morning live reports back home, but they were locking up before the close, so I had to do a rushed return to the hotel in time for 7 a.m. in Britain.

The following day, the tuck shop and the school switchboard both shut down much earlier and a nearby petrol station had to become my studio. How much easier life became with the advent of mobile phones!

Tasmania would be aggrieved to be referred to as 'up-country'. The Bellerive Oval stages Test matches after all, though England have never played one there. When I first went to the island state in 1982, the main Tasmanian Cricket Association ground was up a hill on the edge of Hobart, where a fierce wind made the huge teapot which greeted us in the old wooden press box every morning very welcome indeed. The ABC radio box (which I needed to access for close of play reports) was a hut on tall stilts with a vertical ladder to reach it. Negotiating this in the gale was an interesting exercise, to say the least.

On that tour the three-day match against Tasmania in Hobart was followed by a one-day game in Launceston on the far north side of the island. There, what should have been an enjoyable day's cricket on a delightful ground was rather spoiled by a very sub-standard pitch. Michael Holding was playing for Tasmania at the time and a ball from him reared to take Derek Randall in the face, after which Holding finished his spell bowling at half-pace. The incident inspired Ian Botham to bat in a helmet for the first time.

Meanwhile, in a small wooden hut of a press box, a heap of radio equipment had alarmingly burst into life during the morning session, with a voice demanding, 'Hello, Bruce. Are you there?'

There being no Australians on hand, the members of the British press insisted that I, as the radio man there, shut the thing up. I found the right switch and replied to the studio that I didn't think Bruce was there. The man asked me for a score and subsequent calls followed, which eventually resulted in me making my debut on Radio Launceston with fairly regular reports.

In mid afternoon Bruce turned up and hailed the studio to tell them, 'Sorry, mate, me car went crook.'

The response came back, 'That's all right. Some kind old gentleman's been helping us out.' I was 35.

By my next visit to Tasmania, which was not until 1990, the Tasmanian Cricket Association had moved their main ground to the Hobart suburb of Bellerive, on the other side of the Derwent River from the city centre. It had become a Test venue barely a year before, though it was still fairly short on grandstand accommodation and the press were in a Portakabin.

It has become the practice to have England play 'An Australian XI' in Hobart as the last match before the first Test in Brisbane – as contrasting a pair of climate conditions as the Australian board can come up with. I see that in 1990 on at least one day of the game I went from the city across the harbour by ferry, but the ferry times are more geared to shoppers and workers visiting town than people going the other way, so it was not an ideal arrangement – a pity, because it was a pleasant way to travel.

Here it was that Jonathan Agnew set up a leg-pull on Simon Heffer the columnist who was covering the tour for the *Daily Telegraph*. A feature piece about him had appeared in the *Tasmania Mercury* and so Aggers persuaded all the prettiest girls he could find round the ground to approach Heffer for his autograph, culminating with a fetching lass who we had all admired, who operated the pie van. It was long after she had come into the press box for the great man's signature that he realised that he was the subject of a prank.

For Aggers that tour marked something of a debut. I was splitting the BBC reporting and commentating duties with Christopher Martin-Jenkins, who had just announced that he would be leaving the BBC in the spring to take up the job of *Daily Telegraph* cricket correspondent. So, as I embarked on the tour I was trying to come up with a suitable successor to do that job for the BBC.

In the departure lounge at Heathrow, I was talking to Aggers, who was about to fly out as the *Today* newspaper's new cricket correspondent, only weeks after finishing his playing career. I had used him for a few things on the air and so I suggested that he might like to consider going for the BBC job. 'Oh, no,' he said, 'I've got far too good a deal from *Today*.'

Within a fortnight, the paper had betrayed him by writing a piece he had declined to do and giving it his by-line. I tried again. His reaction had, perhaps unsurprisingly, changed, 'You can put my name in the hat,' he told me.

My actual hand-over to Christopher on the tour was

not perfectly timed. I was quite keen to get back home for Christmas for once, and for similar reasons CMJ was keen to delay his departure. We ended up with a game – against Victoria at Ballarat – falling into the inter-regnum. I turned to my putative cricket correspondent, Aggers, furnishing him with various pieces of equipment, all carefully labelled. I was not too worried, as he had worked at Radio Leicester over a few winters and was fairly technically minded.

In the event, he admitted later, his shyness made him have the BBC phone moved to the groundsman's hut, rather than perform in front of his press colleagues. He ended up sharing the space with a rather ferocious looking dog, but evidently considered this the lesser of two evils.

On England's next tour of Australia, their game against Victoria was played at Bendigo. Thanks to their having been knocked out of the one-day international series, the game was extended to four days. Here I was persuaded to join the commentary by the local radio station, KLFM. They operated from a miniscule box at square leg, where they had also persuaded the former Australian captain, Bill Lawrie, to take part.

On the Sunday evening I was asked if I would go into the KLFM studios to take part in 'a discussion programme'. The host was the station manager, who led the way in his car. I followed in my own vehicle, so that I would have transport for the return journey.

Sunday 22 January 1995

I followed him through a maze of streets to an apparently deserted railway station. It seemed that KLFM inhabited its buildings – ticket office, stationmaster's room and ladies' waiting room. In fact, the ladies' waiting room turned out to be the studio, though I gathered that there were plans for other of the station buildings to be developed.

Brad, my host, pointed out platform 2 across the still-operative Bendigo to Melbourne line. 'That's where we used to be,' he said, indicating a small hut.

The Ladies' Waiting Room had a little old lady in it – waiting. It turned out she was waiting for her husband to finish presenting the 'Christian Hour' of religious music interspersed with homilies. They were the only other people in the place and the 'Christian Hour' had in fact already run to an hour and a quarter, because we were a bit late.

The 'foyer' had a large signal lever emerging from the floor. 'What would happen if we pulled this?' I asked.

'Change the points, I guess,' said Brad.

He invited me to see their 'master control' and opened a cupboard to reveal some technical equipment.

'No engineer?' I asked.

'Aw, there's one on call,' he said. 'He can be here in half an hour.'

Thereafter the two of us were on the air for an hour or so, chatting and playing the odd bit of music.

This sort of one-man operation is not, apparently, unique. On the drive from Melbourne to Sydney one year, I picked up the local station from the small country town of Yass, New South Wales. The presenter from Yass FM apologised to his listeners for a break in transmission. 'I had to go and get some CDs from my ute,' he said.

One night in Bendigo a few of the press were in a local pub when a hen party came in, giving a bride her last night on the town. We gathered that the groom's 'bucks' party' were doing the same. One of our number asked, 'What happens if you run into them?'

'Aw,' said the bride, 'Bendigo's a pretty big place.'

It really isn't.

Queensland have not played a first-class fixture with England at their headquarters, the Gabba, since 1986. For the match in 1994 Simon Mann and I headed a hire car west of Brisbane for about a hundred miles.

We took the steep road up the Great Dividing Range and there, perched on top of the hill, was the pleasant, apparently quiet and conservative city of Toowoomba. After checking in and sending a couple of pieces over to London on the phone, we went out to look for the cricket ground – a venture we were very unsuccessful with, despite stopping a few times to ask. As it was getting dark, we gave up.

Happily, the next day, giving myself an early start, I had less trouble. We all got very excited when a nineteen-year-old called Andrew Symonds made a century for the home side and we discovered he was born in Birmingham. However, he poured cold water on any suggestion of an English affiliation. 'I'm a dinky-di Aussie,' he said. Nevertheless he was happy to take his place the following season in the Gloucestershire team with an England qualification and the England selectors then tested his resolve by picking him for an England 'A' touring team. He withdrew to declare himself again an Aussie.

Also during the game, Mike Gatting – who incidentally made a double hundred in the first innings – took a blow in the face while fielding. He might have expected attention from the physiotherapist back in the dressing room, but as he headed that way it was rather to find that member of the support staff, Dave 'Rooster' Roberts, rushing onto the field as twelfth man.

One other thing I can remember there was waiting to do a live report for Radio 5. The item on the air before me was a harrowing interview on assisted suicide with a woman in America who had helped her daughter to die. After five or ten minutes of this tearful discussion, the presenter said cheerily, 'Now let's catch up with the latest cricket news from Australia ...'

Follow that.

Four years later I joined the tour for the game with Queensland at Cairns. The rebuilding of the Gabba ground in Brisbane had just completed its first phase, so the ramshackle position that I had been rather fond of on the pavilion roof had gone. I took the opportunity en route to check the new arrangements out.

I had originally had a fanciful idea to hire a car and drive on up to Cairns, but when I had got my map of Australia out, I had carried on unfolding it until I found Cairns – a little over a thousand miles to the north. Melbourne, two states away, seemed to be nearer Brisbane than Cairns was. So I took the two-hour flight north to the laid-back tropical holiday town instead.

A pitch that deteriorated sharply gave us an exciting one-wicket win for England there, while John Crawley being mugged in the street aroused the interest of news desks back home, particularly as the England management decided – for reasons best known to themselves – to say that his facial injuries had been caused by slipping in the shower. The clumsy lie made us all much more suspicious, even when the truth did emerge. With the match finishing early on the final day, we retreated to our hotel and as London began to wake up to a new day, Aggers decided that Radio 5 Live's breakfast programme could be served from the jacuzzi. He sat there, broadcasting live with the water bubbling ferociously round him.

For England's next visit, in 2002, the match with Queensland, originally scheduled for the Gabba, was moved to the Allan Border Field near Breakfast Creek, just out of the Brisbane city centre. Queensland Cricket have since moved their headquarters there.

With anything at all out of the ordinary, Australian taxi drivers (very rarely these days actually Australian born) seem to struggle. The London cabbie's 'knowledge' is not a concept that has been adopted in any Australian city. I recorded one exchange.

Monday 4 November 2002

My taxi driver had never heard of the Allan Border Field.

'Just behind Albion racetrack,' I tried. No recognition. 'Do you know Breakfast Creek?'

'Yes.'

'There's a racetrack just behind the hotel there.'

'Oh, is that called Albion? I'm not very good with place names.'

'Bit of a drawback in your line of work,' I suggested.

If itineraries permit it, Don Bradman's childhood home town of Bowral in the New South Wales countryside, about 80 miles from Sydney, is included in major tours of Australia for a game against 'a Bradman XI'. I first went there in 1990 and encountered something that came as a bit of a surprise.

Tuesday 16 December 1990

I arrived over an hour before the start to find the neat little ground packed. The first enquiries from the press established the fact that we would not be permitted to sit anywhere where we could actually see the game. A tent had been provided for our use behind the catering marquee, which was itself behind the pavilion and that was where our telephones had been installed. Eventually we found one official who grudgingly acknowledged that we might find it difficult to report a game we could not see!

England played poorly – particularly in the field – and deservedly lost. They looked thoroughly petulant as Darren Lehmann, who was dropped three times, played an otherwise commanding innings.

After my second visit there, four years later, I drove on to the next fixture in the federal capital, Canberra, by way of the tiny village of Wingello. Having seen Don Bradman's home town it seemed only right to visit the place where his neighbour, Bill O'Reilly, came from, though the two men were never on friendly terms.

The match against the Prime Minister's XI in Canberra is something of a traditional fixture on most major tours. Many Australian prime ministers have taken a keen personal interest in the selection of the teams representing them.

I first went to Canberra in 1990, when elements of the playing side of the tour were unravelling. Gooch was still ruled out with that hand injury and Allan Lamb led the side, despite being not fully fit himself. One could not avoid the feeling that the team management's main aim was to avoid David Gower, who by that stage appeared rather disaffected with the team set-up, taking over the captaincy for this one festival game. The locals and particularly the Prime Minister, Bob Hawke, would have loved it, as Gower was always a popular figure in Australia. They, at least, loved the way he played.

In the event England suffered an embarrassing defeat in that game.

When I first saw it, I was delightfully surprised by the Victorian splendour of the North Sydney Oval, a short taxi ride across the Harbour Bridge from the city centre. The stands are all of the green-roofed nineteenth century colonial style. At the tail end of 1994, though, I saw England go down to two embarrassing defeats on successive days at the hands of the Australian Cricket Academy. Unfortunately, as I was reporting both matches for the ABC as well as the BBC, I found myself being asked questions about what a laughing stock the England team were.

That was the tour in which Australia A were brought into the one-day series to beef up what would otherwise have been a triangular tournament including England and Zimbabwe. Almost inevitably, the finals were played out between the two Australian teams, though the Australian board rendered that even more pointless by failing to appreciate the need for players to be 'cup tied'. The selectors plundered the A side at will to bolster the first team and the bowler who had done most to get Australia A to the finals, Paul Reiffel, was picked for the senior squad for those matches and then left out.

Over the years you get asked which is the best of the tours. I think people expect you to say that it is the West Indies, because of the palm-fringed beaches and all that. But I have always said Australia, because things work and a journey does not have to be a great drama. In fact, you can travel a huge distance and still do something else with your day. Those sort of very basic elements, mundane as they may sound, are hugely important to a radio producer on a long tour.

Maybe it is no coincidence that I eventually married an Australian.

The Cricket Highlights (ii)
Melbourne 1998

In 1998, we came to Melbourne for Christmas with the Ashes already retained by Australia, thanks to big wins in Perth and Adelaide, following a Brisbane thunderstorm saving England in the first Test. An Australian XI had even just inflicted a nine-wicket defeat on England in Hobart.

Boxing Day was cold and wet and, although there was a toss and England were invited to bat, there was no play. Now every day of the Test would start half an hour earlier and finish half an hour later, to make up some of the time lost.

When play did start on the 27th, despite losing Atherton and Butcher in each of McGrath's first two overs, England were 200 for three in the middle of the day, with Alec Stewart having made a hundred. Shane Warne was out of the series injured, but it was his leg-spinning understudy, Stuart MacGill, who took four wickets as they slumped to 270 all out, half an hour after tea. Before the close, though, Darren Gough managed to nick out both Australian openers cheaply.

So Australia began the third day – the second day of actual play – at 59 for two.

As England's spearhead, Gough was magnificent and the fastest bowler in the match. When he removed Matt Nicholson's leg stump with a yorker before tea, he had taken five wickets and Australia were 252 for eight, still eighteen behind.

MacGill now showed his talent with the bat, making half of a stand of 88, which saw Steve Waugh to his hundred. Australia had taken a lead of 70 before Alan Mullally finished them off.

Atherton made it to the second over before he bagged his pair and England were still five runs behind at the close, with two wickets down.

Tuesday 29 December 1998

I heard a radio piece in the morning on the ABC by Tim Lane, suggesting that England were bound for inevitable defeat today or tomorrow, which I thought a little strong. I teased him about it when I got to the ground.

However, he seemed right when England were all out for 244 before tea. Australia needed only 175 to win.

Though Stewart and Hussain had both reached 50, neither had gone on. Hick was batting with the tail to reach 60 before he was ninth out.

With the last wicket falling half an hour before tea, the interval was taken early. With the half hour tacked on to the end of the day already, that left a scheduled three-and-a-half-hour session to play, with even the possibility of extra time. So Australia could get these runs in the session.

They reached 100 with only two wickets down. Ramprakash took a flying one-handed catch at square leg, to dismiss Langer off Mullally, but at 130 for three with the Waugh twins together, the result seemed certain. Then Dean Headley got to work.

He had already removed Michael Slater at the start of the innings. Now he started a devastating spell by having Mark Waugh caught at slip for 43 and over his next 13 balls he took four for four. Lehmann, Healey and Fleming followed Waugh and suddenly it was 140 for seven.

Matthew Nicholson had been brought into the Australian side for this, his only Test match. Now he joined Steve Waugh to stop the rot and help him add 21 crucial runs. The official close of play was reached with fifteen runs needed for an Australian win. England appeared only too willing to go off and the fielders started to head for the dressing room. But Waugh – maybe because of England's obvious reluctance – went to the umpires to claim the extra half hour to finish the match.

The state of the light and a session now heading towards four hours caused Alec Stewart, the captain, to protest. But to no avail.

However, in the first over of the extra half hour, Headley had Nicholson caught behind. It was 161 for eight. On the phone at the back of the commentary box, I got a call from Radio 4's *Today* programme for an update in their sports slot.

Tuesday 29 December 1998

As I was doing the report, Gough bowled MacGill with a yorker. Steve May, presenting the sport, picked up, saying that he was off to listen to the commentary on long wave, which drew a slightly churlish response from Sue MacGregor.

However, a minute later, they were back on (I gather as a result of pressure from James Naughtie) to hear that Gough had just had McGrath lbw and England had won by 13 runs.

At 7.35 in the evening, England had won the Test by that slender margin, after what was quite probably the longest ever day's Test cricket.

Despite a hat trick by Darren Gough on the first day, Australia won the final Test in Sydney, thanks to MacGill's twelve wickets and a remarkable hundred by Michael Slater in a second innings of 184 all out.

3. The Best Tour

In the very small hours of 31 October 1984 David Gower's England team arrived in Delhi and I was with them.

For a variety of reasons, not least that my daughter, Claire, was approaching her first birthday, I had not been very keen to go on this trip. Bizarrely it turned out to be the best tour I have ever been on, even with its ill-starred beginnings. I think all the participants – be they players or press – has remained a good friend ever since

Wednesday 31 October 1984

I had scarcely closed my eyes when the phone was ringing. A voice from London was saying, 'We're putting you through to the Foreign Duty Editor about this Ghandi business.'

I did not have a clue what she was talking about, but the FDE made it clear. 'Mrs Ghandi has been shot. She may even be dead. Could you get down to the BBC office and give Satish Jacob a hand.'

Satish Jacob, Mark Tully's number two, was holding the fort while the legendary BBC Delhi correspondent was out of town covering Princess Anne's visit to Dehra Dun. When I arrived at the office he was in the middle of a live report for Radio 4, while the other phone in the office was forever ringing with enquiries about the situation. Soon I was helping with the scripting of his reports and offering advice on the sort of audience he might be broadcasting to in Britain and what this momentous news might mean to them.

I had not been at the office long when the first agency report of Mrs Ghandi's death came in. We advised London, but remained cautious. Then came a second report and Satish checked the source. It became clear that the Indian prime minister was indeed dead. Down the line from London the Foreign Duty Editor said, 'If you're confident, go with it.'

I took a deep breath and wrote it for Satish's next report.

As the Today programme ended, the word from London was that one of us should be out, gathering material. Satish reckoned that he was better placed by the phone, so I headed off in a taxi. The prime minister's residence was cordoned off, so I felt that the hospital was the best place to start.

Armed only with a BBC identity card and a tape recorder, I walked straight in and it became immediately clear that news of her death was not generally known. I was told that they were still operating on her.

Outside the front of the Medical Institute I found a huge crowd, eerily subdued. Rumours of the death were beginning to circulate, but most people seemed unprepared to accept that as a fact. Government ministers started leaving the hospital without any noticeable reaction from the crowd.

Thus started my second visit to India. From the hospital I went to the Overseas Communication Service, not far from Parliament and the only place in those days from which we could get a studio line to London. There I delivered a report for the Radio 4 one o'clock news and, after waiting at the studios in case there was any further development to report, returned to the BBC office where Mark Tully had now taken over and was pounding at his portable typewriter.

Wednesday 31 October 1984

What of the cricket tour? With difficulty I persuaded a taxi driver to take me back to the hotel. There was, it seemed, trouble in the city, which had started as darkness fell and the news sank in, so we took a circuitous route.

After interviewing the team manager, Tony Brown, I tried to get a taxi back to the OCS studios, but none of the drivers were prepared to do it and the hotel staff advised me to stay put. There were now apparently full-scale riots in the city. I booked a call to London, but was told that overseas lines were 'sealed'.

That seal was broken in the early hours of the morning, at which point my phone started ringing off the hook.

For the next few days we were firmly advised to stay put, as reports of riots in the city came back to us. A helpful member of the hotel staff pointed out to me columns of smoke rising from fires not too far away. 'That's a Sikh-owned garage,' he said, 'and that's a Sikh school.' It was, it seemed, Sikh members of Mrs Ghandi's own bodyguard who had killed her and so vengeance was being taken.

Under our curfew we became a close-knit band of brothers, players and press together, exchanging information in a way that happened on no other tour I went on. My days involved garnering whatever news I could and plenty of waiting for booked telephone calls to and from London.

Thursday 1 November 1984

At 11 p.m., work done, I left my room to see if any developments had occurred late in the day. I immediately ran into an hotel messenger. 'Ah, Mr. Baxter,' he said. 'I have message.'

He handed me a piece of paper. It said 'London rang at 9.30 and will ring again in half an hour.'

'It's a bit late to tell me now,' I said. 'Why didn't I get the original message?'

'No,' he explained. 'This is not original message. This is carbon copy. Original message is in ink.'

Thereafter the British High Commission provided some makeshift practice facilities for the players, though, as I soon found out, leaving the hotel was still not an option for the press. The newsroom in London suggested that I could get to the Overseas Communications Centre to meet a broadcast circuit to London. But no taxi driver was prepared to take me there or to the BBC office, which was a little less central. It was clear that the policy was to keep all foreigners in their hotels.

As early as the day after the assassination the team management had received an offer from Sri Lanka to go there for a short spell until things quietened down. As the Indian Board considered inevitable changes to the tour itinerary, they were clearly not enamoured of any suggestion of the England team leaving the country with the possibility that they might not return. They were quite happy to leave the team with another ten days of net practice while the country was in official mourning.

Saturday 3 November 1984

It seemed that all telephone traffic in and out of the country had been stopped for the funeral of Mrs Ghandi, which we watched on television as it took place about two miles away from the hotel.

By the evening we had news that a new tour itinerary had been drawn up, involving four Tests. In the meantime the tour manager, Tony Brown, had insisted that we leave for Sri Lanka tomorrow, to be out of the way while the official mourning went on.

The team had the offer of a lift on the Sri Lankan president's plane as he returned from the funeral. That left the press corps of eleven to make our own arrangements.

Fortunately we had help from the crew making a television mini-series, 'Mountbatten – the Last Viceroy'. They had just finished all their Indian shots and had a bit more location work to do in Sri Lanka. They had a fairly large aircraft to accommodate themselves and all their equipment.

Sunday 4 November 1984

They were a fascinating, larger-than-life bunch to rattle around with in an airbus for the three-hour flight.

Ian Richardson, who was playing Nehru, was as languid as when he had been a Le Carré spy. Sam Dastor had changed his appearance so much for the part of Ghandi that

Indian officials at the airport had questioned his passport photograph, but were eventually honoured to be in the presence of the man playing the Mahatma.

The American director, Judith de Paul, seemed intrigued by the little band of English cricket writers and we were lined up for her inspection before we boarded. The whole crew were very friendly.

A three-day practice match was followed by a semi-official one-day international, which was designed to pay for the trip, but a torrential downpour at the half-way stage ended that exercise. I visited the dressing room, the door of which was obscured by a torrential curtain of falling water. The players were sitting on tables to keep out of the flood and David Gower proposed the bathroom as the only dry bit of ground for me to interview him on. That became something of a theme for the rest of the tour, as he would mischievously look for a similar studio facility at every opportunity.

The next day, exactly a week after leaving Delhi, we returned to India, arriving this time in Bombay to begin a tour that had been yet again re-scheduled, with three first class games now before the first of five Test matches. A bit of lee-way had been found in the schedule with the cancellation of the proposed leg of the tour in Bangladesh.

Monday 12 November 1984

We had the best part of a day in Bombay before the evening's flight to Jaipur, so I decided to make the best use of it by visiting the Overseas Communications Service.

Once I had tackled the problem of the form-obsessed

receptionist and queued for the overcrowded little lift to the eighth floor, things went extraordinarily well. The director, who I was sent to see, was a handsome woman in a sari, who was immediately sympathetic to my requirements and fully grasped the fact that our circuit bookings had all had to be re-arranged with the itinerary changes in a way that left all her male assistants standing. A meeting, which on past experience I had expected to take over an hour, lasted ten minutes. My confidence was boosted.

India never fails to surprise.

Our run-up to the first Test, back in Bombay, consisted of three-day games in Jaipur and Ahmedabad, with a four-day game in Rajkot.

Jaipur provided a pleasant setting for our re-introduction to India and most of us were able to make some time for sight-seeing in and around the Pink City, which has subsequently become something of a tourist magnet.

Wednesday 14 November 1984

The service to the press tent was attentive and willing, even if command of the English language was not always the strongest suit. The boy with the teatime sandwiches announced his arrival with a shout of, 'Breakfast!' which, for a few of our party, may have been accurate.

I had been to Ahmedabad three years before, but a change of both ground and hotel were certainly not for the better. The new stadium, built on rubbish-strewn waste ground on the outskirts of the city looked unfinished and vultures cruised speculatively past the press box at eye level.

The match there was against an Under-25 XI, captained by Ravi Shastri and included a player new to us, called Mohammed Azharuddin, who made 151. This match gave England their first defeat of the tour – by an innings – and was a rather bad-tempered affair. Towards the end, as England were well into the final slide to defeat, Pat Pocock, the last man in, commented to the over-enthusiastic young wicket-keeper, 'Look, mate, when I nick one, I will walk.'

Big airport welcomes had been a feature of the tour three years before and we witnessed the first of these on this tour at Rajkot, in the far west of the country. They were pushing the boat out for the first visiting team since Douglas Jardine's side in 1933-34. A big airport welcome was followed by a lavish and well-lubricated reception, even in the dry state of Gurarat.

This being the last game before the first Test, on the Saturday it was planned that for Radio 4's *Sport on Four* programme I should have a proper broadcast circuit instead of the very scratchy telephone lines that I had been using.

Friday 23 November 1984

In the morning two All India Radio officials came to me in a great state of excitement, with the usual problem that the next day it would not be possible for me both to hear London and talk to them.

As contributing to a live programme would therefore be impossible, I protested.

I was taken to Rajkot telephone exchange, where I sat in on my first meeting conducted entirely in Gujarati. Eventually I decided to stick in my two pennyworth in English, and it must have carried the day. All would be well tomorrow, I was assured.

Saturday 24 November 1984

It all worked! Apart from my match report and on-air chat
to Cliff Morgan, I heard Tony Lewis in Bombay, reporting on
his golfing activities. Always reassuring to know that the
commentary team is assembling.

The other thing I remember about that match in Rajkot,
played on a shirt-front of a pitch, was that the West Zone's
captain, Dilip Vengsarkar, then one of the rocks of India's batting line-up, made 158 and did not take the field when his side
bowled. Sensing an injury story just before the Test, I went to
ask him what the problem was. 'Oh, I just didn't feel like it,'
was his nonchalant reply.

Rajkot does stick in my memory for a few reasons – not all
good. An intermittently updated scoreboard made live radio
reports a problem, particularly when it refused utterly to post
individual scores. But I did see the following entry in my diary
for the final day.

Saturday 24 November 1984

I had bidden farewell to the helpful and friendly staff of
the telex office in whose company I had spent so much
time waiting for calls to be connected and peering between
policemen's heads to see the scoreboard.

Especially memorable had been the moustachioed messenger
who had come to fetch me from the press box every time
that I received an unscheduled call from London. He would
salute me and address me as 'Peter Sahib' every time our
paths crossed and would guide me with a great air of pomp
to the telephone, indicating to any friends of his who passed

that he was on important business for the BBC. This just
may have had something to do with the several rupees which
had crossed his palm.

And there is one other entry from that leg of the 1984-85 tour,
to highlight the fascination of travel within India.

Sunday 25 November 1984

As we approached Bombay, two of our party were invited
into the plane's cockpit. They were somewhat alarmed when
the captain made the usual request for clearance to land and
there was a stunned silence from the control tower.

Then, 'Who are you? We know nothing of you. Go away!'

In the body of the plane the rest of us knew nothing of
these exchanges, which apparently persisted until the pilot
suggested that his fuel was running low. We just enjoyed
repeated views of the Arabian Gulf, the Bombay suburbs and
the Western Ghats. At last we got down.

And then it was into the usual preparations for the Test, as
the press party swelled. In the evening two days before the
Test we all – players and press – were guests at a very con-
vivial and relaxed drinks party given by the British Deputy
High Commissioner, Percy Norris, at his residence.

Tuesday 27 November 1984

The first engagement of the day was a series of group
photographs – players and press – for the traditional tour
Christmas cards. The gathering was followed by the manager

announcing an unscheduled team meeting for his players just as they were due to be heading off to the nets.

Within a few minutes we heard the news that he was giving them. Percy Norris, our jovial host from last night, had been shot dead on his way to his office this morning.

After our immediate reaction of shock and sadness we started to think about what this meant for the tour. The general consensus was that this was likely to be the final straw. The Test Match should surely at least be delayed and maybe it – and the whole tour – were in doubt.

After reporting the events to the news desk in London, I went to the High Commission to interview the acting replacement deputy HC, Roy Carter, who made the case for continuing the tour.

Despite misgivings among many of the team, the Test went ahead the next day, after one of our photographers had – perhaps unwisely – tested the security arrangements by introducing himself to the increased ranks of police at the stadium gates in an Irish accent with, 'Good morning. I'm from the IRA. Could you show me where the England dressing room is?' He was escorted to it.

Perhaps in the circumstances it is not surprising that England lost that Test match. In a makeshift commentary box, Mike Selvey, newly retired from county cricket, made his *TMS* debut and on the field Chris Cowdrey did so for England.

Thursday 29 November 1984

The sixth Indian wicket fell to Chris Cowdrey in his first over in Test cricket and we soon heard that his father

– Colin – had been in the car listening and had been so
excited by hearing him brought on to bowl, that he had
turned the wrong way into a one-way street. He was just
explaining this to a policeman who had stopped him, when
Chris took his wicket – the not inconsiderable one of Kapil
Dev. The policeman shared Colin's joy and let him off.

On the rest day I used for the first time a piece of kit which was
later to escort me through several tours of the sub-continent.

Friday 30 November 1984

My interview with Gower I put over in the evening by
means of a machine called Comrex, which encodes material
from the cassette recorder to be decoded at the other end.
Apparently it greatly improves the quality. Leaving me, it
sounded as if both David and I had been breathing helium,
but in the studio in London they pronounced themselves
well satisfied.

Later in the tour I was told that this frequently made the difference between being able to broadcast the reports and
interviews and having to reject them and so I became adept
at dismantling telephones in order to attach clips to the termi-
nals inside.

As the Test match came to its end in Bombay, from the city
of Bhopal, four hundred miles to the north-east, came news of
a massive and deadly chemical leak from the Union Carbide
factory there. Soon we heard that the death toll was likely to
be in the thousands. In later years no firm figure has ever
been reached, but subsequent deaths related to the leak could
have taken it past eight thousand.

It was suggested to some of the journalists in our party by their offices that they should try to get there, but understandably the Indian authorities had made that impossible. Nonetheless, one of our number, filing reports from Bombay airport, had his copy in the paper given the by-line 'in Bhopal'.

The cricket tour, meanwhile, continued to Pune, formerly known as Poona, which was what all the locals still seemed to call it, for the first one-day international.

As usual in a new place, I started by visiting the local All India Radio station.

Tuesday 4 December 1984

It had been, I gathered, a Roman Catholic boys' hostel and was rambling and airy, with offices opening onto the balcony which ran the length of the building. I found the Station Engineer's office and there met the most useful person – a smiling, sari-clad lady called Jai Laxmi, who was to look after me.

It seemed, though, that AIR's Delhi or Bombay offices had not told Pune to expect the BBC, so it was just as well I had called in. A small party happily accompanied me to the ground, to show me where they would put me tomorrow. It turned out that the people who install the lines were expecting me, at least, which was a start.

After a long day of travelling and sorting out the logistics I arrived back at the hotel in the early evening from another hairy auto-rickshaw ride as the phone in the hotel reception was ringing. 'That'll be for me,' I said in jest. And it was! I was handed the phone with a matter-of-fact, 'It is the BBC in London.'

The position we were allocated for the match was on the roof of the pavilion, well away from the rest of the press, who were at the far end. I was therefore very grateful for the company of Mike Selvey.

Wednesday 5 December 1984

During the afternoon two men came importantly up to our commentary position. 'Hello,' said one of them, 'I am Sanjay, surgeon. This is my friend Ashok, computer analyst.'

'I didn't think we ordered a surgeon and a computer analyst,' I said.

'No,' said Mike, 'But it's handy to have them on call.'

Jai Laxmi, our engineer, was brilliant, taking no nonsense when dealing with the usual obstructions to our getting on the air. I was to come across her again three years later during the World Cup, when, at the end of a day's commentary, Christopher Martin-Jenkins and I were asked to contribute an item to the *Sports Report* 50th anniversary bash. We set up a scenario in which I was an Indian telephone operator and CMJ was trying to deliver a report, which I kept interrupting to enquire if all was well, or whether he wanted to continue and then usually telling him to 'Speak on', while he reacted with increasing irritation.

As we were recording it, I was embarrassed to see Jai watching, looking rather bemused. Happily this turned to amusement as she appreciated what we were up to. We must have done a reasonable job, because I was told later that when the recording was played at the *Sports Report* celebration party, it was assumed by many that it was genuine.

Significantly, England had their first win of the tour, thanks to a second successive century from Mike Gatting and, perhaps, India's failure to push on, as Vengsarkar seemed to be more concerned about reaching three figures. As England neared victory the crowd showed their displeasure with a shower of bottles and other missiles, which held up play for twenty minutes.

In the aftermath of the assassination of Mrs Ghandi, the tour had thus far avoided going too far north and their game against the North Zone which followed, and had originally been scheduled for Jammu, had been moved to Bombay. It was as if Yorkshire were playing a touring team at Hove and the emptiness of the Wankhede Stadium over the three days of the drawn match reflected that.

Now we did have to return to Delhi, which we had scuttled out of five weeks before. At the All India Radio headquarters I found that an old friend, Jasdev Singh, whom I had first met in 1970 when he was a Hindi language commentator at the Edinburgh Commonwealth Games, was now the Director of Sports Broadcasting. He greeted me like a long lost brother and introduced me to all our technical back-up. One of these gentlemen, when we arrived at the Ferosz Shah Kotla ground where the Second Test would start next day, proudly produced a thick cable which erupted in multi-coloured wires, like a bunch of flowers and announced, 'This is your line to London.' I don't know why I was not reassured.

When I arrived the next day I found that they had set up their equipment over the whole of the front desk of the commentary box, leaving no room for the commentators themselves. It took some persuading to get them to see why this was not very practical.

Victory in this second Test, set up by a Tim Robinson

century and driven home by the spin of Pocock and Edmonds, brought England excitingly right back into the series, which, for those of us who had been here three years before, was both a surprise and a relief. During the course of the match I made two notes in my diary of incidents which may have had a bearing on the future of *Test Match Special*.

Saturday 15 December 1984

In the commentary box, in the absence of our Indian summariser, Abbas Ali Baig, who had gone to Bombay on business, we had the help of the manager, Tony Brown, and a new recruit, Vic Marks, who was very impressive, with a delightful sense of humour.

Sunday 16 December 1984

The news was broken during the day that Paul Allott was to return home, as the back complaint which had kept him out of both Tests so far was showing no sign of improving. Jonathan Agnew will be his replacement.

Throughout the latter stages of the match came various bits of news that made it clear that there were difficulties with our next venue, Gauhati in Assam. There were a few problems there, mostly as a result of immigration from Bangladesh, immediately to the south of the state, having got out of control. Tales of a very uncertain security situation were being bandied about and the first edict said that while the team could go to fulfil the fixture with the East Zone, no press would be allowed into Assam.

Tony Brown, however, was adamant. If the press were banned, the team would not travel. So special permits were issued to us and we were told that we would have to sign declarations that we would report only on cricket and nothing else. Our misgivings about doing that were never put to the test, as no such document ever materialised.

The flight east took all morning, touching down at Patna and Bagdogra, the nearest airfield to Darjeeling. It gave us fantastic views of the Himalayas, Everest and all.

Gauhati is a place of forested hills, on a bank of the wide Brahmaputra River, which traverses Assam before sweeping down through Bangladesh to the Bay of Bengal. For all the worries about permits to come here, it turned out to be – to our eyes at least – delightfully relaxed.

I took a rickshaw down into the town from our hillside hotel overlooking the river to reconnoitre the ground. I was dumped at a sports ground, which turned out to be the wrong one, but I had a pleasant walk through the streets, following several mis-directions (including one from a man who pointed in two directions at the same time) before I found the ground, with its grey dusted outfield and grey plasticine-looking pitch. I gathered that this was because of the river silt which is used in its preparation.

The hotel on the elevated river bank, at a point where the river was over a mile wide, was called the Bellevue, but known to rickshaw drivers as 'the Belly View'. Here the drain in my bathroom smelled so foul that I had to smoke a cigar in the room before bed each night to counteract the stench.

There were no phones in the rooms, so my daily reports from the hotel in the evenings had to be done from the manager's office. I would wait for these to come through each night, while conducting a game of Scrabble with Mike Carey of the *Daily Telegraph*. These contests drew quite an audience of hotel staff, so that when the inevitable power cuts came a burning torch would immediately be provided in a wall bracket, to illuminate the action.

Then an excited messenger from the manager would arrive. 'Mr Peter! Please come. London is on line.' The manager would sit there unperturbed as I dismantled his precious Bakelite telephone to connect the wires from my Comrex.

The Test win in Delhi, squaring the series at one-all, was followed by an innings victory over East Zone in Gauhati, in which Vic Marks found that the Brahmaputra river mud very much suited his off-spin. As a result the whole party was in good spirits as we moved on to Calcutta for Christmas – there to find the hotel bar shuttered and barred for three days because of local elections. Unfortunately the same regulation also meant that the wine that was being imported for our Christmas celebration was not allowed to be moved from the airport's bonded warehouse.

Determined efforts were made to ensure that the latter consignment would reach our hotel in time for Christmas Day.

Monday 24 December 1984

At 11.30 at night I headed off down Chowringhee Road to the Victorian Gothic splendour of Calcutta's St Paul's Cathedral for the midnight service. At one point during this, I had a tremendous feeling of the familiarity of home. The candles flickered and were reflected in the stained glass windows. Until I raised my eyes to the ceiling fans hanging down on their long shafts, it could have been England. The plaques on the walls showed British names, dead long before their time in an alien land.

Tuesday 25 December 1984

My third Christmas on tour was far and away the most
enjoyable. The traditional party given in the morning for
the players by the press had been better organised, despite
the panics over the last few days over moving in our
consignment of wine and beer.

The press contingent, with a few notable absentees who
were shy of their singing abilities, lined up for a rendition of
the Christmas carols that Mike Carey and I, fuelled by a few
reasonable sized whiskies, had been putting together over
the last couple of days. Lyrics were credited to Carey, Baxter
and Johnny Walker.

Two of the carols recalled umpires who had made their
presence felt in the series, 'God Rest You, Swaroop Kishen'
and 'Dohtiwallah's Coming to Town'. There was also 'The
First L.B.', but the most popular with the players was not
really a carol at all. It surprised and delighted its subject,
Tim Robinson.

Sung to the tune of 'Old Man River', it went:

Here we all work on the Brahmaputra.
Here we all work while the white folk play.
Wielding them bats from the dawn till sunset,
Getting no rest till the close of play.

Don't hook up or put a catch down,
'Cos that upsets Mr Tony Brown.
Play right forward or get right back –
That's the only way on this sort of track.

Old Man Robbo, that Old Man Robbo,

He must know something. He don't say nothing.
That Old Man Robbo, he just keeps batting along.

He's not like Gower; he's not like Gatting,
For some strange reason he keeps on batting.
That Old Man Robbo, he just keeps batting along.

You and me, we sweat and strain
On really good pitches or affected by rain.
Guard those stumps, defend that bail;
If you get bowled you get a rocket in the Mail.

We gets weary and sick of touring,
Just like Boycott, it's bloody boring,
But Old Man Robbo, he just keeps batting along.

India had just acquired a new leg-spinner, so we finished our
little concert with a parody of White Christmas:

I'm dreaming of Sivaramakrishnan,
With every paragraph I write.
Will they pick his googly on the banks of the Hoogly,
Or simply appeal against the light?

I'm dreaming of Sivaramakrishnan
Just like the ones we used to know.
Was it Abdul Qadir or Robin Marlar,
Who couldn't turn it in the snow.

I'm dreaming of Sivaramakrishnan,
With every paragraph I write.
May his spells be merry and bright
And may you continue to smash him out of sight.

The team departed in good spirits and returned to present
their fancy dress to us. We gave our vote to Neil Foster in

a sari. Other outfits included Paul Downton as a turbaned security guard, the social committee of Vic Marks, Chris Cowdrey and Graeme Fowler as the three wise men and Phil Edmonds as an oil sheikh. The captain, David Gower, came as a tiger.

On Boxing Day we flew south to Bhubaneswar, the usual base for a fixture in Cuttack, where the following day we had the second one-day international. Needless to say, we had a delayed flight and, it being Boxing Day, I had a scheduled live contribution to make to the afternoon sports programme at home.

Wednesday 26 December 1984

As soon as we arrived I went to the hotel's telephone operator. 'I'm expecting a call from London,' I said.

The man looked surprised. 'You want laundry?' he asked.

I tried to explain and, as he seemed to think that calls from London were unlikely to succeed, I asked about calls out.

'Oh yes,' he said, proudly. 'I can get you one in only twelve hours.'

I did not take part in that edition of Sport on 2.

The next day England's winning roll continued, though not without some drama, as they chased a substantial Indian total in rapidly gathering gloom. The batsmen were offered the light several times in the last hour, but, by referring to Graeme Fowler's wife's pocket calculator, kept finding themselves behind the required run-rate. As soon as they were ahead of it, Paul Downton and Richard Ellison let the umpires know they were happy to accept the offer, but were kept out there to survive another over before the umpires agreed.

By that time disappointed fans were lighting protest fires in the concrete stands, providing useful light. I had to deliver my final report under a handy security lamp and I saw one journalist writing his piece with a candle mounted on the carriage of his typewriter.

At least by this time we had developed a modus operandi in which I would record the close of play interview in the dressing room and then play it to the press box before sending it to London. It seemed to suit all parties in what were difficult conditions, but I cannot imagine it would have been accepted on subsequent tours.

The run-up to the third Test in Calcutta was dominated by one issue. The great Kapil Dev had been dropped by India after Delhi, for disobeying his captain's orders. The selectors stuck to their guns in the face of considerable pressure and I thought I detected pleased surprise in the captain, Sunil Gavaskar, when he invited me to interview him in his hotel room while his wife was putting the children to bed.

Strangely the Test started on New Year's Eve, which meant that we ushered in 1985 in fairly muted form. On the rest day, though, I had an invitation out.

Wednesday 2 January 1985

I had been invited by Kiran Mavani, our scorer, to his flat a few miles south of Calcutta at the Caledonian Jute Mills, where he works. The simple company flat had a splendid position on the bank of the Hoogly River at a point where it widens as it approaches the sea several miles further downstream.

Kiran took me across the river in a 'country boat', which had the shape of a large canoe. It was propelled with some effort by a single oar at the stern in the hands of a bearded character in a loin cloth, who later produced what looked like a table cloth to act as a sail for the return journey.

Smog, rain and probably a lack of will on the part of India in the absence of Kapil Dev, condemned the third Test to a draw.

Friday 4 January 1985

A remarkable day for the fact that Gavaskar decided to bat on to lunch and beyond. He was finally shamed into a declaration twenty minutes after the interval, when Gower brought himself on to bowl. Edmonds had been seen reading a newspaper at square leg and the crowd had hooted their derision at their own side.

When Gavaskar led his side onto the field at the start of England's reply, he was pelted with fruit, which took another ten minutes to clear up.

There was some discussion between the captains over Vengsarkar's continual appealing for catches off the pad. It ended with a handshake. Gower's comment later was, 'Well, Sunny's not got many friends these days.'

So we moved south to Hyderabad for a four-day game against the South Zone. A circle of temporary stands had created a cosy stadium on an open ground in the suburb of Secunderabad.

The press box was on the roof of the dressing rooms, which formed the only permanent building on the ground.

Monday 7 January 1985

My first contact was with the camp telegraph office, which I found in the usual gaily-coloured tent. 'Can I have a collect call to London, please?' I asked the official.

'In many countries you cannot make a collect call,' came the answer.

'But you can in India,' I said.

'Yes'.

'How long will it take?'

'Four hours.'

'Can you direct dial it if I pay you?'

'Oh yes!' – this with a big smile.

I gave him the number.

'I will book it with operator.'

'I thought you said you could direct dial.'

'Oh, you can direct dial to England – from Bombay, Delhi and Madras.'

It was another forty minutes before I got through to London, where I was told, 'Can you ring the other studio?' I had to explain that I was not calling from Birmingham.

It was a sign of how good the press/team relations were on

this tour that on my birthday, which fell during this match, the team manager, Tony Brown, came to the press box to present me with a cake.

An ironic story reached us from Bombay while we were there. Ravi Shastri, who had made a painfully slow hundred in Calcutta, had just hit six sixes in an over for Bombay against Baroda. The unfortunate bowler was the left arm spinner, Tilak Raj.

The first day in Madras (known these days as Chennai) was all action, again in contrast with Calcutta.

Sunday 13 January 1985

We had a day of ninety-mile-an-hour cricket. Runs came quickly, but so did wickets. India were dismissed for 272 in 68 overs, with Neil Foster taking six for 104 on his return to the side. He visited us in the commentary box during the last ten overs of the day, from which England reached 32 for no wicket.

Monday 14 January 1985

Yet again it was a heartening story we brought to those who tuned in to *Test Match Special* from a snowbound Britain. Robinson and Fowler created a new first wicket record for England against India – 178. Robinson made 74 and Fowler carried on to his third Test hundred. He looked shattered when I talked to him in the dressing room. He is such a perky character that I was delighted for him.

As for those listeners in snowbound Britain, a newspaper cartoon was saved for my return. It showed a man angrily shovelling deep snow from his front doorstep as a radio says, 'Another four for Fowler, pluckily toiling away in this heat.'

The next day both Fowler and Gatting went on to double hundreds.

Thursday 17 January 1985

A half-hour thrash by England in the morning saw the score pass 650 and they declared at 652 for seven – a new post-war record for them. India needed 380 to avoid an innings defeat and they started disastrously, thanks to Neil Foster again.

Azharuddin and Amarnath held England up, with Azharuddin making his second Test hundred in as many matches, but the spinners made the breakthrough on the final morning. They were all out before tea for 412 and England needed only 33 to win. Neil Foster finished with eleven wickets in the match and England lost only Fowler in their pursuit of a nine-wicket win. England had – remarkably – come from behind to lead the Test series 2-1 with one to play.

A third one-day defeat for India in Bangalore brought with it yet another bout of bottle throwing, which held up play for a while and threatened to see the game abandoned.

The fourth one-day international followed immediately in Nagpur. Arriving in the evening, I discovered that I had been selected to share the honeymoon room with Mike Carey, complete with mirrored ceiling above a double bed. Fortunately a twin bedded alternative was found.

From previous tours Nagpur had a poor reputation, but the ground was pleasant enough, in the shadow of an

English-looking church. My commentary position (even though I was only doing telephoned reports) was excellent and the calls worked perfectly. However, as soon as India had secured a three-wicket win, a telephone engineer started ripping wires out with gay abandon. I had to restrain him and completed my match reports with him holding the operation together with his thumb.

The final one-day international was in Chandigarh, 150 miles to the north of Delhi. We arrived early in the morning on the day before the match and as it was a Saturday a proper broadcasting circuit had been booked from the local All India radio station.

Saturday 26 January 1985

I arrived at 9.30 a.m., to be met by blank looks and an all too familiar phrase. 'It has not been intimated to us that you are coming.'

It was India's Republic Day, so nobody of authority was there. I was asked to return at eleven, to see the station engineer.

In the meantime I went to have a look at the ground and found the press box situated behind the sight screen. The explanation was simple. 'We were asked to put it as straight behind the bowler's arm as possible.' I did point out that there might have to be a slight alteration to the plan.

At eleven o'clock I was back at AIR.

'The engineer will be here in two minutes.'

Sure enough, in just over an hour and a half he turned up.

After telling me that my visit had not been intimated to him, either, he asked me to wait. But the programme, Sport on Four, was due on the air within the hour.

'Will I get my circuit to London in time?' I asked.

'Please sit down and wait.'

'No. Please tell me now. Will it appear for this live programme?'

He looked me in the eyes for a moment and then, against all his instincts to prevaricate, gravely said, 'No.'

I thanked him for his unique honesty and went back to the hotel to try to use the phone.

I did not manage to get onto the programme, but I heard later that Tony Lewis, presenting it in London, had read out my telex message telling of hopeless communications.

Saturday 26 January 1985

By the evening the hotel foyer looked like the set of a farce. All those doing pieces for Sunday papers, as well as me, were trying to get through on a switchboard that coped with the excess traffic by cutting off those already talking. My match preview was finally dispatched at the fifth attempt.

The next day the final one-day international was restricted by a waterlogged ground to fifteen overs a side. Considering the unfit conditions it was probably only played at all because a huge crowd had been crammed into the ground well before the scheduled start.

The delay gave us time to sort out the press box problem,

with the solution being the roof of the pavilion, up a 50-foot aluminium ladder with an awkward twist to it. It was particularly problematic if you had to negotiate it every half hour to meet a phone call from London in the secretary's office. However, the char-wallah incredibly made the climb with an enormous tray of tea balanced on one hand.

The game came down to a dramatic final over bowled by Chris Cowdrey in which he took one for three to give England a seven-run win.

The next day I handed on the baton of tour coverage to Christopher Martin-Jenkins, who had just been re-appointed for his second spell as BBC cricket correspondent. I headed for home, leaving him to deal with the final Test and a one-day tournament in Australia.

I had been reluctant to go on the tour, but, by the end I was sorry not to be seeing it through to the final Test. By drawing that match, England achieved a unique feat in coming from behind to win a Test series in India.

The Cricket Highlights (iii)

Delhi 1984

At the beginning of December 1984, India won the first Test match of England's tour in Bombay. Those of us who had been in India three years before had seen England lose the first Test similarly there before going on to suffer five interminable draws. One thing had changed since – and possibly partly because of – that series. A minimum number of overs was now set to be bowled in a day's Test cricket, though interpretation of what might be bad light, as the shadows of stands came across the grounds was still open to debate and might curtail a day.

One encouraging sign that came out of the Bombay Test

was that Mike Gatting, in his 54th Test innings, at last made a rearguard hundred, as England, not without the help of some strange umpiring decisions, slid towards defeat.

So David Gower's team came to Delhi one down, but they started encouragingly enough, with Sunil Gavaskar out in the second over and two more falling to the spin of Pat Pocock and Phil Edmonds before lunch on the first day. Between them they snared another three before tea was taken at 144 for six.

Kapil Dev and the wicket-keeper, Syed Kirmani, got stuck in and made sure there were no more losses on the first day, which ended with India 208 for six.

Kapil was caught behind off Richard Ellison from the second ball of the second day. It was a golden opportunity for England, but each member of the Indian tail got into the twenties and it was half an hour after lunch when their innings ended at 307.

At the heart of England's reply was Tim Robinson, opening the innings. He became the rock. By the end of the second day he had reached a half century out of England's 107 for two.

Continuing after the rest day with Allan Lamb, he went on to add 110 for the third wicket. By the time he reached his first Test hundred in mid-afternoon, England were five wickets down and he had been batting a little over six hours.

His partner now was Paul Downton and the pair reached their hundred partnership at the close of the third day, with England now very handily placed, 30 runs ahead, with five wickets still in hand.

Everyone seemed in euphoric mood at the way England dominated the day. Even the three wickets that did fall were shrouded in controversy, but the situation made the evening's party at the British High Commission even more enjoyable.

In the third over next morning, however, Manoj Prabhakar made Robinson his first Test victim, caught at slip for 160. But England's innings still had legs, with Downton batting with the tail. He was eighth out, one of six wickets for the leg spinner, Sivaramakrishnan, for 74. His four wickets after lunch finished England off for 418, a lead of 111.

Starting their second innings mid-way through the fourth day, India's priority was safety. So losing two wickets to Norman Cowans inside the first seven overs was not the ideal start for them. But Gavaskar was still there and with him was Mohinder Amarnath. Together they batted through to the close of play, by which time they had taken India into a slender lead of 17. It was a platform at least, with only two wickets down, from which they should make the game safe on the final day.

Sunday 16 December 1984

England's hold on the game has loosened slightly. The lead wasn't quite as big as they would have liked and then, despite getting two early Indian wickets, they found Gavaskar and Amarnath immovable in the evening. A draw looks the most likely result.

In the second over of the last day Edmonds got one to turn sharply and bowl Amarnath for 64. An hour later Gavaskar was bowled by Pocock for 65. Four wickets were down with the lead 61.

But time was running out for England. Sandeep Patil and Ravi Shastri took it up to lunch and the lead to 93. It was

96 when Patil was caught at mid-wicket, sweeping Edmonds, for 41.

Kapil Dev, the new batsman, had been told by his captain to delay playing his big shots until the match was absolutely safe. The next over it became apparent that Kapil reckoned that a lead of 97, with five wickets in hand and three hours left in the match, was safety enough. He hit Pocock for a big six, to take the lead past 100 and then next ball he tried to do it again. Allan Lamb held the skied catch at mid-off. It was 214 for six.

Three overs later it was 216 for seven, with Gaekwad out. Kirmani followed at 225 and Yadav at 234. When Pocock held a return catch off Sivaramakrishnan, India were all out for 235, leaving Shastri high and dry on 25. In 26 overs since lunch, they had lost six wickets for 31. The two England spinners, Pocock the off-spinner and Edmonds the left armer, had each taken four.

England needed 125 in two hours. In the tenth over they lost Robinson, thrown out from silly point by Vengsarkar. The mandatory last twenty overs started with 74 needed and only one wicket down. Two overs later, Vengsarkar swooped again, this time for a catch off Fowler, who had made 29.

But the momentum was very much with England and Lamb, coming in to join Gatting, was not going to let it slacken. By the time they were half way through the last twenty overs, they were only thirteen from victory and they won by eight wickets, with eight and a half overs to spare. From being one down in the series, they had come back at the first opportunity to get on level terms.

In India, despite his massive charisma, it was Kapil Dev who was held up as the villain of the piece. The selectors dropped him for the third Test in Calcutta, due to start on New

Year's Eve. They even resisted an attempt from the Board to add him to the squad, which, in the politics of Indian cricket, represented quite a triumph for the captain, Sunil Gavaskar.

In Kapil's absence, though, there was no urgency in India's approach to the match. Even the umpires never seemed particularly keen to get on with the game when the Calcutta smog settled over Eden Gardens. The elements played their part in providing rain and the Indian first innings drifted into a fourth day.

The match could only be a draw, but the fourth Test in Madras provided plenty of action, with Graeme Fowler and Mike Gatting both making double hundreds and Neil Foster taking eleven wickets in the match to give England a two-nil series lead, which they preserved with a draw in the final Test in Kanpur.

Uniquely England had come from behind to win a Test series in India.

4. The Caribbean

I sometimes think the great secret, known by people who have toured the West Indies but not always fully comprehended by those who have not, is that they are all different countries who come together really only for cricket (and as far as some partisan supporters are concerned, barely for that – at home, at least). This certainly makes the travelling more arduous, with each journey being an international flight, involving a change of currency, customs and all the rest.

On a Caribbean tour it is noticeable how little sympathy and support you will receive from those confined to offices and studios in London. Tell them you are in the West Indies and all they can imagine is a sun-kissed beach. That is inevitable, but it's not really fair. Not all the West Indian locations are holiday resorts and anyway working in a holiday environment is always difficult. Hotels, and indeed sometimes whole islands, are simply not geared up for their visitors to be on business.

That said, I am not calling for any sympathy for having been able to get my toes on the sandy beaches of the likes of Barbados and Antigua. The West Indies can charm you, even when you are trying to get things done in an environment where mañana can seem like indecent haste.

My first landfall in the West Indies was far from the

traditional view of palm trees on a beach. It was in the thriving, bustling city of Port-of-Spain.

Monday 12 February 1990

My first sight of the West Indies was impressive. I was lucky to be at a window on the left of the BWIA plane to see the island of Tobago and then the northern coast of Trinidad, with thickly wooded mountains, which almost seemed to brush the wing-tips. Then Port-of-Spain appeared under the left wing and we passed right over the Queen's Park Oval on the way into Piarco airport.

A wall of heat hit us in the face as the plane doors opened and the sights and smells as the taxi took me into the city were more reminiscent of the Indian sub-continent than I had expected from the Caribbean.

This was the first occasion that we had sent a producer on a tour of the West Indies. Up to that point any commentary that had been taken by the BBC had come from whichever the local station was, with our man added to the team. The quality had been patchy. In advance of this tour, I had – I hoped discreetly – consulted with contacts in the West Indies about which radio stations would be best to join forces with and in which countries it would be best to do our own thing. I was to find out how touchy the various islands can be on this sort of issue and in retrospect it would have been wiser to have committed us to one or the other policy throughout. In fact, after this experience, that is what we did.

Trinidad was one place where we were combining forces. This occasionally presented the odd problem.

Wednesday 14 February 1990

I was at the ground just over an hour before we were due on the air for the first one-day international, in order to do the first report on conditions for Radio 2. Unfortunately no one from Radio Trinidad was there to unlock the box and I had the frustrating sound of my phone ringing inside, without being able to get at it.

After the game was abandoned to the rain, our post-match duties were quite light but as I was having dinner later I was told that all our conversation with London as we waited to record at the close of play had been transmitted live over Radio Trinidad. I hope we were restrained in our language.

Both the Trinidad one-day internationals were rained off. I was to discover over future trips that this was not at all unusual for this island.

The Test match there on this tour was also affected by the weather in its latter stages. A tight game left England with only 151 to make in the best part of the whole of the last day.

The West Indies bowling was as hostile as ever, but progress was encouraging until Gooch was hit painfully on the left hand by a ball from Ezra Moseley. He retired hurt and went off to hospital for an X-ray. Then, half an hour before lunch, rain brought them off at 73 for one, with 78 more needed.

We waited through a frustrating afternoon. When conditions were again declared fit by the umpires, it was fairly clear that the West Indies players – and, indeed, a fairly lethargic groundstaff – did not agree.

Wednesday 28 March 1990

Because of a deplorable over-rate in the morning, there were
still ten overs to go before the statutory last twenty started.
Gooch's hand had been announced as only 'bruised', but,
having seen his agony, we did not expect him to bat.

The West Indies bowlers started on a session of the slowest
progression through overs I have ever seen. Those first ten
overs took an hour and a quarter. You could barely see Ezra
Moseley moving as he walked back to his mark.

The light was fading, with the last twenty overs being started
fifteen minutes after the scheduled close of play. And then
wickets started to fall to Walsh and Bishop.

Eventually, with only 31 runs needed, David Capel and
Jack Russell, the batsmen, had to concede that it was now
dangerously dark in the face of that fast attack and in these
conditions, with five wickets down and Gooch injured they
could even lose. So they accepted the third offer of bad light
and the match was drawn

As I walked down the ground to the pavilion for close of
play interviews, I could appreciate that the bowlers' run-ups
were indeed, quite wet.

Wednesday 28 March 1990

In the usual bedlam at the end, I interviewed Gooch and
Malcolm and discovered that Gooch's hand really was
broken, but he had not wanted either the West Indies or
his own side to know. But he confirmed that, even with the
injury, he would have come in next.

Returning to the commentary box, I had to relay this to CMJ, who had recorded all his pieces and was ready to leave, but now had to re-do the lot. It was very dark when we left the Queen's Park Oval.

Four years later I was to leave the same ground in a state of shock after a devastating piece of fast bowling had shattered England's aspirations.

For most of the course of that 1994 Test, England had the upper hand. They had already suffered heavy defeats in Jamaica and Guyana, but here in Trinidad Chris Lewis and Angus Fraser first dismissed the West Indies for 252 and then saw the batsmen take a lead of 76, with Graham Thorpe to the fore. Six second innings wickets for Andrew Caddick meant that England needed just 194 to win. It should have been less, but for a late rally by the West Indies, helped by a couple of dropped catches.

I was doing the commentary as England's second innings started, after a brief shower had left fifteen overs of the fourth day's play to go. I can still vividly remember my horror as Atherton propped half forward to the first ball from Ambrose and was lbw. And my cry of 'Oh, no!' is in the archives, as I watched the inevitability of the run out of Ramprakash in the same over. It was one for two and I was happy to pass the microphone to Vic Marks.

Curtly Ambrose was bowling like a man possessed. Courtney Walsh was just his support act on this occasion, but the pride of these two great fast bowlers seemed like a force of nature, utterly determined to deny England their comeback victory. Robin Smith was bowled leg stump in Ambrose's second over, Hick went in his fourth and Stewart in his fifth.

Walsh at last got in on the act by removing Ian Salisbury, but Ambrose was back to dispose of Russell and, in the last over of the day, Thorpe. I was back on commentary for that one and I can still remember clearly the shell-shocked look on Graham Thorpe's face as he was bowled by the sheer, blinding pace. In those fifteen overs the match had effectively been lost. England were 40 for eight at the close of play.

The only question now was whether they could avoid their lowest ever score of 45. They did, but only by one, when Walsh cleaned up the last two wickets within twenty minutes on the final morning. The West Indies had secured the series – three-nil up, with two to play.

England's next performance was almost more horrible, as they slid to defeat at the hands of a West Indies Board XI in Grenada. With the Barbados Test to come next – on a ground where the West Indies had not lost a Test since 1935 – no one had any great expectations.

Over the last twenty years, for England at least, playing in Barbados has become almost like playing at home, as far as support goes. This is also the part of the tour when the families arrive. Who can say whether it was this, or shame at what had gone before, but suddenly it was a different team.

After the collapses in Trinidad and Grenada, England were put in to bat, understandably, by Brian Lara. It was well over half way through the day before they lost their first wicket. Atherton and Stewart had started with a stand of 171, Stewart going on to a century when Atherton had gone for 85.

A burst of Ambrose on the second morning kept the total to 355. But now came Angus Fraser's finest hour. He recorded the best figures ever by an England bowler against the West Indies, who could have been out for a lot less than their 304. But, as in Trinidad, Chanderpaul, batting with the tail, helped to see too many runs added by the last two wickets. The innings ended with Phil Tufnell, never traditionally the safest pair of hands, waiting under a skier. He caught it and it gave Fraser his eighth wicket, for 75.

Angus Fraser is known for a slightly gloomy expression and that might owe something to occasions like this, when his great bowling effort was pushed out of the limelight by Alec Stewart's second century of the match – the first England batsman to achieve that feat against the West Indies. With the contributions of Thorpe and Hick, England were able to declare shortly after tea on the fourth day and set the West Indies 446 to win.

This time it was Andrew Caddick who took the honours, with five wickets. Tufnell took three and after 59 years, England had at last won in Barbados

The two countries where we decided to mount our own commentary in 1990 were Guyana and Antigua, both places where the politics seemed to be closely woven into everything, radio broadcasting being no exception.

We came to Guyana from Jamaica, where a shared commentary with Jamaica Broadcasting Corporation had worked very well. England had not visited the South American country since their enforced exit in 1981, following the row over Robin Jackman's inclusion in the team, so this was a big moment. Tales about the country were not encouraging, but the welcome we received was genuine and the Pegasus hotel on the sea front turned out to be much better than anticipated, even if it did have the world's worst pianist in its restaurant.

Communications were still fraught, with (we were told) only eight international telephone lines out of the country. Getting a call on one of them was a hit-or-miss business and required a lot of patience. And trying to get through from the hotel was, we quickly discovered, a waste of time, because all the eight international lines had been transferred to the cricket ground for the duration of our stay.

Money changing was to be another interesting business. The official government rate for Guyanese dollars was wholly unrealistic, so illegal deals had to be struck with taxi drivers in a remote corner of the hotel car park.

One other thing marked the start of our time in Guyana – for me, at least. Our journey from Jamaica had been tortuous. While a direct flight might perhaps have taken a couple of hours, we landed at Puerto Rico, Antigua and Barbados in turn, before having to overnight in a rudimentary airport hotel in Trinidad. Then early next morning it was the short hop to Georgetown.

Just to spice up proceedings, as we backed off the stand at Kingston I had seen a number of cases left on the tarmac and recognised mine among them. The passenger sitting immediately in front of me had also seen his. His name was Viv Richards, so the cabin crew were instantly alerted and they reassured us that our cases would catch up with us. It was to take a fairly unpleasantly sweaty 36 hours, however, before they did so.

The hotel was a pleasant surprise – as indeed Georgetown was after its build-up. I even had the press liaison officer at the airport come up to me and say, 'We must meet at the ground this afternoon, to site your commentary position'. I was greatly encouraged.

My optimism was entirely misplaced, as the man failed to turn up at all and the local radio sports producer who was going to be in charge of GBC's broadcast seemed unaware of our intentions, although we had corresponded on the subject long before I left England. The politics kicked in on the following afternoon, when I was taken to the GBC offices to meet the general manager.

She denied that they had heard anything from us about our plans, even though I was holding a copy of their letter of reply. Eventually their line was that they had passed everything on to the cricket board. The Georgetown Cricket Club themselves, the owners of the Bourda ground, turned out to be much more helpful. They allocated me my preferred space and I engaged a carpenter to make the required alterations.

However, GBC were to have the last laugh when the one-day international started. We were still dependent on their technical support and the engineer arrived late and with no idea how to work their equipment. Then I was told there were no lines. Then that 'There is some question of payment', that 'There are negotiations' and finally, 'There has been no booking'.

Meanwhile, on a lucky hit with a call to London, I discovered that on the line that we had been told did not exist, intermittent GBC commentary was being heard.

The local telecom company promised better things for the Test match which followed. In the event, it didn't follow. Days of rain caused the ground in what is a city below sea level to flood. Fish were found swimming on the outfield as the drainage ditches round the ground overflowed.

Sunday 11 March 1990

I have never seen a wetter cricket ground than this. More rain all night had left the press box and commentary box marooned. It was impossible to get to the press box without wading through water at least six inches deep. The commentary box could be approached – with difficulty

– along the stands. The engineer arrived, wired up the mixer
and then disappeared. I discovered how to connect the
solitary microphone and switch the antique equipment on
and we gathered round CMJ to do a half hour's chat for *TMS*,
before returning to the rather drier hotel.

Eventually the Test was abandoned to an extra one-day international on what should have been the last day.

On subsequent Caribbean tours I was to grow quite fond of
Georgetown, which is a unique place. The government was to
change before our next visit, which seemed to open the place
up. Certainly communications improved beyond all measure.
The city is defended from flooding by a sea wall, built by the
Dutch, and by a system of drainage canals. The buildings are
mainly of wood, using the greenheart hard wood from the
abundant rainforests.

Since my last visit there, Bourda has been replaced
as the main cricket ground by a new stadium, built with
Indian money for the 2007 World Cup, but the old wood-built
ground had so much charm, particularly in its large, airy
pavilion.

On that last visit, in 2004, for a one-day international, our
usual hotel was full and, along with three other journalists, I
was placed in a remarkable hotel on the sea wall called the
Emba-Sea. The significance of the name did not strike me until
I discovered that it was a former part of the Russian Embassy.
This enormous compound – needed, I suppose, in the Cold
War days – had been divided by a chain link fence and what
had once been diplomats' apartments were now hotel rooms.
It was austere but roomy and throughout our four or five days
there the rain lashed down, completing the impression of the
Soviet era. As I set up the small satellite dish to broadcast,

directing it over the embassy roof, I could imagine suspicious eyes watching me.

With all the rain that had fallen, the secretary of the Guyana Cricket Board assured me 36 hours before the event that there was no chance of play in the one-day international. Next morning, looking at the ground and talking to the West Indies stand-in captain, Ramnaresh Sarwan, I could only agree, and my reports reflected this situation.

Saturday 17 April 2004

Late in the afternoon I had a call from Reds Pereira about the postponement of some awards ceremony.

'Sorry if it's a bit noisy,' he said. 'It's the helicopter.'

'What helicopter?' I asked.

'They're drying the ground with it.'

'But surely there's no chance of play?'

'Oh, yes,' he said, 'They'll play tomorrow.'

After my own inspection, I was hastily on the line to London to change my previous assessment of the situation.

Amazingly, after another intervention from the helicopter, they did play and gave us an exciting finish, with England winning with three balls to spare from an unpromising position.

After our Guyanese experiences on the 1990 tour, I decided that we needed to be more self-sufficient for our next separate commentary, scheduled for the final Test in Antigua. My wife was due to join me in Barbados just before that, so I arranged for her to bring the necessary extra kit. Ultimately it proved to be an advantage for her at Gatwick, when she was asked at check-in what it was. 'I don't know,' she said and to calm her distress at this, British Airways upgraded her to business class.

In Antigua the obstruction to our doing our own commentary was more open, involving both the Antigua Cricket Association and the Antigua Broadcasting Service. I had to get the cooperation of my colleagues in the written press to allow us to take over the front row of the press box as a commentary position, which is never a popular idea, but on this occasion they could appreciate the crisis. (They probably also hoped there might be some lively diplomatic action played out in front of them.)

Having arrived early and set up my equipment I had a visit from the vice president of the Antigua Cricket Association.

Thursday 12 April 1990

People had mentioned to me from previous tours a rather difficult individual called Victor Michael, who now appeared, in order to tell me that I would not be allowed to broadcast from anywhere inside the ground. 'You would not allow it at Lord's,' he declared.

'We frequently do,' I told him. 'In fact in two months time we shall be laying on full commentary facilities there for All India Radio.' He also seemed genuinely surprised to be told that we have a substantial contract with the West Indies Cricket Board to broadcast this series.

'I will check on that,' he said.

He was back a few minutes later to tell me that there was no contract. I told him that was rubbish, but he was now into telling me that he didn't like us because he hadn't liked CMJ's attitude on the previous tour.

We had done the deal for the broadcasting rights – at the time the biggest rights deal we had ever done for an overseas tour – with an American executive of Trans World International (TWI), Bill Sinrich. He had made the mistake, once the deal had been done, of telling me to come to him with any problems on the tour. This seemed like one, so I sought him out.

Thursday 12 April 1990

Bill presented himself to Victor Michael, as our rather undignified meeting continued in the car park behind the pavilion.

Michael was not prepared to believe him as he had never met him, so we had to await the arrival of Steve Camacho, the secretary of the West Indies Board.

In the meantime I spoke to the Cable and Wireless operations room, who were not prepared to make the final connection to our line without the Antigua Cricket Association's permission.

So the Test Match started with CMJ on the phone in the press box and me being hauled off to yet another meeting behind the pavilion, on the fringes of which stood the local Cable and Wireless director, with a walkie-talkie.

Steve Camacho knew the local politics and I realised that his speech was to please the locals, rather than to worry me.

'There was no agreement for your own commentary,' he said, 'only feeds of local commentary.'

'Not so,' I said. 'It was specifically mentioned and I was told it would make no difference to the contract.' TWI were able immediately to confirm that.

So, apparently grudgingly and with a further remark that we would never allow it in England, which was easy to dismiss, we were given the go-ahead.

The Cable and Wireless man muttered, 'It's on' into his walkie-talkie and by the time I got back to the press box the line was through to London.

A few nights later, I had dinner with Steve Camacho, who was as genial as ever. I had no further contact with Mr Victor Michael, though.

It was unfortunate that this was my first encounter with Antigua. It took another couple of tours before I warmed to the place at all.

There was one other incident during that Test, when the West Indies took the field on the second morning as their captain, Viv Richards, still in T-shirt and black jeans, was in the press box remonstrating with Jim Lawton of the *Daily Express* about something he had written the previous day. Viv was fortunate that after a few balls had been bowled a shower brought the players off and he was able to lead the team out on the resumption.

Two days later, the West Indies clinched the series two-one.

A week before all this we had been in the throes of another diplomatic incident.

We had arrived in Barbados for the fourth Test, with England remarkably one-nil up, after a surprise win in Jamaica, the abandoned Guyana Test and a tense draw in Trinidad. In fortress Barbados, though, the West Indies had not lost a Test match since the Second World War and they now flexed their muscles, declaring on the fourth evening, leaving England a theoretical 356 to win. But by the close of play, in failing light, England were 15 for three.

Sunday 8 April 1990

When the second wicket fell, I was already in the passage outside the dressing room, waiting to snatch a quick interview with Gladstone Small after his eight wickets in the match. I was aware of what seemed like a very delayed decision to give Rob Bailey out after a huge appeal and then Bailey himself came past me, muttering darkly. A helmeted Small emerged from the dressing room to go out as night watchman. I returned to the commentary box just in time to see him out too, and then to hear Michael Holding's opinion that Bailey had been given out caught down the leg side off his thigh pad.

It sounded like just an unfortunate mistake by a usually good umpire, Lloyd Barker, but I also heard that what seemed to have been a change in his decision might have been the result of a charge down the wicket, with arm twirling, by Viv Richards.

I heard further that Barker had actually handed the bowler his cap at the end of the over before he raised his finger.

In the usual shopping list of reports that we were always asked for at the close of play for different programmes, Christopher Martin-Jenkins was commissioned to do a reflective piece for next morning's Radio 4 *Today* programme. He wrote this carefully. In the course of it he built up to talking about the Bailey decision by saying that both sides had cheated each other over the business of over-rates. He went on to say that this evening a previously good umpire had been pressured into changing his decision.

What we did not consider was that, to make things easier, the World Service sports unit then based in Bush House, always had a feed of our line from the West Indies, so that they could record whatever they needed. The next morning they used the piece that had been directed at a Radio Four audience on their sports bulletin beamed back to the Caribbean, which is frequently re-broadcast by the local stations there.

Strangely, it was the rest day of the Test – after four days' play. Early in the morning I received a phone call from Reds Pereira, one of the Voice of Barbados commentary team. He suggested that I should listen to the station.

Monday 9 April 1990

I was astonished to hear that the report that CMJ had done for the Today programme was the leading topic of the news. It seemed that it had been picked up from the World Service, used all morning and then been interpreted as an attack on a Bajan umpire, Lloyd Barker.

I listened to a phone-in being conducted by the VOB Sports Editor, Erskine King, another member of the commentary team. He seemed to be relishing stirring up what was being referred to as 'the Martin-Jenkins affair'.

Christopher, when I saw him, was understandably very apprehensive about the whole business. We went together to the England team hotel for the rest-day press conference and he managed to get himself involved in the VOB discussion programme, which was again being chaired by

Erskine King, to explain remarks which seemed to have been totally misconstrued. By this time, though, the controversy was blazing nicely and no one was inclined to douse the flames.

The problem seemed to be that the word 'cheat' had been used in the same piece as the reference to the umpire. The fact that it did not refer to the umpire was of no concern to those who wanted to make mischief.

As chance would have it, I was a guest that day of the Caribbean Broadcasting Union at a lunch. I had to deal with the topic of the day with as much diplomacy as I could muster.

Further radio programmes that I heard during the afternoon made me realise that for the final day of the Test it would be impossible to share commentary with a local station. Eventually, in the evening, I spoke to VOB's general manager and we agreed that we would set up our own commentary position. He promised any technical help we needed. At this point I was particularly glad that my wife had brought the extra equipment out with her.

During the day, as we described England fighting to stave off defeat – and failing to do so – there was a knock on the commentary box door. I found a large man outside with 'BAILIFF' handwritten on a badge on his lapel. 'Is Christopher Martin-Jenkins here?' he wanted to know.

I told him he was on the air and he stayed outside, but as I took over from Christopher, I whispered a warning. A minute or two later CMJ was served with a summons for libelling Lloyd Barker.

Over the next four years the case rumbled on with no resolution until the BBC, taking local legal advice that, however things might appear to us, they could not hope to win such a sensitive case in Barbados, settled out of court.

On subsequent tours Barbados was always the jewel in the crown. Usually coming towards the end of the trip, the Test match there is something to look forward to. For once the jealous comments down the line from London might be justified.

Like Georgetown and Port-of-Spain, Kingston, Jamaica, is a city far from anyone's idea of a holiday venue. Close to Sabina Park, the Test ground in the capital, is Gun Court, the prison for those convicted of crimes involving firearms. The advice to visitors is not to wander the streets.

I naively thought before I went there that I would not recognise the sweet smell of ganja. That was before I walked across the small grassy hill at Sabina Park that used to be beside the press box stand, where the air was thick with the smoke from spliffs and I realised what it was I was smelling.

Indeed, on the 1998 tour, when England played the West Indies 'A' at Chedwin Park near Spanish Town, not far from Kingston, I walked round the ground enjoying a contemplative smoke of my pipe. The trees beyond the walls of the ground, which was surrounded by cane fields, contained spectators sitting in the branches, as is something of a Caribbean custom. As I walked by, puffing away, a voice from one tree called, 'Hey, man. Come over here an' I put something more interestin' in dat pipe.'

I hasten to say I did not accept the offer.

That 1998 visit to Jamaica was famously to be cut dramatically short. On that tour we had rented a circuit on the Sky television satellite that was sending their pictures and sound. They had room for one out-going line and so I had to run a cable from our box to the TV control room in each place and put together another complicated arrangement for our other broadcast requirements with a slightly poorer quality line. My luggage for the tour included a hundred-metre drum of cable, which drew a cheer from my colleagues whenever it emerged on to airport baggage belts. This all made for a fairly lengthy day's rigging and negotiating before each of the Tests and one-day internationals on that tour.

One other matter intruded into the preparations for this first Test. Just before I had left home, the papers had been full of a court case in France, where Geoff Boycott had been convicted of an assault on his girlfriend. Boycott was due to be part of the *Test Match Special* team in the West Indies and looking at the lurid headlines, I thought we might have a problem. I rang the head of sport and was advised that he would consult others and get back to me.

A fortnight after this, three days before the first Test, I received a call from London instructing me to drop Boycott from our team. The matter had gone as high as the Director General of the BBC. It took me half a day to track down Geoffrey and break the bad news to him. It is possible that at that moment the seeds were sown for the future tours when Talk Sport secured the broadcasting rights, with Geoffrey at the heart of their team.

With that and the lengthy technical set up, it was a relief when the action started and, with everything apparently working, I could concentrate on the cricket.

Thursday 29 January 1998

England had chosen to bat and it soon became apparent that this was not an easy surface on which to do that. Stewart was hit on the shoulder in the second over and in the third

Atherton and Butcher – to his first ball of the tour – were caught at gully and third slip.

The physio started coming on frequently as the ball reared unexpectedly. Then Hussain was caught at second slip and it was 9 for three.

After an hour – and six visits from the physio, Wayne Morton – the drinks were called on and Atherton and the referee, Barry Jarman, came out to talk to the umpires and to Brian Lara.

After ten minutes, both teams left the field and three-quarters of an hour later came the announcement that the Test had been abandoned because the pitch was too dangerous.

Now the work really did start, with reports for every BBC network and, even a call from Radio New Zealand, wanting a live contribution to their breakfast programme.

Reports continued on the phone from the hotel way into the night, by which time we had a press handout with a new schedule, which would include an extra Test in Trinidad, but with so many people to move, I noted in my diary:

Now, how to get to Trinidad?

Friday 30 January 1998

I was woken at 6.30 by the phone and John Snow (our travel agent) saying, 'I can get you on a flight to Trinidad at midday. The flight's full, so don't be late.'

Aggers is staying to fly with the team tomorrow, but I rushed

off to be charged huge sums of money for excess baggage
and then we had a three-hour delay because of an electrical
fault with the aircraft.

Eventually we were hurried onto the plane, which was to do
the usual round of the islands en route to Trinidad. On the
first leg of this, the pilot announced himself on the intercom.
'Good news and bad news,' he said. 'The electrical fault has
returned. If we land in Antigua or Barbados, they won't let
me take off again, so my head office in Trinidad has told
me to go straight to Port-of-Spain.' There were groans from
those in the plane who were bound for the other islands, but
it was a great result for me!

The hastily arranged extra Test match – officially the second
– turned out to be a gripping, comparatively low-scoring affair.
The West Indies had to make the highest total of the match in
the fourth innings to win, which they did – by three wickets.

The new arrangements gave us two Test matches on the
same ground back to back and on the first day of the second
of these we made a bit of broadcasting history.

Friday 13 February 1998

In the afternoon I asked Donna Symmonds to do a session of
commentary. I have seen and heard her operating on a few
Tests on previous tours. She is very experienced and Victor
and Selve have both been working with her on Radio 610
here and reckon she's very good. I await the response from
England with interest.

Thus did *Test Match Special* launch its first female commentator. And on her home island of Barbados she was with us

again on that tour, and also joined us in England for the World Cup the following year.

That second Trinidad Test match also had a three-wicket winning margin – but this time to England. The batting of Chanderpaul and Lara made the difference in Guyana and the Barbados Test was largely washed out.

In Antigua, too, the weather took a hand. A lot of time was lost over the first two days, when England were batting – and only making 127. With better conditions, the West Indies ran up 500 and left England five and a half sessions of play to save the game. At the end of the fourth day they were 173 for three.

Tuesday 24 March 1998

There was obviously rain around and it began in earnest just before the start of this last day's play, so that there was no play before lunch. However it was fine to start at 12.45, with two sessions to go.

Hussain and Thorpe batted until they were almost safe. Then Thorpe set off for a suicidal single and Hussain was run out by three-quarters of the length of the pitch.

And with that the collapse started. They were all out in the ninth over of the last fifteen and the West Indies had won by an innings and 52 runs, to take the series three-one.

Instead of going into the usual intolerably noisy corridor outside the dressing room for the post match interviews we were led up the stairs to a VIP lounge, which had been set up for a press conference. As television cameras arrived, I had an inkling that this was going to be more than just end-of-series remarks.

Mike Atherton came in with a piece of paper in his hand.

Ready to lead off the press conference as I was, I asked quietly, 'Are you reading a statement?'

'Yes,' he said. It could only be the resignation of the captaincy. And it was.

Jonathan Agnew had booked his flight home for that evening and in fact had his suitcase at the ground ready to go straight to the airport, so his reports on this momentous announcement had to be fairly swiftly delivered. I heard later that he had to do more when he disembarked at Gatwick the next morning.

On the previous tour to the West Indies, the final Test in Antigua had belonged to one man – Brian Lara. On the flattest of pitches, he was 164 at the end of the first day and 320 at the end of the second day. I wanted a word with him early on the third morning, but was told he had gone for a round of golf. Clearly Sobers' 365 record was in danger of falling and duly at 11.45 on the morning of 18 April 1994 Lara pulled a ball from Lewis for four to set up a new record. The game stopped for several minutes while well-wishers, including Sir Garry himself, came out to shake his hand. To be honest, after the first day it had just seemed inevitable.

Lara's record innings of 375 stood for nine and a half years. Matthew Hayden was the man who broke it – by five runs against Zimbabwe. Brian Lara's recapture of the title six months later seemed almost more inevitable than his 375 had. This time he made it to 400 not out, before he declared at 751 for five. Antiguans were just as keen, though, to celebrate the unbeaten hundred made by their man, Ridley Jacobs.

Monday 12 April 2004

Just after the close of play, our phone rang and a voice
announced himself as Matthew Hayden. He was after a
number for Brian Lara. There was a moment when I thought
it might be a leg-pull, but he convinced me he was genuine,
so I gave him Simon Mann's mobile number, as Simon was
at the other end of the round, covering the Lara press
conference.

I discovered later that it had worked and Simon had handed
the phone to Lara in the West Indies dressing room. It was a
pity we had no way of getting Hayden on the air.

While the laid-back attitude that pervades the Caribbean can
infuriate a producer trying to get his show on the air, it is, of
course, the essence of the charm of the region. On one tour
the press contingent were invited to drinks at the residence of
the prime minister of St Vincent. It was a fairly ordinary house
in a nice hilltop location and we found the PM with his shoes
off in an armchair in front of his television. I thought maybe
we had made a mistake and got the wrong evening, but, no,
he was expecting us.

As the only Test-playing area to the west of Britain, the
pressures of the time difference are not the same as the rest
of the cricket world. Here, instead of getting most of the day's
work done before the office at home is functioning, they are
liable to be champing at the bit to talk to you first thing, but
have lost interest by the close of play. It does, though, make
for very good audience figures.

And then there is the music of a West Indies tour. Trinidad
is the most musical island, particularly in the run-up to
Carnival, but whatever song is popular at the time will be in

your ears throughout the tour. David Rudder or maybe Destra and always the evocative sounds of Bob Marley will be belted out through the public address systems at the grounds or just heard in the streets.

Tours seemed to come to a crescendo with the final Test at the old ground in Antigua – the Recreation Ground in St John's, with the prison on one side and the cathedral on the other – which used to rock with the sounds of Chickie's disco and rejoice at the antics of Gravy, the extravagant cross-dresser who would cavort on a platform at the front of the stand.

Now, that really wouldn't happen at Lord's.

The Cricket Highlights (iv)
Jamaica 1990
For a remarkable and unexpected change of fortune, it is hard to think of better than 1990 in Jamaica. England started that tour having failed to win a single Test match against the West Indies for sixteen years. Their previous Jamaica Test, four years earlier, had seen them annihilated by fast bowling on an uneven pitch, which had given Patrick Patterson seven wickets on his debut. If the team expected any very different outcome from the first Test this time, they were probably the only people in the world who did.

In the run-up to the Test there was a big dinner at the hotel to celebrate the approaching fortieth anniversary of the famous 1950 Test at Lord's, when the 'little pals of mine', Ramadhin and Valentine, had bowled the West Indies to their first ever win in England. Twelve of the players who had taken part in the game were there, including Sir Len Hutton, who was one of the speakers and who had a delightfully under-stated dry wit.

Two days later I was interviewing the coach Micky Stewart about the team selection, which included for the first time Nasser Hussain and Micky's own son, Alec. As usual, Micky would only refer to him as 'Stewart', but when I really pushed for some sort of personal feeling, he at last conceded, 'His mother will be very pleased.'

The amount of the cricket that I wrote up in my diary at the time emphasises what a big game this was.

Saturday 24 February 1990

I can't remember being so tense on the morning of a Test Match for a long time. And, judging by a very distracted 'good morning' from the normally effusive Allan Lamb, I was not alone. This was a very big day.

We rather groaned when the West Indies won the toss and, despite some hesitation from Richards, decided to bat. The feeling of déjà vu was greater still, when Greenidge and Haynes had reached 60 quickly, even though England had not bowled badly, after deciding on a four-man seam attack and an extra batsman, rather than a spinner.

The breakthrough came when Greenidge misjudged the power of Malcolm's throw, after he had fumbled a stop in the outfield, and was run out. That was the only wicket of the morning, but four more in the afternoon put England right on top, particularly as one of them was Richards.

Then after tea, Fraser took the last five, conceding six runs in six overs and the West Indies were all out for 164.

It left England 24 overs to go in the day and they lost first Gooch and then Stewart, after getting a four from his first

ball in Test cricket, out for 13 to an unplayable lifter from
Bishop. It's going to be a tense day tomorrow.

England had ended the day at 80 for two.

Next day Allan Lamb, first with Wayne Larkins and then
with Robin Smith consolidated England's position and they
took the lead with only three wickets down.

Sunday 25 February 1990

Lamb's century was celebrated twice. The main scoreboard
of the three was alone in having him on 96, when he hit a
four and raised his bat to the applause. But hasty checking
showed that the boundary had taken him to 99, so in the
next over, when he hooked Bishop for another four, he raised
both arms in triumph. It was his first overseas Test hundred
and he certainly deserved the chance to celebrate it twice
and the applause that even Viv Richards gave him.

He was out an hour from the eventual close of play for 132
and England subsided a bit to 342 for eight by the time the
inevitable bad light ended the day.

Still, that was a lead of 178 and on the third morning they took
it to 200 exactly.

Monday 26 February 1990

Now, could the bowlers do it again? After half an hour
Haynes saw his leg stump uprooted by a yorker from
Malcolm. But that was the only wicket before lunch.

Three more in the afternoon brought in Richards to join Best
just before tea and after that interval we started to worry

that these two might just make things very different, as they took command in a stand of 80. Richards was determined to attack Malcolm and it proved his downfall. Just as it seemed the West Indies would take the lead with only four wickets down, Malcolm bowled him with a yorker for 37.

Just after five o'clock they did pass the 200, but double nelson struck twice and Bishop was eighth out at 227. At the close they were only 29 ahead. I went across the ground to ask the manager, Peter Lush, if I could interview any of the England fast bowlers, but he said, 'Not until the job is done.'

I see from the diary that I woke the next morning – the rest day – to the news that Les Ames, the great Kent and England wicket-keeper/batsman and manager of quite a few England tours, had died. I remembered him telling me about batting with Andrew Sandham here in Jamaica in 1930, when Sandham made 325. The young Ames joined him when he was past 200 and started calling sharp singles and twos. The 39-year-old Sandham called him down the wicket to indicate the scoreboard and the fact that, at his time of life and in that heat, he was not inclined to do so much scampering up and down.

After making 849, England drew that 1930 Test match. The threat to this one in 1990 was coming from the heavens. Rain started to fall on Kingston that afternoon and persisted heavily through the night. It washed out the fourth day's play entirely. Surely England's great chance of a win could not be denied them now, we thought.

Thursday 1 March 1990

Nervous early glances through the curtains were rewarded with clear skies. They were evidently anxious in London, too.

I got a call at 7.30 a.m., asking if I could get to the ground early to do a weather piece for the two o'clock Sports Desk, at 9 a.m. our time. That had been my intention anyway.

I found the bowler's run-up at one end still pretty soggy, but it had only just been exposed to the sun and I was reasonably confident that an hour of that would bring a dramatic improvement.

In the end, neither the weather nor the West Indies tail could deny England an historic win by nine wickets. I remember both captains being quite awkward to interview. Graham Gooch seemed belligerent over the apparent universal surprise that his team could beat the West Indies and Viv Richards' pride had clearly been wounded by this defeat. Happily both men were to become good friends in the commentary box.

I had to gather one other interview for my regular Saturday *Sport on Four* despatch. Tony Cozier had written beforehand that for England to win one Test, let alone the series, would be 'a catastrophe too calamitous to contemplate'. I really had to record his view now. He chuckled and said that he had always been a fan of alliteration.

That Test was followed by the washed out match in Guyana and then in Trinidad England found themselves in a strong position to go two up, but the weather denied them at the last gasp.

From that heady position, they moved on to Barbados and Antigua, where the West Indies returned to their usual form and took the series 2-1.

5. The African Experience

In November 2004 England embarked on a winter tour of southern Africa. They were to start with two one-day internationals in Namibia before moving on to five more in Zimbabwe and a full tour of South Africa.

It was the Zimbabwe element that was the concern. Trapped between politicians and the ICC, the cricketers were uneasy while, with the BBC banned from the country by the Robert Mugabe regime, we had our own problems to contend with.

We believed that they had been resolved when Jonathan Agnew and I, detached from the rest of the press and the England team, caught an evening flight from Johannesburg to Harare.

Thursday 25 November 2004

Aggers approached the immigration desk first. He saw his name on a list on the wall beside the official.

'That's good news,' he said, cheerily.

'No,' said the immigration officer, 'It is bad news. You are banned.'

My name was there too and I was handed a deportation order and invited to sign it, an invitation which I declined.

A shadowy plain-clothes man was hovering and clearly
making the immigration officer nervous. He suggested to the
man in uniform that we should spend the night in the cells
before leaving on the first plane back to Johannesburg in the
morning. We suggested that on the whole we would prefer
the transit lounge.

The previous few days had been beset by uncertainty as this
leg of the tour approached. I had been in Namibia, covering
the two games there. At the conclusion of the second one-
day international in Windhoek, I interviewed the man of the
match, Vikram Solanki, and was leaving the press conference
to send the recording to London when the England media liaison officer, Andrew Walpole, told the assembled press men
that he had an announcement.

Tuesday 23 November 2004

Some of us, he announced, had been declared unacceptable
by the Government of Zimbabwe. He read out a list of
proscribed organisations. 'The BBC, *The Times*, the *Daily
Telegraph*, the *Sun*, the *Mirror*, the *Sunday Telegraph*, *The
Sunday Times* and the *News of the World*.' With that and no
added advice or comment, he went to board the team bus
back to their hotel.

I asked for an interview with him or someone from the team
management, but that was refused.

After reporting the facts to London I returned to the team
hotel and found the players in the foyer, waiting to go out,
but anxious to hear what was going on. It was slightly odd to
find myself giving them a press conference.

There followed an evening of many reports for several radio networks late into the night, while packing in between times, ready for an early departure.

In the preparation for the tour I had made sure that I had cleared our way with the Zimbabwean cricket board, who had indicated that despite the BBC being banned from the country we would be allowed in for the purpose of covering the cricket. To that end I had sent off all the visa paperwork to Harare. While the BBC was, we knew, banned, there was a random nature about the selection of papers also listed as being excluded. For instance, the *Daily Mail*, possibly Mugabe's most outspoken critic, was, it seemed, acceptable.

The original plan had been to meet Aggers at Johannesburg airport in the morning for our onward flight to Zimbabwe. Now it was clear that there was no point in doing that and we met instead at the Johannesburg hotel in which I had over-nighted en route for Namibia.

During the afternoon came news that the England team had decided, in the circumstances, not to continue their journey to Harare and were staying in an airport hotel in Johannesburg. Twenty-four hours of rumour and confusion followed. Aggers and I booked ourselves on flights back to England, as the Zimbabwean government seemed utterly intransigent.

Meanwhile, the team, it seemed, were refusing to go to Zimbabwe unless all the press were granted entry, so the five one-day internationals would have to be cancelled. Discussions bounced back and forth. The chairman of the England and Wales Cricket Board and his deputy were both in Zimbabwe already and the ICC were also taking a keen interest and exerting what influence they could.

At around lunchtime in Johannesburg the deadlock broke.

There was plenty of additional rhetoric from the Zimbabwean government, but essentially the word was that all the accredited media with the team would be allowed in after all. The team would fly to Harare in the morning for a series of one-day internationals, now reduced from five matches to four.

Flights had to be re-booked and so Aggers and I found ourselves on the 7.30 p.m. departure from Johannesburg – evidently arriving in Harare in advance not only of the team, but also of any notification of the change of policy.

Thursday 25 November 2004

The British Embassy man who had come to help us reported that Lovemore Banda of the Zimbabwe Cricket Union was on his way to the airport with the paperwork, though the sinister plain-clothes man declared that it would do no good unless the documents had been issued by the correct ministry.

It was an hour's anxious wait before the papers did arrive and suddenly the mood changed. A car and driver were waiting for us and, as we checked into our hotel, we were told that the chairman and vice-chairman of the ECB – David Morgan and Mike Soper – were waiting for us in the restaurant. The first glass they offered went down very well indeed!

The next morning we were broadcasting live from the roof of the hotel and then were off to get our press accreditation to operate in Zimbabwe. Everyone seemed to know about us, but we were still relieved of US$600 each for the privilege.

Then it was back to the airport, where a luggage trolley became our broadcasting base for live coverage of the team's flight arriving. Aggers tried to explain to a bemused security guard that if he stood in front of the small satellite dish he might find himself accidentally sterilised – 'No more kids!' he warned. After going away and thinking for a moment, the man returned, recognising a golden opportunity. With a huge grin, he spread himself in front of the dish.

The accreditation people had told me that I must also report to the Broadcasting Authority of Zimbabwe. They were on the thirteenth floor of a building whose lifts were out of order, which was a good start. It turned out that they knew about the satellite equipment and required prohibitively vast amounts of money – in US dollars of course – on a daily basis to permit it to be used. I thought it prudent to omit the information that we had already been using the kit.

Fortunately a BBC television news team had also arrived and had not been told about this licence demand, so my satellite equipment stayed in my room where the policeman down the corridor (who searched the room every day when I left it) could see it there unused. Meanwhile we used the television team's kit, though the man who had given me the original order rang a couple of times to check that I was not using our dish clandestinely. It seemed it was a good deal more than his life was worth to let me slip through the net.

On our last evening in Harare, before moving on to Bulawayo, the press were invited to a cocktail party given in our hotel by Zanu Patriotic Front, the ruling political party. It was a rather strange and heavy-handed charm offensive by the very people who a week before had placed a ban on half of us entering the country. The atmosphere was strained and in between the painted-on smiles, we were treated to several thinly veiled harangues about British policy towards their country.

Broadcasting arrangements for the four one-day internationals – two each in Harare and Bulawayo – were fairly Heath Robinson, as most of the booked circuitry failed to turn up. At least we were only doing reports, rather than ball-by-ball commentary. By the time we reached the more relaxed atmosphere of Bulawayo, any tension had been dispelled and the TV crew, with no reporting to do during play, arranged for a magnificent tea to be supplied at the ground by their hotel – best china and all.

As we departed Bulawayo to return to Johannesburg I reflected that the first fortnight of this particular African adventure had been more eventful than most – and we still had a full tour of South Africa to go.

The saddest thing about this, my third trip to Zimbabwe, was the contrast with the previous two, or at least the first, when small hitches were there to be overcome. On such a short visit we had limited opportunity to see the full extent of the decline of the country, but it was still clear that it was not the happy place it had been in 1996, when land seizures and other restrictions were only a distant threat. Back then there were some hints of what was to come, though.

Tuesday 26 November 1996

Harare's immigration officers seemed none too keen on letting journalists into the country, but issued each of us with 48-hour temporary visas, to be extended at the Ministry of Information within that time.

I was in something of a quandary over the equipment I was carrying and whether I could walk in with it, after hearing horror stories of Zimbabwe customs. The photographers were in a similar position. Graham Morris approached one of the Zimbabwe Cricket Union officials, who were there to greet the team. 'Go to the Red Channel and see what they want to do with you,' was his advice.

Despite all my equipment – not exactly hidden, in a steel case labelled 'BBC Outside Broadcasts' – I decided to breeze through the Green Channel and see what happened. Nothing did.

I went to pick up my hire car. Showing me round it, the man from the Avis desk proudly indicated the spare tyre in the boot.

'Not exactly over-burdened with tread, is it?' I commented.

'Oh no, sah!' he said proudly.

I had offered Graham a lift into town and it was two hours before he emerged with no cameras and an enormous amount of paperwork. I had to get him and two other snappers to the British High Commission for documentation to guarantee that the cameras and even all the film would be removed from the country at the end of the tour.

That tour was memorable more for England's public relations disaster than for the problems of Zimbabwe, which were not yet very obvious on the surface, even though Robert Mugabe had already begun to clear his throat on the question of taking over white-owned land.

On the second evening in Harare the team and those of the press who had arrived so far were invited to a cocktail party on the splendid lawns of the British High Commissioner's residence. I witnessed the team coach, David Lloyd, being asked by some of the guests if the team would be able to visit a few schools and hospitals. 'We're here to work,' was the rather sharp response. It did bother me slightly, because a first full England tour to Zimbabwe must surely have something of a missionary role as well as the purely cricketing one.

A policy of no wives on tour had been decreed for the team in this spirit of being on business and with an all-too fresh memory of the previous winter's family attendance in South Africa. It did seem counter-productive, however, particularly over the Christmas period. For the first time in my touring experience, the traditional invitation from the press to the team for Christmas Day drinks was rejected by the management and (at least on any tour that I've been on) it has not been revived since.

(Incidentally, the presence of two David Lloyds – one the correspondent first of the Press Association and then the Evening Standard and the other the England coach – on the tours of this period gave rise to a few inevitable misunderstandings, with hotel rooms or airline seats being sometimes cancelled because officials would think they had mistakenly recorded the same name twice. In the way of things we all just used their nicknames. 'Bumble' for the England coach, who would go on to become a Sky commentator, and 'Toff' for the journalist.)

The Zimbabwe captain, Alistair Campbell, seemed to realise quite early on that there was a public relations advantage to be gained over the old colonial power. And he was shrewd enough to grasp it, with an early informal chat with the British journalists in which he subtly played on the relative approaches, implying a heavy-handedness about the England camp in contrast with his own side's more casual attitude. There were some on-field gifts presented to him, with England losing a couple of games in the run-up to the first international encounters. England's management did at least succeed in warning photographers off capturing their image in the team bus in Bulawayo, which bore the legend 'BULAWAYO GIRLS HIGH SCHOOL'.

The nadir for England came with the coach's notorious reaction to the end of the first Test in Bulawayo – what was then a unique outcome in Test cricket, being a draw with the scores level. 'We murdered 'em,' declared Bumble, over and over again. He supposedly went on to have an angry spat with a member of the club hosting the match.

David Lloyd had at that time only recently left the *Test Match Special* team to become England coach and therefore was a good friend. This had the potential to make the situation difficult. I was also doing a book on this tour with him and Jonathan Agnew (the latter was covering the second half of the trip, which was to New Zealand). Some issues did need careful handling, but we got through without any personal rancour, even though *Out of the Rough* may not have entered the bestsellers lists.

On the fourth day of what turned out to be a rain-ruined second Test in Harare, there was a visit from the patron of the Zimbabwe Cricket Union – none other than the president, Robert Mugabe. The presidential palace is just across the narrow lane off which the Harare Sports Club opens.

The teams were presented to him on the outfield in the lunch interval and then the word came that he would like to meet the British press. I asked, more in hope than expectation, if we would be allowed to interview him. To my surprise, the request was approved. Henry Blofeld immediately said that he would like to do the interview. 'How do you think I should address him?' he asked.

'How about "My dear old Excellency"?' I suggested. As I say, relations with the UK were not quite as strained as they were to become.

By the end of the decade I doubt that Henry would either have made that request or have conducted such an amiable chat if he had. But at that time much was being made of a quote from Mugabe on the subject of cricket. He had said that, 'It civilises people and creates good gentlemen. I want everyone to play cricket in Zimbabwe.' It was felt by some that this might mean that he was not such a bad fellow after all. The world would soon learn otherwise.

I had cousins living in Zimbabwe and was able to enjoy a Christmas dinner in a farmhouse 50 miles from Harare, surrounded by family. Then, when a grumpy England team had departed for New Zealand, I had a wonderful driving tour with my wife, Sue, round what is a very beautiful country.

When I returned to Zimbabwe five years later – for a tour consisting only of five one-day internationals, which England won comfortably enough – I naively tried to hire a car again to go out to the farm. I discovered that to do that I would virtually have to buy the vehicle. I struck a deal with the taxi driver who was ferrying us to and from the ground each day, part of which was that I had to start the journey by getting his cab filled with petrol.

On that trip I was appalled to find, on walking round Harare, how little there was in the shops that had been quite well stocked only five years earlier. On my cousin's farm I was shown the so-called 'war veterans' who were recruited to start the occupation of land, scuttling round the edge of the fields. In due course, like so many others, my cousin was forced off the farm he had put so much of his life into.

In 2001, as in 2004, press visas had to be bought, a fact that only came to our notice the day after the first match.

Thursday 4 October 2001

During yesterday's match apparently Mavis Gumbo, of
the Ministry of Information, had visited the TV trucks
demanding to see visas. The Sky crew had been told to
report to her office. At breakfast today came word that the
BBC team must report to her today as well, or be thrown out
of the country.

So, at ten o'clock, we six all pitched up at the ministry. Our
presence was reported to Ms Gumbo, but we were of course
made to wait for an hour – her way of getting her own back
for our failure to do things by the book.

When we did arrive at her office she was in a fierce mood,
demanding to know how we had been given 30-day visas in
our passports. Still, she eventually made up our press cards
before leading us to the accounts department where we had
to hand over US$100 each. As we left the building we saw
her scuttling out of it. Could our dollars have been funding a
shopping spree?

Despite the oppressive regime in Zimbabwe, I never felt at all
uncomfortable in the streets of Harare or Bulawayo, with individual Zimbabweans being very friendly, whatever their race.
By contrast, South Africa could seem threatening in places.

England, of course, did not tour South Africa from 1965
until 1995, while that country languished under the apartheid regime, so it was a real voyage of discovery when I first
went there. I arrived in November 1995, to find the country in
something of a 1960s time warp in many areas. That feeling
may have been accentuated by the fact of my first port of call
being Kimberly, where the taxi driver at the airport told me

disarmingly that I was lucky to get him, as his was one of only two taxis in town. It became a valuable lesson for future South African tours that you always needed to hire cars.

Everywhere on that 1995 tour was a new experience, of course, though the dawn landing in Johannesburg that started each trip was to become extraordinarily familiar over the next ten years. On each tour, we stayed in the sanitised Johannesburg suburb of Sandton, even for matches at Centurion, an hour's drive up the motorway, on the southern edge of Pretoria, where the first Test of that tour took place.

That Test match was probably Graeme Hick's finest hour, as he made an excellent century under a considerable amount of pressure, but the rain that washed the match out after two days meant that few remember it. Unfortunately, rain is an abiding memory for me of that ground, which in good weather is a splendid place to watch cricket. The main stand is in a crescent at the northern end of the ground, while the other two-thirds of the circle is made up of grass banks with a few huts on stilts for corporate sponsors to look over the heads of the picnickers with their barbecues (the ubiquitous South African 'braais').

The elevated stand, which affords a view over the High Veldt towards Johannesburg, often gives you the chance to watch the next spectacular thunderstorm marching towards you at speed.

My first arrival in the rather more picturesque city of Cape Town was fraught with local difficulties. England's game was to be at Paarl, in the Cape wine region, and most of the press contingent would be commuting from Cape Town. To this end, our travel agent had made elaborate car sharing arrangements which didn't work out particularly well.

Tuesday 5 December 1995

As it was the first visit to Cape Town for most of us, Jack
Bannister, a frequent visitor, had offered to lead a convoy
of hire cars from the airport to our hotel in the suburb of
Claremont. My position in the column, with two other press
men as my passengers, was behind Jack and in front of
Mr and Mrs Agnew.

After a few hundred yards I became aware of Aggers
flashing me and I stopped, to be told that one of my wheels
was wobbling alarmingly. The convoy moved on, while my
passengers and I returned to the airport.

The car was changed. All the luggage for three people was
moved from one vehicle to the other. And then we found that
the boot could not be closed. It looked as if the replacement
car had had a shunt recently and damaged the catch. Out
came all the luggage again and a rather nicer car was
produced. It had only one problem – all four tyres were flat.
It was a twenty-minute wait for it to be taken away and
inflated.

That first introduction to the Cape area saw us commuting
to the vineyards of Paarl, which is overlooked dramatically
by the Drakenstein Mountains. The dusty ground and perfect batting pitch set the match on course for an inevitable
high-scoring draw, which meant that – uniquely in my experience – a first class match was abandoned after three days at
the suggestion of the tour manager, Ray Illingworth, due to
lack of interest. Instead a one-day game was arranged for the
scheduled fourth day.

Generally my first impression of South Africa was duller

than I expected it to be. On hearing that we were off to his home town of Bloemfontein for the best part of a week, Allan Donald remarked, 'I hope you've got a good book'. On subsequent visits I found that the place had become a great deal more lively, so I attribute the subdued nature of that first visit to the fact that the country was still recovering from the dead hand of apartheid.

In Bloemfontein I was doing a Radio 5 report, which ended with the presenter asking what the local papers were saying about events. I had to tell her that no English language papers reached the town until the afternoon and that my Afrikaans was not good enough to enlighten her. (However, I did discover to my delight, that runs are 'lopies'.)

A great friend in the South African Broadcasting Corporation team was their technical producer, Gawie Swart, who I had met first in England. His family came from Bloemfontein and so he invited me to a party at his uncle's large house. When I arrived there I found him working at the fish braai, preparing a robust sea fish with spices, before sewing it up and putting it on the flames. He recommended a peppery South African Shiraz to accompany it. Fish and red wine is a combination that I would not usually make, but on this occasion I found that he was quite right.

Christmas on that tour was celebrated in a particularly bleak hotel, set back from the sand dunes on the outskirts of Port Elizabeth. We usually have to work a bit on Christmas morning, with a Test match starting next day. In 1995, returning from duties at St George's Park, we were dismayed to find that most of the hotel's buffet Christmas lunch had been consumed by the influx of England supporters.

There was something of the air of a prison compound about that hotel, which is a pity, because there are things about

Port Elizabeth to recommend it, not least the Test ground, St George's Park, which I rather like. It is good to be able to refer to 'the Duck Pond End', in commentary and we also rather took to the raucous brass band which would periodically strike up in one of the stands.

The BBC is usually placed in a ground level conservatory, which is right alongside the brick path which leads off the field to the dressing room staircase. Thus we were in an almost dangerously perfect position to witness a furious Mike Atherton storming off after a particularly poor decision and taking a swipe at a plastic armchair, placed there for the security guard (who fortunately had temporarily vacated it). A leg was sheered off the chair with a single swing of the bat.

Christmas 1995 saw the team entourage swelled by the arrival of players' wives and children, along with nannies and grandparents. This was a source of some disaffection for the coach/manager, Ray Illingworth, who was inevitably finding things rather different from his day. The party that had to be moved by the team management from Port Elizabeth to Cape Town after the Test match numbered around 90. The logistical nightmare that ensued probably had a great deal to do with the decision to ban players' wives from the next winter's tour.

Nearly a month later, the tour would actually end in Port Elizabeth as well, with the seventh one-day international, which South Africa won to complete a 6-1 series victory.

Sunday 21 January 1996

Nelson Mandela had arrived to see the final rites and, as I gathered he was going to speak, I got myself near a loudspeaker with recorder in hand.

There was a praise singer first, but then came the great
man. He was heavily protected by security guards, all armed,
and there was a sniper helicopter overhead, so I decided to
make no sudden movements.

Even though there was a wall of guards between me and him,
I was close enough to be able to appreciate the aura of the
man and what he means to this country today.

Christmas 1995 was in Port Elizabeth, but subsequently it
seems to have become traditional for the Boxing Day Test to
be played in Durban. In 1999 I was lucky enough to have my
children join me for the week to enjoy the strange experience
of a touring Christmas, which on this occasion included a midnight service where some of the carols on the hymn sheet
were printed in Zulu.

They also rather enjoyed the Barmy Army at the Test
match and especially one rather embittered reaction to one of
their songs. To the tune of 'The Whole World in His Hands',
the song started with, 'You get one rand to the pound', building by a rand each time to a *rallentando* final verse of 'You get
ten rand to the pound.' At that point a large man sitting in front
of them commented in a clipped Afrikaner accent, 'Nine point
six, actually.' Incidentally, the last time I looked, it was nearer
twelve. (Eleven point eight, actually.)

On my last tour of South Africa it became apparent that
the local officials' reaction to the Barmy Army was to try to
develop their own version. But, like Graeme Smith aping
moves that Michael Vaughan might make in the field, it just
did not quite work.

Durban's sea front rather flatters to deceive, with its
broad esplanade and piers. A stroll along it in daylight is very

pleasant, but the advice on my later tours there was to avoid going out on foot at night. It was considered far too dangerous. The Durban weather, too, can be surprisingly unpleasant and has affected England's cricket on more than one occasion. The 1995 Test there was ruined by rain, and several one-day internationals have been as well.

Following the 1995 Test, England were playing a match against the South African Universities at Pietermaritzberg, about 50 miles up the road from Durban. Aggers and I were sharing reporting duties on the match, but I got a commission from a Radio 4 programme to record some players on the subject of being away on tour for Christmas. I had tapped up a few of them in advance and they had agreed to talk during what promised to be a fairly relaxed game.

Maybe the rain had got into my system, because I had developed a bad cold which made the drive through the wet even more of a trial. At the game, play was being severely disrupted by the weather, which should have been good for my chances of getting my recordings done quickly – with the players twiddling their fingers in the pavilion it was an ideal opportunity to do the interviews. This was obvious to me, but not to the militaristic security guards.

Wednesday 20 December 1995

Turned away from approaching the front of the pavilion, I went round the back, where two security men in dark glasses – very obviously Afrikaner – were posted. I showed my press pass.

'Is your name on the list?' I was asked.

'I doubt it.'

'Then you can't come in.'

I explained my mission and that I already had the agreement of the players concerned.

'You can't come in.'

I asked if they could take a message in.

'No.'

I tried again but was told, 'You are making the mistake of thinking you are speaking to someone who cares.'

I assured the man that I had fully appreciated the level of his concern.

Fortunately, late in the day, I found some of the relevant players away from that protected fortress and was able to take my hard-won recording back to Durban.

After my earlier ride in 50 per cent of the taxi strength of Kimberley, I took to driving myself from place to place in South Africa whenever time allowed. South African Airways were never very sympathetic on the question of excess baggage, which was a major problem given all the broadcasting equipment I necessarily had to have with me, so it usually made economic sense, too. It had the great advantage of giving me the chance to see more of the country. Having been advised that the direct drive between Port Elizabeth and Durban, through the Transkei, was hazardous – generally, it must be said, by people who had not done it – I was given more encouraging descriptions by some who had and, taking to that road in 2004, found it a delightful journey.

In the course of covering the huge distances involved in

getting around South Africa, I have to confess that I have twice been stopped for minor infringements of the speed limit.

Friday 17 December 1999

Approaching Johannesburg on the motorway from Bloemfontein, I was stopped by a charming and diminutive policewoman with a huge pistol on her hip. I was 10 kph over the 120 limit. I was surprised she had bothered, as huge Mercedes had been thundering past me all the way.

'They going too fast to stop,' she said. 'Can you get to a police station?' she asked, when she had seen my British driving licence and consulted her sergeant.

'Can't I just give you the 50 rand?' I offered.

She thought that was a good idea and smiled hugely as I handed her the equivalent of £5. We wished each other a Happy Christmas very cheerily.

During the 2003 World Cup, on the road from Cape Town to Port Elizabeth I was again pulled over in the middle of nowhere, by a police unit that was strategically placed at the bottom of a long hill. This time there was paperwork and, having established in conversation what I was doing in the country, the policeman watched my face when he had written his name on the form. He was PC Cronje. He obviously expected me to ask.

'Any relation?'

'Hansie was my first cousin,' he said and was then able to point to the mountainside where the former South African captain had died in a plane crash. The question of his disgrace I did not go into with his obviously devoted cousin.

I think it is fair to say that I like all the Test grounds of South Africa, which each have their own character. Generally, even for the two tours I did there when we were not allowed to bid for the commentary rights, we managed to sort out reasonable positions to operate from. My first arrival at the Wanderers in Johannesburg, though, brought me up against one of those press liaison men who can be the bane of a broadcaster's life.

These are the men who have come to the job after a career in newspapers. That might not necessarily be a bad thing, but you occasionally meet newspaper men who have a chip on their shoulder about the broadcast media. Television is usually too big and self-contained for them to cause much disruption, so they turn their attentions to making life difficult for radio, oblivious to the fact that, unlike the writers, the broadcasters have paid for rights. The difficulties usually start with seating allocations, moving on to press conference access.

On my first arrival at the Wanderers I discovered that our Radio 5 reporting position, from which Pat Murphy was to operate, had been put in the back row. I pointed out to the intransigent official how impractical this was for a number of reasons. However, it was not until I pointed out how annoying his buddies in the press, who he thought he was trying to favour, would find Murphy's voice booming from the back every quarter of an hour, that he finally relented.

The lofty Wanderers media area, if too high to be ideal for covering the game, does give a fine view across the golf course towards the northern suburbs. But the view most people celebrate is the one from Newlands in Cape Town, with its backdrop of Table Mountain. That is certainly spectacular, but it is difficult to ignore the rather less magnificent Castle Brewery

– all pipes and steam – in the foreground. Even if it produced decent beer, it would detract from the view.

The legacy of South Africa's history – its complex racial mix and the politics which attend that – is obvious to anyone working there. They have come a long way, but I cannot help feeling that it will take at least a generation, and possibly more, for attitudes to change completely.

The Cricket Highlights (v)
Johannesburg 1995

It's one of those questions that all of us in this business get asked regularly. 'What's the greatest Test match you've ever seen?'

It is never easy to answer that. But I could start with probably the greatest Test innings I saw. It was played by Mike Atherton at the Wanderers in Johannesburg over 3 and 4 December 1995.

England were in a deal of trouble when it began. They had put South Africa in and bowled them out on the second morning for 332. When South Africa passed 200 with only two wickets down, they would probably have settled for that. With no specialist spinner in the side, they had to rely on Graeme Hick's occasional off-spin to break a third-wicket stand of 137 between Cullinan and Kirsten. Though Kirsten went on to his century, five wickets after tea brought England back into the game on the first evening, which ended with South Africa 278 for seven.

Cork and Malcolm finished the innings off on the second day after some lively batting from Shaun Pollock, in his second Test. Dominic Cork's fifth wicket gave Jack Russell his sixth catch of the innings. But by the close of that second day they'd been bundled out themselves for 200, with the rot starting in the third over, when Atherton left a ball from Allan Donald alone and lost his off stump, to be out for nine.

Three more wickets fell between lunch and tea, but at 116 for four, England did at least have Hick – who had made a century in the last Test – and Robin Smith together. However, the early loss of Hick to Clive Eksteen's left-arm spin left Smith batting with the lower order. He was last out shortly before the close.

So, South Africa batted through the third day, taking their lead past 400, with Brian McMillan 76 not out.

Sunday 3 December 1995

It was quite conceivable that England could lose the match within this fourth day, so my main practical concern was to have the magnum of Veuve Clicquot ready for the Champagne Moment presentation. But South Africa delayed their declaration until McMillan had reached his hundred. He then removed Stewart and Ramprakash and England were in trouble. At the end of the day they were only four wickets down, but nobody is in any doubt that it will take rain for them to save the game.

Still, Mike Atherton is still there with 82 and among my post-match interviews Allan Donald paid effusive compliments to him.

The delaying of the declaration for Brian McMillan's hundred was a small tactical triumph for England. His last 24 runs to the landmark took him an hour and a half, during which time England captured three more wickets, Eksteen giving Russell a record eleventh catch of the match. It meant that South Africa had only four overs to bowl at the England openers before lunch. No one expected that to make much difference.

Robin Smith started the final day in partnership with Atherton. They had already been together for an hour on the fourth evening. They were nine overs from the new ball, which, particularly in the hands of Allan Donald, might just be decisive.

When it was taken, in its fourth over Atherton on 99 was missed from what seemed like a relatively straightforward chance to short leg. He hooked Donald's next ball for four to bring up his hundred.

That ball was eight overs old when Smith top-edged a cut off Donald to third man. Was this the end of the brave resistance? As it turned out that was the only wicket South Africa were to take all day. Atherton found a new partner as obdurate and stubborn as himself in Jack Russell.

The two of them stayed together for seventy-five overs, occupying over four and a half hours. They added 119 for the unbeaten sixth wicket and, as the stand went on, the usually vocal South African close fielders were largely silenced.

Monday 4 December 1995

I think I have just seen one of the great Test innings. Mike Atherton, having come in before lunch on Sunday, was still there at the end – 187 not out. England only lost one wicket in the day and the match was saved.

It was an amazing escape and much more nerve-wracking for us onlookers after tea, when we realised that there was a chance of getting away with it.

I have pasted in my notebook a South African newspaper

cartoon of Atherton standing in front of his wicket, with a union flag flying from his bat handle, resisting shot and shell in the form of cricket balls, saying, 'Is that all you've got?'

I see from my diary that I didn't forget to present the traditional *TMS* award for the champagne moment of the match – funnily enough, not to Atherton, but to Jack Russell, whose eleven catches in the match passed Bob Taylor's world record – though it might have been earned just as much for the way he encouraged and cajoled his captain in his finest hour.

6. The East Revisited

My third arrival in India was for the cricket World Cup in 1987. That tournament also took me to Pakistan for the first time. And then, after the Calcutta final, we went back to Pakistan for a Test series which became notorious for the conflict between the England captain, Mike Gatting, and an umpire called Shakoor Rana.

I was extremely apprehensive about Pakistan, because previous travellers' tales on the cricket circuit did not paint a very rosy picture. Later in my experience of touring, however, I was to find it rather easier to work there than in India. But it did not seem that way when I first put *Test Match Special* on the air from Lahore. After a comparatively efficient operation during the recently completed World Cup, things were considerably less organised.

Wednesday 25 November 1987

As the match started, we still had not got our circuits to London, though the engineers were talking, I gathered, to Karachi. I went to the telegraph office in the corridor behind the commentary boxes, where they were only just starting to install the telephones.

I tried to get a call through to London – eventually successfully – and I was plunged straight into ball-by-ball commentary, with a very restricted view of the ground and an even more restricted one of the scoreboard, through four sheets of wonky glass.

After half an hour, Jack Bannister relieved me and I retreated to the commentary position I had selected on the balcony. Miraculously, ten minutes later the broadcast circuit appeared. It seemed that it had been booked via Karachi from this end and via Islamabad from London.

One other minor crisis that had struck me that morning was that the scorer promised by Radio Pakistan had failed to turn up. One of the journalists, Ted Corbett, aware of this, mentioned that his girlfriend was a capable scorer, so between chasing communications I hired Jo King for her first broadcast engagement.

In the days leading up to the first Test, England had won the one-day series three-nil. Now they were reaping the whirlwind.

As I made my way back to the hotel in Peshawar after the third Pakistani defeat, I saw their team heading out of town on the road to Islamabad, crammed into two minibuses. The story was told later that they had been carpeted by the President, General Zia ul Haq, along with officials of the cricket board. They had been told, we heard, that they had to win the Test series, whatever it took.

Now the Lahore pitch was very clearly roughed up for the spinners, notably Abdul Qadir, and even on that first morning it became clear that the umpires felt they ought to lend a hand, too. These were the days before neutral country umpires were introduced, and this series was to go some way towards their adoption.

Wednesday 25 November 1987

Abdul Qadir, the first of Pakistan's three spinners, was on after half an hour and got his first wicket – Gooch – in his third over. By lunch he had four, with the addition of Robinson, Gatting and Athey, though at least two looked rather dubious decisions.

England were 50 for four and they lost another four wickets in the afternoon session.

They were all out half an hour before the close for 175. The umpiring looks likely to become a sensitive issue.

Well, I got that one right. Two days later, when Pakistan had taken a first innings lead of 217, Chris Broad refused to leave the field for some time after being given out caught behind off the left-arm spinner, Iqbal Qasim. He was persuaded to go by the non-striker, Graham Gooch, who then suffered a similar fate.

Friday 27 November 1987

In the evening a grim faced pair, the manager, Peter Lush, and coach, Micky Stewart, came to our hotel to give a statement to us, first about Chris Broad, who had been reprimanded for his conduct, and also a general comment about umpiring. They protested that a visiting side needed to be allowed to compete on equal terms.

It was a clear accusation of sharp practice, which seemed an astonishing declaration from a touring manager.

Next day Pakistan wrapped up the match by an innings and 87 runs, with a day and a half to spare.

Saturday 28 November 1987

Afterwards I interviewed a desperate Mike Gatting, who talked about 'blatant' conduct by Pakistan in the preparation of the pitch and in the umpiring. It had been a very sad match for cricket.

And at that stage I did not know what was to come next, though I did also interview the Pakistan captain, Javed Minadad, who affected astonishment that there was any suggestion of controversy about the match.

Immediately, there was a three-day game to be played a hundred miles away in Sahiwal. We had been warned of a shortage of hotel accommodation and difficult communications, so only seven of the press party set off in the minibus.

Tuesday 1 December 1987

The team were to be accommodated in the local biscuit factory and we had to report there to find out where we had been billeted. It turned out to be in the government rest house – no frills, but comfortable enough. However I totally failed to find a telephone to do a piece for the Radio 2 Sports Desk.

The lack of any outgoing telephone at the ground made me enquire about a central telegraph office in the town. I was given some Urdu scrawled on a scrap of paper to show to a rickshaw driver, who deposited me at a busy crossroads, where I found a man peering out of a ragged hole in the wall at a queue of people. This, apparently, was the telegraph office. The man gestured me to get into it round the back of the building.

I picked my way down a dusty alley, with chickens running wild, washing drying and rickshaw drivers resting on their charpoys to find the way into what looked like a Victorian coal-hole. The man who had peered though the aperture at the front was perched on a tall stool like a Dickensian clerk. I gave him the studio number and my name and settled down for a long wait. But he was through to London almost before I had got my tape recorder and notebook out of my briefcase and he did not turn a hair when I dismantled his precious antique telephone to connect my wires.

The match was notable for the appearance of a seventeen-year-old leg spinner called Mushtaq Ahmed. He took six wickets on the first day, but after a visit from the Pakistan selectors, no doubt not keen for England to practice too much against such bowling, he took less of a part.

Don Mosey had never had a good word to say about Pakistan and his two tours there had reached their lowest ebb in Faisalabad, our next destination, where he had stayed in Ray's Hotel. Apparently the choice there lay between a room with no window at the back and a room with a window at the front opening onto the main road. Having made the mistake of choosing the latter, Don recorded the noise outside his window at three in the morning – a cacophony of lorry engines, blaring horns and loudly complaining animals and people. This, he insisted, continued at the same decibel level 24 hours a day.

Out of curiosity, I went to see Ray's Hotel just before the second Test match and found a visitors' book, in which generations of unhappy foreign journalists had recorded messages like 'Unforgettable', 'A remarkable experience' and

'Execrable'. The proprietor felt these were favourable endorsements of his establishment and was particularly proud of the praise he felt lay in the last word.

After a quick look round I was very glad that one of the Aga Khan's Serena Hotels had been built in the city by that time – it was a comfortable oasis.

It was also very handy for the Iqbal Stadium, which was about to stage one of the most notorious Test matches of all time. On first inspection, the pitch there looked as cracked and crumbling as had the one in Lahore, but the afternoon before the Test – remarkably coinciding with news that Abdul Qadir might not be fit because of a bad back – it changed in character completely, with a good dousing of water.

In the early stages of the match, England were doing well. Broad made a splendidly patient century, but losing their last eight wickets for 51 was a big disappointment for England. Nonetheless, their 292 was looking good when Pakistan were 77 for five on the second afternoon.

Criticism of umpiring decisions from the press had led to television monitors being removed, including from the *Test Match Special* box. That certainly hampered us from appreciating fully what happened at the end of the day. In a strong position, England were pushing through Eddie Hemmings' over, in the hope of getting one more in before the close. We then became aware of an argument between the square leg umpire and the captain, Mike Gatting, though we had no idea of its cause.

With the players leaving the ground quickly at the end of play for the comfort of the hotel, and reports and interviews keeping us busy at the ground for an hour or so, it was some time after our return that the story started to unfold. The catalyst was the arrival of the television news pictures in London.

There was then no live TV coverage back home and the news reporters had been forced to send the shots they gleaned from Pakistan television from Lahore, as no suitable facilities existed in Faisalabad.

Tuesday 8 December 1987

As the evening went on, the reasons for the row gradually came out. Umpire Shakoor Rana had objected to Gatting moving his field late and had shouted at him. Gatting had apparently felt that it was none of the umpire's business. I re-did my reports on my return to the hotel, as the impact of the row became clearer.

Later I had to do them again, because the crisis seemed to have deepened, with Shakoor Rana's statement that, unless he received a full apology from Gatting, he would not stand in the Test tomorrow.

Wednesday 9 December 1987

We all arrived early at the ground to see what the morning would bring. There was no sign of the umpires at the starting time of ten o'clock, when Mike Gatting led his side out onto the field. The ground staff were still in the middle with the roller and the mower both immobile beside the pitch and the stumps lying in a heap at one end. No Pakistani batsmen emerged.

It transpired that Gatting had said he would apologise, but only if the umpire apologised to him for what, we gathered, had been the first abusive part of the exchange. There was a great deal of coming and going amongst the offices two floors below us, but it seemed that the Pakistan Board

themselves were not pushing too hard for a settlement, even
though that had seemed a possibility in mid morning.

The crisis deepened. Peter Lush could make no contact with
the president of the Board of Control for Cricket in Pakistan,
General Safdar Butt, in Lahore. When he and Micky Stewart
returned from the hotel where they had gone to talk to
Lord's, they found that Ijaz Butt, the Board secretary,
had left for Lahore without a word. So Peter decided to go
there too.

TMS had gone on all day, but by mid-afternoon it was obvious
that there would be no play. Luckily, CMJ has been in the
studio in London to keep us going.

During the evening, news came of a further snub to Peter
Lush. When he reached Lahore, the general had been 'out to
dinner'. Peter has decided to stay the night and see him in
the morning.

The next day was the official rest day, during which I stayed
by the phone to update any BBC radio or television network
that rang, with only brief breaks to find out any new developments. The Serena hotel was laid out like some labyrinthine
eastern sultan's palace, with nooks and crannies and small
courtyards, which seemed purpose built for conspiratorial
whispered conversations. The fact that both teams were staying there added to the intrigue, though we saw little of the
Pakistan team during the day.

Friday 11 December 1987

Everyone arrived early at the ground – except the England
team. We found out why when they did arrive. Lord's had

issued the edict that Gatting must apologise unconditionally.
And, fifteen minutes after the scheduled start of play, Peter
Lush made a prepared statement to that effect, which
seemed to imply that they deplored the need for this climb
down.

Ralph Dellor, who is part of the commentary team for these
last two Tests, played a blinder with interviews and even got
a few words from Shakoor Rana himself. They did not make
him sound like the easiest of people to deal with.

Later in the day the players issued a statement of their
own, deploring in strong terms the actions of both boards in
the dispute. The mood was very morose – and the weather
matched it.

That weather curtailed what playing time was left still further,
though England did dismiss Pakistan, to give themselves
a lead of 101. They set up a declaration next day, leaving
Pakistan 40 overs to make 239. They were not interested and
Javed Miandad seemed to take the decision on himself to call
it a draw before the final 20 overs had even started. Nobody
argued.

When I interviewed him at the end, Mike Gatting said
that he would never play in Pakistan again after the final
Test.

It was only when I returned home a couple of days before
Christmas that I realised the impact all this had made. On occasions I had been leading news bulletins – sometimes vying for
top billing with the meeting between presidents Reagan and
Gorbachev. The demand for more and more on the subject
continued right into the third and final Test in Karachi. Two
days before that match the Chairman and Secretary of the

Test and County Cricket Board, Raman Subba Row and Alan
Smith, both arrived.

Monday 14 December 1987

We waited through the afternoon as they met Gatting and
Stewart, then the whole team. They looked a bit shaken when
they arrived at a press conference, flanked by Messrs Lush
and Stewart and they were given a fairly rough ride there,
too.

Raman, when I interviewed him afterwards, seemed a bit
surprised at the strength of feeling they had encountered.
When I spoke to Gatting later, he seemed grimly satisfied
that they had got their point across.

Unfortunately, a lot of sympathy was to be lost when it
emerged that a hardship payment was to be made to the team.

The final Test was negotiated as a draw, with no more controversy, and everyone headed home for Christmas.

England would not play another Test match in Pakistan for
thirteen years, only going there in between for the World Cup
in 1996. In the meantime, we were back in India in 1993.

On this occasion it was Jonathan Agnew, not quite two
years into the job of BBC cricket correspondent, who started
the tour with the warm-up matches, while I was to join him
for the international cricket. In the early days we encountered
two major problems.

Hindu-Muslim clashes over a shrine in Ayodhya, not too
far from Lucknow, where the second warm-up game was
played, eventually caused the first one-day international to be
cancelled, as it was scheduled for Ahmedabad, where there
had also been unrest.

Then there was an airline pilots' strike. This made what were already arduous travel plans even worse. The Indian government's solution was to draft in pilots and aircraft from various countries around Asia. This might just explain why, when I reported to All India Radio for my appointment with the head of sport, I was asked, 'You are from Uzbekistan?'

Thus we went from Delhi to Jaipur by coach, for what became the first one-day international, and to Chandigarh by train for the second.

It was in Chandigarh that Aggers was forced to change his hotel room after hearing a rat in his air conditioning ducts. Our travel courier, Raghu, was adamant, 'Is not rat. Is pigeon,' he said.

'I've never heard a pigeon gnawing concrete,' insisted Aggers.

After the second one-day international, the series stood at one all and we returned to Delhi that evening by road. The bulk of the writers went on a bus as soon as the game finished, while we broadcasters and a few photographers were allocated seats in two of what were described as 'fast cars', because we had to do more work at the ground before we left.

After dismantling equipment, I got into the second of these cars to leave.

Thursday 21 January 1993

Our driver was splendid. He spent a lot of time on the wrong side of the road, overtaking, and we began to revise the estimate of a six-hour journey to Delhi. We overtook the first 'fast car' with a cheery wave and then passed the bus.

We'd been going for about an hour when our car's engine cut

out and we coasted to a halt. It refused all efforts to restart it. As it was a newish vehicle, the driver probably became the first man in India to use hazard warning lights.

It was just as well that we had overtaken our colleagues – and imperative that they saw us in the dark beside the ridiculously overcrowded Grand Trunk Road.

Fortunately, they did and we were able to cram onto the press bus for a very late arrival in Delhi.

Though a plane was found to get us to our next destination, Bhubaneswar in the east, there were none available for the 300 mile onward journey north to Calcutta for the first Test. The Indian board, it seemed, reckoned that it was England's problem how they got there. Eventually the tour manager, Bob Bennett, managed to arrange for an extra coach to be added to the Puri to Howrah night express train, which would stop at Bhubaneswar specially to pick us up.

Monday 25 January 1993

We scrambled onto our second-class sleeper carriage. The bunks were slightly padded plastic-covered shelves. As the train rattled off to its top speed of maybe 25 miles an hour, card schools started. Cans of beer and hoarded bottles of whisky were opened. Aggers fell asleep – amazingly – on the top shelf above our heads, after deciding that his sheet was best employed stuffed into the air conditioning vent by his head, and we all decided to ignore the mouse scuttling round our feet.

We arrived in the extremely faded Victorian splendour of Howrah station, Calcutta, at five in the morning. Inevitably the photographers among us took pictures of the players disembarking from their night on the train.

Unfortunately, by this time a condemnatory attitude towards the England team was growing at home, and newspaper picture editors were quick to caption these shots as depicting an unacceptably scruffy arrival for the Test match. When I heard about that, I immediately felt that pictures of the press party would have looked far more ramshackle.

And other such unfair comments were made.

Graham Gooch had been shown early on running round a training ground in – naturally enough – shorts and T-shirt. But outrage was expressed in some quarters that an England captain should dress like this. Later in the tour, Bob Bennett was suffering from a bad back. He was therefore half-lying on a sofa in Gooch's room for a meeting between captain and coach. That meeting was followed by Graham agreeing to see the press for an informal briefing. Bob made to get up as we came in but, appreciating his pain, everyone told him to stay put.

As Gooch was answering our questions, though, snaps were taken of him with the manager sprawled beside him and these were then published as further evidence of the disarray of the tour.

In Calcutta, Ted Dexter, the chairman of the England committee, which included team selection, joined the party. Comments he made about the pollution in that city (which is admittedly undeniable and leaves most who visit it with a sore throat) and about the players' tendency to forgo shaving on hot mornings were given a great deal of prominence.

Of course, if this had been a winning England tour, attitudes might have been a bit different, but all three Tests were won by India by a distance.

In Calcutta the All India Radio station is a splendid building, as so many are in that city (or would be if they were maintained). It is handily placed right next door to the Test ground, Eden Gardens. On this, as on previous tours, I passed through its marbled entrance hall for a meeting with my opposite numbers, on my way to check out the commentary box a couple of days before the Test.

The AIR building's position did mean that it was convenient for them to approach looking after the BBC as a bit of a treat. Our engineering staff would often change for every session of play, which made building a rapport a bit tricky, particularly contending with what seemed to be a generally declining use of English.

In my thank you letter to the station controller after the 1993 Calcutta Test I did express my gratitude, especially for the only day when we had an engineer who spoke a little English. But then I have to admit that my Bengali is not up to much.

Tuesday 2 February 1993

As I was leaving the hotel for the ground, Bob Bennett was doing the same and expressed an interest in the walk across the Maidan, which he had never attempted. So I advised him to take his blazer off and fold it to hide the England badge to avoid being mobbed and off we went, across Chowringhee Road, through the alley to the bus and train station and onto the Maidan. We crossed the foul-smelling ditch by the shack that is the Calcutta Sports Journalists' Club, arriving at a busy junction.

Yesterday, when I was trying to cross this junction, I queried

Watching the clock: the author reporting for Radio 2 from the exposed gantry at Brisbane in 1982.

The distinctly impressive clock tower commentary position in Cuttack.

The England team in Melbourne on Christmas Day 1994: Mike Gatting, Henry VIII; Graham Thorpe, centurion; manager M.J.K. Smith, court jester; Mike Atherton, Robin Hood; Darren Gough, Uncle Sam; Alec Stewart, Elvis; physio Dave Roberts, fairy; Craig White, mobster; Chris Lewis, musketeer; Angus Fraser, Munster; Phil DeFreitas, Batman; Steve Rhodes, convict; coach Keith Fletcher; selector Ray Illingworth, Fu Manchu; Shaun Udal, Austrian in lederhosen.

The Remarkable Mountains provide a stunning setting for Queenstown's first ever first-class game – Otago v England, March 2002.

'The Best Tour': The England team and press combine in Bombay in November 1984.
Back row: Graeme Fowler, Richard Streeton (*The Times*), Vic Marks, Paul Downton,
Martyn Moxon, Richard Ellison, Neil Foster, Norman Cowans, Chris Cowdrey,
Tim Robinson, Bruce French, Geoffrey Saulez (scorer), John Thicknesse (*Evening
Standard*). Seated: Bernard Thomas (physio), Allan Lamb, Pat Pocock, Mike Gatting,
David Gower (captain), Tony Brown (manager), Phil Edmonds, Paul Allott, Norman
Gifford (coach). In front: Charlie Pinto (travel courier), Graham Morris (photographer),
Colin Bateman (*Daily Express*), Matthew Engel (*Guardian*), Chris Lander (*Mirror*),
Michael Carey (*Telegraph*), Peter Smith (*Mail*), Peter Baxter (*BBC*), Ted Corbett (*Star*),
Paul Weaver (*News of the World*), Graham Otway (*Press Association*).
Photograph reproduced by kind permission of Graham Morris.

Zimbabwe v England at the Harare Sports Club
with the jacarandas in bloom, 2001.

Every vantage point is used to watch a one-day international in Kanpur in 2002.

The *Test Match Special* commentary position in Faisalabad 1987,
with Ralph Dellor and Mike Selvey in action.

India 1993: coach Keith Fletcher, Alec Stewart and Robin Smith follow the luggage as the England team embark on another train journey.

The author in the commentary box at Eden Gardens, Calcutta, in 1993.

Will anyone hear us? Our engineers in Calcutta, 1993.

Aggers at work in his rooftop 'studio' surrounded by the hotel laundry:
Multan, 2005.

The *TMS* team in Lahore, 2005. From the left: the author, Jonathan Agnew,
Ramiz Raja, Christopher Martin-Jenkins, Geoff Boycott, Mike Selvey,
Vic Marks, Arlo White, Jo King (scorer), Deepak Patel and Alison Mitchell
(BBC Asian Network).

An impressive backdrop for Duncan Fletcher and Marcus Trescothick
at net practice in Lahore, 2005.

(*above*) Spectators at Kurunegala in Sri Lanka, 2001.

Engineers in Jaipur amid a mass of wires trying to put us in touch with London during the 1987 World Cup in India.

with a policeman the use of the traffic lights. 'What does red mean?' I asked.

'It means stop,' he told me.

'Why does nobody stop?'

'Because all Calcutta's traffic is controlled by hand.'

Thankfully we got across without delay today and Bob thanked me for the experience as we arrived at Eden Gardens.

Passes are always a problem in India, because everyone seems to be after them. On recent tours one accreditation from the board has usually been sufficient for all matches, but in 1993 every game required hours of negotiation and trying to establish who the key person for issuing passes was.

By the time we got to the third Test in Bombay I had had enough.

Wednesday 17 February 1993

In the search for our passes, I was sent from room to room in the Bombay Cricket Association clubhouse. Eventually, in 'Room 27', I found a crowd of people yelling. Further investigation established that they were surrounding a man at a desk.

I fought my way to the front and asked for the BBC Radio passes. 'Come back tomorrow,' was the reply, which sounded as if it had become his standard response.

I flipped. 'No, I will not come back tomorrow. We have paid

many lakhs of rupees in rights for this series and have been given the run-around from start to finish.'

He put his hand in the desk and pulled out five passes.
'Sorry,' he said. It was quite deflating.

India never fails to surprise.

In Madras on that 1993 tour I had spent just such a frustrating day at Chepauk Stadium, with the added problem of having to stand over a carpenter who I had paid to make some modifications to the box.

Thus it was after half past nine in the evening when I regained the hotel, sweaty and filthy after twelve hours at the ground. I went straight to the bar for refreshment. An England supporter, already apparently well refreshed, turned to me as I waited to be served. 'It's all right for you lot,' he said, 'You get paid for your holidays.'

His friends sensed that he might not have picked the best moment for such a remark. And swiftly removed him from harm's way.

Two memorable events marked that Test match. First Graham Gooch was unfit with a stomach upset (later several other players left the field with the same complaint). Secondly, we welcomed Brian Johnston for his first experience of cricket in India. He was anxious about getting ill and a hair-raising drive from Delhi to Agra to see the Taj Mahal on his first day in India had done nothing for his nerves. Still, he was hoping that a daily tot of whisky – which he detested – would keep any bugs at bay. Nonetheless, I don't think he ever felt entirely well during his stay.

On one of these tours you just have to accept that there will be a day when you are laid low. It is also inevitable that the timing of the affliction will be the least convenient it could possibly be. I remember one day in 1993 when I had suffered a particularly bad night. We were due to fly from Bangalore in the south to Jamshedpur, some way inland from Calcutta, a journey which I now anticipated with dread. However, to my profound relief the flight was delayed, and I found myself, for once, feeling grateful for the inefficiency of Indian travel.

Eventually, however, we did get underway. The first leg of the journey was the two-hour flight north along the coast, which gave the mad pilot the chance to announce, 'If you look out of the right-hand side, you will see the shadow of my beautiful aeroplane on the sea.' He let out a yell – of either terror or relief, it was impossible to guess which – as we landed rather heavily at Calcutta a little later.

The next phase of that journey was a bus-ride 200 miles east to Jamshedpur.

Saturday 27 February 1993

It was getting dark as we came out of the Calcutta suburbs into the countryside. We thundered on into the night on a surprisingly clear road for India, with many of us dozing off. Eventually we pulled up at a roadside shack, where drinks and snacks were on sale. At the sight of a party of English journalists coming in out of the night, the proprietors looked as astonished as if they had been invaded by Martians.

On many miles of the next stretch it seemed the road surface had been completely eroded. We lurched along at walking pace, with expletives coming from the back seat, where Aggers had stretched himself at full length. Then the oil filter came off.

There were a few stops to sort that out and then we found our road blocked by a tree trunk. The bus was then surrounded – apparently by bandits. Our courier, Raghu, who claims his uncle is a maharaja, went down the steps to talk to them. After ten minutes, we were allowed to move on. We asked Raghu how he had saved our lives.

'I told them to fuck off!' he announced proudly. 'They were only minor dacoits,' he told us.

We overshot the turning to Jamshedpur by about ten miles, which added to an already very long journey – in total the bus ride took ten hours.

Some of the town, as we drove into it, looked quite pleasant, but that certainly did not include the Hotel Natraj. However, such a journey makes even a grubby, dimly-lit room with frosted windows and a rock-hard bed seem welcome, though I drifted off to sleep to the sound of the Brummie tones of one of our number in the corridor, protesting, 'You're treating us like animals!'

At the ground next day, I was introduced to the man selected to do the scoring for the BBC at the one-day international. 'This is Mr Mukerjhee. He is the second-best scorer in all of West Bengal.'

It begged a question. 'Who is the best?' I asked.

'I am,' said the proud official.

Mr Mukerjhee's local knowledge was tested next day by Aggers. The weather seemed unsettled, so his help was sought. 'Is it going to rain, Mr Mukerjhee?'

'Oh no.'

Within minutes it was pouring.

As the rain continued, Aggers turned again to Mr Mukerjhee. 'Is this going to carry on all day?'

'Oh yes,' came the confident reply.

The rain quickly stopped, the players re-emerged and finished the game.

As India were going down to defeat, the crowd got hold of the metal numbers from the scoreboard and started skimming them head-high at the Indian fielders with lethal intent. The result – remarkably – gave England a three-one lead in the six match series.

That tour finished with two one-day internationals in as many days at Gwalior, about 250 miles south of Delhi. Although accommodation had been booked and confirmed months before, the president of the Indian board of control, Madavrao Scindia (who just happened to be also Maharaja of Gwalior), cancelled all the bookings in order to keep rooms for guests of the board. The rumour was that the British press would be put up instead at Agra, 90 miles away. As I had to be there the day before and then early on each match day to set up, this was not going to work.

Together with the press photographer, Graham Morris, I took the train down from Delhi the day before the first match. The hotel manager confirmed that there were no rooms for us. Though he refused to say how that had come about, he did advise going to the ground to see members of the cricket board.

Wednesday 3 March 1993

Happily the first person I found at the ground was Cammie Smith, the match referee, who asked how things were going. When I told him, he took me to Mr Nagaraj, the board secretary, and made it clear that the ICC would be interested in how this was resolved.

It took time, and when I returned the hotel manager seemed nervous to go against the wishes of 'His Highness', but eventually we were given a couple of rooms.

India won the two back-to-back matches, to square the one-day series.

It was a slightly depleted party that went on to Sri Lanka after that. No Graham Gooch for England and no Jonathan Agnew for the BBC, after both had opted to skip that leg of the tour. Two one-day internationals were played, either side of a Test match. In mid-March Colombo was as hot as I have ever been in my life and Sri Lanka made short work of beating England in all three games.

In the second one-day international in Moratuwa, a chaotic ground just south of Colombo, the wheels really came off the England effort, with batting, bowling and fielding all falling apart. A measure of how badly the news had been going down at home came in an interview with Bob Bennett, conducted down the line from London by Mark Saggers. Bob had to defend himself against a fairly savage bit of questioning, some of it rather ill-informed, based as it was on the mischievous picture-led stories from India.

Despite the fact that my next visit to Sri Lanka had its trials, wrestling with the problems of covering a series with no commentary rights, I have always been very fond of the beautiful island. I was back there in 2002 for an enjoyable little trip to cover the Champions Trophy, split between two grounds in Colombo.

A run of tours for which Talk Sport had secured the

broadcasting rights was broken in 2001, when England went to India for three Tests before Christmas and then returned in the new year for a one-day series. After Talk's coverage of three successive tours, we were suddenly flavour of the month in the BBC, even with people who had never been our allies.

As a result, I was allowed to take an engineer on both legs of the Indian tour for the first time, and on to New Zealand afterwards. For me it was untold luxury, not that, as I see from my diary, it prevented me doing all the jobs at times – commentator, on the phone when the line went down; engineer, when he was called away to look after Pat Murphy on Radio 5; scorer, when our man for that tour, John Brown, was taken ill. In Ahmedabad I was even, to my considerable surprise, asked to do a couple of commentary shifts on All India Radio.

But although having an engineer – Andy Leslie – was enormously helpful it did not mean that we completely avoided the usual hiccups. As, for instance, on the eve of the first one-day international in Calcutta.

Friday 18 January 2002

I had become aware that we would need different passes for this match from those issued by the Board of Control. When I went to the ground to secure these, though, I was initially refused entry by a senior policeman. Eventually an official said that I would get my passes if I came with a list of names at 3 o'clock.

Now for the ISDN lines. I found a telecom official who insisted, 'You have no booking. Delhi has no record of any booking.' But after an hour or two of this stand off, a couple of engineers arrived who knew all about it, and twenty minutes later Andy was talking to London.

Now I was back to the Bengal Cricket Association with my list of names for the passes. I was told to come back at 7, when the passes would be issued.

When I did return, I found utter mayhem. The treasurer and assistant secretary were sitting in an office with a mountain of tickets, screaming hysterically at a large crowd of people, who were screaming equally hysterically back at them. This continued for another four hours.

Hardly anyone was issued with any passes, and they tried to get me to go away with half the number I needed. It then became apparent that all the passes had to be taken to the police headquarters to be signed by the commissioner and of the last batch of 80, only ten had been returned, while 70 had been retained by the police.

At 11 p.m. the TV people, waiting for 60 passes, were awarded 40. I left with six of the nine I had asked for and left a note with the cricket association treasurer of three carefully selected – and I hoped impressive – names who were still without: Sunil Gavaskar, Henry Blofeld and Angus Fraser. The treasurer promised to ring me overnight and amazingly at 1 a.m. he did so, telling me where the passes would be in the morning.

In fact next day it was the secretary of the Indian board who had to sort out the remaining passes for me. That was the worst – but not the last – of the battles for passes on that tour.

It was while awaiting a delayed flight during that same tour that Aggers and I were told that producing our boarding passes would get us a free meal. Hungry as we were, we hurried to take advantage of this offer, hoping to be presented with a delicious hot repast. We were somewhat crestfallen, then, when the man in charge of this bounty reached into a drawer of his desk and produced a grubby, unwrapped cheese sandwich, curling at the corners. We both declined, and he replaced it in the drawer, ready for the next victim.

In that trip of six one-day internationals we zig-zagged round India on a routine of travel one day, practice and preparation the next and the match itself on the day after. Then the three-day cycle would start again. On the field, with four matches played, India were three-one up. Then England won by two runs in Delhi, where Nick Knight made a hundred and Ashley Giles took five wickets. In the last match in Bombay England won again, this time by five runs, with Flintoff pulling off his shirt to run round bare-chested after taking the last wicket to tie the series.

Towards the end of the following year, England had their first Test tour of Bangladesh.

Wednesday 8 October 2003

We came at last through the rain clouds a long way into our descent into Dhaka. As a result, my first sight of Bangladesh was from little more than a thousand feet and my first impression was of an awful lot of water. There were swollen rivers everywhere, linked by flooded fields. Could there be 22 dry yards anywhere?

An agent with not much English was there to meet us and take a small group of us press through the downpour to a minibus. When we pulled up at a fairly basic-looking hotel we all cried 'Wrong one!' but the driver spoke no English.

It took some discussion at the hotel before we discovered

that our agents in London had been told that until the
Commonwealth Parliamentary Association had finished
their conference in the city, this was the best we were going
to get. It was a pity they had not bothered to tell us.

With Dhaka being statistically the most densely populated
city in the world, being in an hotel any distance from where
the team were staying presented problems – and a lot of time
stationary in traffic jams. In fact, estimating the time for any
journey was an impossibility. It was quite normal for a theoretical five-minute trip to the Test ground to take an hour and
a half. Thus it was good, not just from a comfort point of view,
that we moved hotels within three days.

The rain fortunately eased up before the business of the
tour began. England were just given a little bit of a fright in
their first ever Test against Bangladesh in Dhaka. They displayed some familiar frailty against sub-continental spin, so
that, although they had taken a first innings lead of 92, by the
fourth evening, when Bangladesh were 153 ahead with four
wickets in hand, England were looking at the possibility of an
awkward run chase on the last day.

Saturday 25 October 2003

A mournful youth was ushered into our little box first thing,
proudly bearing on his pass the handwritten legend 'BBC
BOY'. He was there to help us, we were told, but a) it was the
last day and b) he spoke not one word of English, so c) he
was useless. Poor chap.

We need not have worried about the win. It was wrapped up
efficiently, taking another nine overs to bowl them out, with

Harmison and Hoggard sharing the spoils. That left 164 to win and it took only 40 overs to get them.

It had been decided by the programme planners before the tour that we should not mount a *Test Match Special* commentary on either this leg in Bangladesh or the one in Sri Lanka that England were moving straight on to. I had protested this, asking what I would say to the high commissioner of either country if they were to visit the commentary box during the Oval Test (not a completely unlikely event) and ask the reason for this snub.

There was a partial climb-down, but only for the Sri Lankan Tests and initially only to go on the fledgling 5 Live Sports Extra, the digital network, though Radio 4 did subsequently take the commentary.

In Bangladesh I did encounter some disappointment (and a little affront) that we were not doing commentary, not least from the local commentary team, one of whom came into the little hutch that Simon Mann and I were operating from in Dhaka. He announced himself as 'Bangladesh's John Arlott' and stood behind us, muttering a running commentary to demonstrate how good he was.

Local officials told me that if we were not going to buy rights, we could not use the satellite dish to broadcast our reports at the ground. I therefore concocted an elaborate system using two telephones wired into our equipment, which thankfully was a modified success.

From home, Jonathan Agnew rang to ask why our broadcast line did not sound as good as the one Jack Bannister was using on Talk Sport.

'Because he's not here,' I said. 'He must be reporting from his living room in Wales.'

After the congestion of Dhaka, Chittagong felt pleasantly relaxed, though Simon Mann and I were billeted in a gloomy hotel called the Harbour View – a misnomer on both counts. We did at least find a rooftop terrace from which we could set up our portable satellite dish and get a good signal for our post-match reports. We had had to do the same in Dhaka, where the hotel manager had shown us the way through the plumbing in the loft to gain access to the flat roof. I thought there that we might have a problem when Bangladesh's prime minister visited the hotel and the roof also became a vantage point for police marksmen. However, they seemed to be dis-armingly trusting of us.

That tour saw the start of the build-up to the winning of the Ashes in England in 2005. After that historic victory over Australia, England were off to Pakistan. That country was in the aftermath of the earthquake that had struck Kashmir a fortnight before England arrived. Practice sessions and the opening match at the Pindi Stadium were played under the flight path of relief helicopters heading north.

The captain, Michael Vaughan, and his vice-captain, Marcus Trescothick, went on one of these missions in an RAF Chinook helicopter and the team visited the Islamabad hospi-tal where injured survivors were being treated.

Previous unrest and the situation in Afghanistan meant that the tour was largely confined to the Punjab, though there was a foray to Karachi for a one-day international. The first Test was in Multan, a new venue for most of us, which meant some more interesting hotel accommodation.

Most of the press were in the Shiza Inn. Aggers and I checked in to adjacent rooms and, seconds after entering his, he gave a cry of anguish and was out again quickly enough to accost the porter who had guided us upstairs. Aggers had inspected the bathroom and found that instead of a European-style lavatory bowl he had been blessed with a hole in the floor. I checked mine while he was explaining to the porter that he was not up to using this arrangement for a week.

His room was changed, but a few days later the correspondent of the *Sunday Telegraph* arrived and was offered this room as the only one still available. On finding that I was next door he enquired, 'Are you a squatter or a sitter?' The next day I saw him hurry towards me with a pained expression and so, without the need for an exchange of words, I handed him my room key.

The Shiza Inn, finding itself under the considerable pressure of accommodating a large number of western journalists, went out of their way to try to help. As well-intentioned as their hospitality was, it would sometimes have been better if they hadn't bothered. Spotting the fact that many of us were keen on an omelette for breakfast to get us through the day, they took to making a large quantity of the things and stacking them in a cold, rubbery pile well in advance of anyone arriving for the meal.

Friday 11 November 2005

At breakfast I struggled to get a warm omelette. Seeing my eventual relative success on this front, CMJ thought that he, too, would go for a freshly made one. 'Without the bits, though,' he said, eyeing the chopped up onions, peppers and chillies in mine.

'Oh, sir, bits are complimentary,' said the head waiter.

When it arrived it had bits. 'Bits are compulsory, Christopher,' I told him.

The hotel had a small, sparsely grassed courtyard from which we found that we could just get a bead on the satellite to broadcast. We were even able to run a power cable from a nearby washroom. The only problem was that it was infested with mosquitoes. I was required by Aggers and anyone else using the equipment in the evening to light up my pipe as an insect repellent.

After a couple of days, however, this courtyard was taken over to erect a great coloured canopy for a wedding party. The hotel management were most solicitous in showing us to the roof and laying on electricity, chairs and a table, creating a new studio for us amid the drying laundry.

The glory of the little satellite dish was our ability to broadcast from anywhere. When the team visited a local orphanage, we put Kevin Pietersen on to talk to Radio 5 Live from the playground; when Marcus Trescothick had to take over the captaincy from an injured Michael Vaughan in Multan, he was put on the air live from the stadium nets and when a domestic crisis threatened his continuation on the tour while we were en route from Multan to Faisalabad, we stopped the convoy of press minibuses (despite an unsympathetic group of writers) for Aggers to broadcast from the roadside.

England collapsed in their second innings at Multan, when they looked certain to win. Shoaib Akhtar was the destroyer on the last day as they chased a modest target.

In Faisalabad our accommodation was the Chenab Club. It is a relic of colonial times and not hugely updated, but they went to enormous lengths to provide wi-fi computer access for their journalist guests. It was perhaps reassuring to see the notice on the door of the dining room: 'MAID/ MALE SERVANTS, GUNMEN AND DRIVERS ARE NOT ALLOWED'.

That second Test was drawn, but some big batting from Pakistan in Lahore took the final Test away from England.

My final tour of India for the BBC began in February 2006, covering warm-up matches at the Brabourne Stadium in Bombay and in Baroda. A number of place names in India have been officially changed over the years since independence. Some have caught on and some have not. Baroda is officially 'Vadodara', but I never met anyone who called it that and, as soon as you arrive you are greeted by a sign advertising The Bank of Baroda.

When Bombay was officially changed to 'Mumbai' I was about to set off on a tour to India. I checked BBC policy on this and no one – including the Delhi office – seemed inclined to rule, indeed, all seemed surprised to be asked. What I have found in subsequent visits to India is that no one – at least nobody I dealt with – calls Bombay 'Mumbai', although one Indian commentator told me that he grew up calling it Mumbai, but then his family spoke Marathi. Most, on the other hand, do call what was Madras, 'Chennai', so I suppose one should go along with that.

It was in Baroda that we first became aware of problems with Marcus Trescothick, though their nature was a closely guarded secret. The fact that the rest of a fairly substantial sick list was being given to us in gruesome detail, meant the vague remarks about Trescothick sparked wild speculation. It wasn't until several months later that his depression became public knowledge.

Michael Vaughan was already on the injured list, with a recurrence of the knee problem that had kept him out of the first Test in Pakistan.

Saturday 25 February 2006

England lost the match to the BCCI President's XI by eight wickets and by the close of play we had also lost Trescothick from the tour – on his way home for an undisclosed reason. England finished the match with Flintoff in charge.

The injury list was obviously of some concern, because I saw the manager, Phil Neale, having a net. Afterwards it was Michael Vaughan who faced the press, wryly finishing his interview with me with, 'If this carries on, you could get a game.'

Tomorrow we're off to Nagpur for the first Test.

Two days later, Vaughan's knee had not improved and Flintoff was confirmed as the captain for the Test. Further, they had sent for a batsman from the England 'A' side in the Caribbean – Alastair Cook. The day after arriving on the tour, he was opening the batting for England – and doing remarkably well.

Arriving at the hotel in Nagpur, I searched early on for a suitable site for the satellite dish. Swimming pool areas are often a good idea for this and – remarkably – this hotel said it had one.

Sunday 16 February 2006

The pool was – quite literally – a rubbish dump, full of builder's rubble, including broken lavatory pedestals and old bits of pipe work, with a pig snuffling through it to see what he could turn up. Thankfully I found 'the lounge' – a room with not a single stick of furniture in it, but a handy terrace outside which faced the right way for the satellite.

England had the best of most of the drawn first Test, but in Chandigarh they suffered an all-too-familiar second innings collapse and lost.

While the also all-too-familiar problems of communications and passes had been moderately chaotic in Nagpur, in what purported to be the more sophisticated surroundings of the Punjab Cricket Association at Mohali, they were more deliberately obstructive. Passes were released gradually with great reluctance, and only when they had put the recipient up against a wall to photograph him. I had to go online to find pictures of those who were not making an early visit to the ground.

While the telecom tests on the day before the Test match were ultimately successful, no line appeared on the first morning. We had a problem, because the line of sight for transmission to the satellite, if we needed that back-up, was directly behind us and there was no window or balcony on that side of the building nearer than three floors below our box. My cables simply would not stretch that far. However, we realised that the press box was way below us and I could just about reach a satellite point from the front desk of that.

So we went on the air like that, with cables at full stretch down corridors and across gangways, protected by an abundance of the outside broadcast producer's friend – gaffer tape. There was one other niggling worry with this arrangement, though, because the box on the satellite dish had only an hour and a half's worth of battery.

It took far too long to establish that the problem with our booked broadcast lines was not a fault but a deliberate block put on by the Punjab Cricket Association, who wanted some cash up front. Fifteen thousand rupees was suggested by an elusive official – and it had to be cash. That was the equivalent of about two hundred pounds and a great deal more than I had in my back pocket. I persuaded him to take a promissory note and said I would sort some cash out for him for the next morning.

Thursday 9 March 2006

He took my letter on BBC headed paper to be counter-signed by five other officials, before reluctantly agreeing that the lines would be opened 'after some time'. In fact it only took a quarter of an hour.

The London studio suggested waiting until lunchtime to make the switch of commentary positions, but I was not sure we had that much battery time left. When we did change onto the regular ISDN broadcast line, I packed up the dish and found it saying there was one minute left on it!

Before the third Test in Bombay, I got on to the head office of the television company, Nimbus, from whom we had bought the series rights, to ensure that this sort of thing did not happen again. Two days before the Test I was at the Wankhede Stadium.

Thursday 16 March 2006

I got a call from Salil, the man from Nimbus, who said he would be at the ground at 2.30 to discuss the accreditation and the ISDNs. I went down for the second time in the day to meet him. He turned up at 5.30 and knew nothing about ISDNs.

Friday 17 March 2006

I had been assured that the telecom men would be at the ground by 10 a.m. and Salil had promised to be there 'first thing'. He came at 4.30 p.m. The telecom engineers started work at 6.30 p.m. and at 7.45 decided that it was not going to work tonight.

Saturday 18 March 2006

The first day of the Test.

Last night the telecom engineers had said they would be at the ground at 8 a.m., 'without fail'.

They weren't, of course, but I was there early to get the satellite dish fixed up. I found a narrow ledge on which I could lash it with copious quantities of gaffer tape.

The telecom men arrived at 9.40, ten minutes before we were due on the air. By lunchtime they had Radio 5 and the Asian network positions working and had sorted out *TMS* just before tea.

While all this was going on, we had a rare – indeed unique in my experience – visit from a member of the BBC Sport management, who was appalled at the filth and conditions we were working in, particularly as he was the man who had negotiated the far from cheap rights.

England won that Test match and in the celebration that they had, after all, squared the series, we were joined at the hotel by Stephen Fry, a previous frequent visitor to the commentary box at home.

He came out with us for what was, for some of our party, an end-of-tour dinner at a nearby restaurant. Amazingly, as we were tucking in, the restaurant door opened and Griff Rhys-Jones walked in. The two comedy legends were amazed to see each other and Griff joined the table.

The evening was not so happy for Christopher Martin-Jenkins, who was the man on whose recommendation we had come to the restaurant. He was, as is his wont, not ready to accompany us when we set off, but said he would join us soon. The evening was then punctuated by a series of text messages of increasing desperation. He had been taken by taxi to another restaurant of the same name and even shown in to a private room where some British businessmen were dining. They were naturally very surprised to see him. Now his driver was lost and confused and from the agitated nature of the texts, so was Christopher. He arrived as we were paying the bill, but a couple of kind-hearted souls agreed to stay with him as he bolted a meal.

Unfortunately, there was almost literally a sting in the tail for CMJ, as that hasty meal laid him low.

This was my eighth trip to India and my last, for the BBC at least. Every time I got on the plane home after one of these trips there would be an inevitable feeling of relief. But there would also be a strong feeling that I would be very disappointed if I never saw this amazing place again.

The Cricket Highlights (vi)
Bombay 2006

On Saturday 25 February 2006, Marcus Trescothick left the England team playing its warm-up match in Baroda and flew home. At the time the reasons for this sudden departure were not disclosed. Michael Vaughan was suffering a recurrence of his knee problems and he, too, would shortly be told that his tour was over. Simon Jones followed hard on his heels with a similar complaint.

England moved to Nagpur for the first Test in apparent disarray. With captain and vice captain both out, Andrew

Flintoff would lead the side. As already mentioned, they sent for a replacement opening batsman from the 'A' tour in the Caribbean – hardly a quick journey to Nagpur. This was the 21-year-old Alastair Cook. The day after arriving in India and getting himself to Nagpur, he was opening the batting for England. His 60 in the first innings and unbeaten century in the second played a large part in England having much the better of a draw.

He had less fortune in the second Test in Chandigarh, where a second innings batting collapse cost England the match.

And so to Bombay, with India leading the three match series one-nil. The start of the match was ill-starred. Steve Harmison was out with an injured shin and Cook had picked up a stomach bug. Ian Bell would have to open the batting with Andrew Strauss.

Maybe these problems in the opposition camp were what inspired the Indian captain, Rahul Dravid, to put England in when he won the toss. It was a big mistake.

By tea on the first day, India had removed only Bell, after which Strauss and Owais Shah had added 106 together. Shah, who had just reached 50, had to retire hurt at the interval, with cramp in the hands, but the runs just came faster in the last session – 114 of them, for the loss of Strauss for 128 and Pietersen for 39. It was 272 for three at the end of the first day.

Shah returned to the wicket next morning when Paul Collingwood was caught behind off Sreesanth for 39. Flintoff, whose presence at the head of the team in Nagpur had seemed to stiffen their resolve, was caught on the boundary for 50 and they also lost Geraint Jones before lunch, which was taken at 345 for six. Ninth out, caught at slip off Harbhajan for 88, Shah helped three members of the tail-enders club add 52, of which he made 34.

England were all out half an hour before tea for exactly 400 and soon after the interval, Hoggard had removed both openers. Anderson got Tendulkar caught behind for one and India were 28 for three. By the end of the second day, Dravid and Yuvraj Singh had steadied things a little, but they were still 311 behind at 89 for three.

In the second over the next day, Geraint Jones took a diving catch to dismiss Yuvraj off Flintoff for 37, but England approached lunch with little more encouragement and Anderson had both Dravid and Dhoni dropped off his bowling. Then, in the last half hour of the morning, one stuck, with Dravid at last nicking a ball to Jones for 55. With half the side out, India were still 258 behind.

Now it was up to Dhoni. He lost Irfan Pathan soon after lunch for 26 and then was himself run out by a direct throw from Anderson for 64. It was 212 for seven. That India eventually got up to 279 was thanks to a lively ninth wicket partnership between Anil Kumble, who made 30, and Sree Sreesanth, who was 29 not out at the end.

But India's deficit as England started their second innings late on the third day was 121. With both openers out and only 21 on the board, it didn't look so bad for the home side. They would need a further breakthrough in the morning, though.

But the fourth morning only gave them two England scalps, one of them the nightwatchman, Udal. Still, losing Shah run out in the first over after lunch, meant that half the side were out with the lead only just past 200. So the sixth wicket stand that took them into the final session of the day was invaluable. Collingwood and Flintoff put on a watchful 66 together.

Harbhajan had Collingwood caught and bowled for 32 and

Geraint Jones followed, holing out at backward square leg for three. But Flintoff rode his luck in the face of the spinners, shepherded the tail and got to his 50 before he was ninth out, stumped off Kumble.

England's demise for 191, with Kumble taking four for 49, left India a possible 313 to win and still eight overs of the fourth day to go. But it was Anderson who took advantage of those few overs to bowl the makeshift opener, Irfan Pathan. India were 18 for one at the close of play. While a rate of three and a quarter runs an over was faster than the match had been seeing, it was not an obviously impossible task to make 295 on the last day.

It looked harder at 35 for three after 50 minutes, with Wasim Jaffer and the nightwatchman, Kumble, both out. But Tendulkar and Dravid were still there at lunch and, even with the great Sachin in a lean patch, that represented the potential, at least, to save the match.

The inspiration that England called on in their dressing room during the lunch interval came from an unexpected source. For the men in white, it was the man in black – Johnny Cash. They raucously joined in with 'Ring of Fire', to ignite themselves for the next session of play.

It worked. Flintoff had Dravid caught behind in the first over after the interval. Tendulkar followed in the next, caught at short leg by Bell off Udal. Sehwag had had to bat down the order after being off the field injured. He only lasted five overs before Anderson had him lbw. In seven overs since lunch, India had lost three wickets for two runs.

Now Yuvraj Singh and M.S. Dhoni were the last realistic line of defence. Defence, though, did not seem on Dhoni's mind when he went for a huge hit down the ground off Udal. The fielder under the skier was Monty Panesar. He did not get a hand on it. We could be sure that Dhoni would not have another such rush of blood.

Or could we? Two balls later, he did it again to the same wretched long-off fielder. We held our breath. Shaun Udal had plenty of time to contemplate the chances.

When Panesar held onto the catch there was an explosion of relief in every Englishman. For all the Dravids, Tendulkars and Sehwags who had gone before, it seemed the most significant moment of the day. India were 92 for seven.

They lasted only another quarter of an hour. Flintoff, the captain, took his third wicket, when he dismissed Yuvraj for 12 – the second top score in the innings – and Udal, whose 35th birthday had been the first day of the match, wrapped up the rest, for figures of four for 14.

Since lunch India had lost seven wickets for 25 in the space of fifteen overs and two balls. Flintoff was man of the match and man of the series. England had won by 212 runs and squared the series.

7. The Commentaries

'Time spent in reconnaissance is never wasted' is an old military adage much beloved of my father. On returning from a few of these overseas tours, I was able to tell him that it is sometimes totally wasted.

On the sub-continent in particular, whole stadia, let alone commentary boxes can be altered overnight to the point that what you inspected the previous day is no longer recognisable. My first *TMS* production in India was a case in point. On the day before the first one-day international in 1981–82, I had seen the barren concrete cave at the back of the stand at the Sardar Patel Stadium in Ahmedabad. The next morning it was totally transformed by heavy, dusty hangings and an expanse of scratched perspex that not only obscured the view but had the additional effect of making the box completely airless.

One place where reconnaissance might have been unnecessary was the Wankhede Stadium in Bombay. Nothing ever seemed to change at the ground that was built by the Indian cricket board to cock a snook at the Cricket Club of India, custodians of the Brabourne Stadium just round the corner. (An English equivalent would have been the ECB having a row with MCC and building a big ground in Hampstead out of spite.) It may be in the financial capital of India, but the Wankhede was scruffy when I first went there in 1981. When

I returned for my eighth visit in 2006 it appeared to have had no maintenance or even cleaning since my first visit.

Saturday 18 March 2006

Aggers opened his commentary with remarks with which we all agreed. 'There are grounds whose names reflect their grandeur, like Lord's, or their beauty, like the Rose Bowl. The name of the Wankhede Stadium is just as appropriate.'

I am told by my former colleagues, who covered the World Cup final there in 2011, that the rebuilt version is much improved. I hope the authorities will maintain it in that condition and not allow it to become a national disgrace again.

There are commentary boxes in India that I remember with some affection. On my first tour those in Madras and Bangalore were both slung high under the roof of the stadium. At the time I reckoned the Madras one to be the highest I had worked in, but I had not then been to the Wanderers in Johannesburg, which must claim that honour – though with stiff competition from the new media centre at Lord's.

When I was last in Madras – or Chennai, as it is now known – the commentary box was not much bigger than a phone box, but happily then we were only covering a one-day international so the sardine-like confinement was not too prolonged.

The old Madras box's main drawback was the distance to the telegraph office in the bowels of the stand for my regular updates on Radio 2. I would have to edge along rows of seats, which had been packed so tightly that there was scarcely room for the occupants' knees, let alone someone trying to find a gangway. The trick was to vary the route, in order to annoy different people each time. All this to arrive in a caged area near the dressing room. England players passing by would push nuts at me through the bars.

On my first two visits to Calcutta, we operated from a box very high up at the back of the stand. With many rows of seats stretching down in front of us, we were a long way from the playing area. I did my first *TMS* commentary in Calcutta, starting on the last day of 1984. Being at the back of the stand, there were a couple of large pillars one had to try to see round. With a fairly wide-fronted commentary box, our method was to separate commentator and expert summariser by a great enough distance that between them they had the outfield covered.

Early on while I was commentating, the ball was played into the dead area behind one of the pillars, which could hide as many as three fielders. As it did not emerge, I suggested that it must have been fielded. Jack Bannister, who was with me said, 'Actually, it was a dropped catch.' Not a good start.

That stand had been rebuilt by the time I next went to Eden Gardens and the boxes were at a much better height for commentary, and open-fronted, which I prefer for radio. Unfortunately they were also a great deal smaller. Changing commentators was an exercise in contortion beneath a large wall-mounted television. Thus, when Mike Gatting was out to the first ball of an over in the 1987 World Cup final, the commentary on the actual ball was done by the summariser, Peter Roebuck, because the business of getting CMJ out and Blowers in had not been completed in time.

In the recce of a commentary box, you have to look at all the practical logistics, such as where it would be best to put the scorer, for instance, so that commentators, who change every twenty minutes, do not fall over him or her. You have to check the view of the scoreboard, though on some grounds the fact that you can see it does not mean that it will be reliable.

In Nagpur in 2006 I found when I first inspected our quite spacious greenhouse of a box, that the commentary desk of black polished granite became hot enough to fry an egg on when the sun shone on it. Thin bits of sheet that I found at the back of the box provided little protection and were best deployed as sunshades, hung from the top of the windows. I advised each member of the commentary team to bring a towel from the hotel, to avoid scorched elbows.

Thursday 2 March 2006

The first clouds we'd seen appeared and the BBC World Service forecast even suggested there might be some rain.

'If it rains in Nagpur,' scoffed Geoff Boycott, 'I'll buy that weather girl dinner.'

And, as we were packing up at the end of the day, the first spots of rain came.

Friday 3 March 2006

After some pretty heavy overnight rain, the commentary box had been filled with all the chairs from outside. Rain had trickled down the terracing on which our greenhouse was perched and soaked the red hessian matting on the floor, which now smelt terrible. I started the day trying to dry out anything and everything that had been left on the floor.

Aggers persuaded Geoffrey to admit on the air that he had been wrong about the weather. The moment was recorded

and dropped in later – 'I were wrong.' It's doubtful, though, if
the weather girl will ever get her dinner.

As I feared, the rain triggered power cuts, so we had to
spend most of the day operating on batteries.

On the first day of the Test there, we were intrigued that a
crowded All India Radio box next door seemed to be inac-
tive. I discovered that they had not acquired the broadcasting rights. I remembered a conversation with the AIR head
of sport some years before, when he was amazed that we had
had to pay any rights fee to cover a series in India. The Indian
government had instructed the cricket board that AIR should
be given the rights for nothing. It was a state of affairs he was
sure would continue in perpetuity.

Now, though, cricket in India was big business and it took
until the eve of the second Test to bridge the yawning gap
between the fee demanded and that which AIR felt they could
afford.

The eventual solving of the crisis, in Chandigarh, did give
me a headache. We had been allocated a narrow commentary
box there and, as I set up the day before the Test (making
the best of limited space to accommodate *TMS*, Radio 5 Live,
the BBC Asian network and a reserve position for reports to
Radio 4, Radio Wales and anyone else who needed something)
I was told that All India Radio would be arriving in force to do
their commentary alongside us. With major communication
problems next morning, delicate negotiations for territory
with AIR were just an extra problem.

It was there, during a lengthy rain break, that Aggers –
in jocular fashion – came out with the time-honoured line, 'I
didn't get where I am today...' I reminded him that where

he was today was in a cramped pigeon loft in the rain in Chandigarh.

On my first tour to India, the commentary team had been built round Don Mosey, the crotchety Yorkshireman, who did not suffer fools and included anyone either born south of the Trent or privately educated in that category. There were many other targets in his list of hates, which did not leave much leeway.

We started that tour with Tony Lewis sharing the ball-by-ball descriptions. A successful former Glamorgan captain, Tony had also captained England in India in 1972–73 and his radio essay on the subject later for a one-off Radio 4 sports programme had been so good that when the programme's success had led to the weekly Saturday morning slot, *Sport on Four*, he became its first presenter. Meanwhile, I had been looking for a few new commentators for the 1979 World Cup and so had tried him out.

After he had joined the radio team, he also did some Tests for television. Changing between the two media is not easy for someone doing the radio ball-by-ball commentary. But Tony coped with this switching back and forwards with a spare method to his commentary and a delightfully observant sense of humour.

Eventually, of course, he did move completely to television, becoming the principal front man for the BBC, but he returned to us for a one-off Test match in Calcutta in the nineties as a summariser. Aggers, not having worked alongside him before, immediately commented on how good he was. During his commentary days, he was also cricket correspondent for the *Sunday Telegraph* and went on to the presidency of MCC.

We had an Indian commentator with us for the 1981 series in the person of Ashis Ray, an experienced journalist, who had done quite a bit of broadcasting for the BBC World Service. He was to be with us also on the next tour, in 1984–85, as was Tony Lewis, again for the first two Tests.

On later tours of India we have been joined by Harsha Bhogle, whose talents were brought to my attention by the ABC in Australia, when he was part of their team for a series. In Indian broadcasting he has moved on from the haphazard selection of commentators for AIR to a high profile position on television, doing commentary and hosting quiz shows. Indeed, he is such a recognisable figure that when he was with us in India in 2006 we found him being mobbed by fans just as much, if not more, than Sunil Gavaskar.

In 1984, knowing that I was trying to assemble possible commentary teams in advance of the tour of India, I was contacted by Ralph Dellor. I had known him for some time as a competent freelance broadcaster, who used to do a lot of Sunday afternoon commentaries on BBC Radio London. I had used him in the extensive coverage we had mounted on the 1983 World Cup in England and I was therefore confident that he was someone I could rely on.

He asked me if, should he find himself in Madras around the time of the Test match there (he was en route to Sri Lanka at about that time), I would use him in the commentary team. I said that I would – and what a Test match he had for his debut, with England winning in devastating form. He joined us again three years later in Pakistan for the last two Tests, starting with the infamous match in Faisalabad. There he played a crucial role, even getting what was certainly at the time an exclusive interview with the umpire, Shakoor Rana.

Finding ball-by-ball commentators is always more difficult than finding summarisers. The radio commentator is the camera, describing the action as he sees it unfold.

The summariser, always a former first-class player, acts more like the television commentator, adding colour to the picture that has been painted. In 1981, we relied – probably too much – on a good relationship with the England dressing room for our summarising effort. The manager, Raman Subba Row, who had played thirteen Tests, encouraged the practice and did several stints himself.

I remember Mike Brearley arriving on the tour as an observer and taking me aside to express his reservations. He felt that it had the potential to put the players in a difficult position. I can certainly appreciate that point of view more now than I could as an anxious producer with a small budget, who had to keep the programme going. Not only might it make things tricky for the players sometimes, but the programme itself might be in danger of becoming sycophantic.

Happily, though, the players seemed to enjoy doing it – most of the time.

Sunday 29 November 1981

We had a stream of willing volunteers from the dressing room to act as summarisers. First came Mike Gatting, followed by the manager, Raman Subba Row, who is turning out to be a natural in this business. Then came Paul Allott and Jack Richards, neither of whom have had much cricket on tour.

All had some insight into the problems of broadcasting here. Mike Gatting's chair collapsed when he was mid-sentence, while Paul Allott was greeted with a shower of pigeon droppings coming through the roof and then had to chase a jumping spider across the desktop.

Part of the original plan on that tour had been to use the *Daily Telegraph*'s correspondent, Michael Carey. He was due to make his first appearance for the second one-day international in Jullunder, in the Punjab. However, during the week before, when contact with the UK had been difficult, the BBC's head of sport and the *Telegraph* sports editor had managed to have a row and permission to use Carey had been withdrawn by the paper.

The first we knew of this was the telex he received when we arrived in Jullunder the day before the match. It presented something of a problem. I had done some commentaries on the odd Saturday afternoon county match which had been well enough received and so my sharing the burden with Mosey seemed to be the obvious solution. Predictably, Mosey would not hear of it and the hierarchy in London were too scared of their lord of the north to tell him to get on with it.

Instead he talked himself hoarse for the day, while I tried to get a rotation of players from the dressing room to come and mount the rickety ladder to our open platform of a commentary position.

Following this, one of the press, Steve Whiting of the *Sun*, offered his services as a commentator. Don's immediate reaction to this was a snort of derision. However, when he started to realise that he might be in danger of having me imposed on him as a co-commentator Don declared him to be perfectly adequate.

Steve made his debut in Cuttack, for the third one-day international, in a most unusual commentary box.

Tuesday 26 January 1982

One feature of the Barabati Stadium was a multi-balconied clocktower at one end. As I walked onto the ground with the

players for our first look around, John Lever, came up beside
me and muttered drily, 'And coming in from the lighthouse
end ...'

I found an official to ask where the commentary
boxes were likely to be and he pointed at once to the
lighthouse-cum-clocktower. On the third balcony up the tower
I found the AIR engineers actually setting up our position. It
certainly gave us a splendid view.

A quarter of a century later the clock tower was still there,
and still acting as a perch for broadcasters and photographers. It became rather a favourite of mine over the three
one-day internationals and a four-day game I covered there
on various tours.

My lack of common ground with Don Mosey finally came
to a head in Colombo, at the end of the tour. We had a very
limited commentary team and very limited space too, having
been moved from a position where our view had been completely obstructed by a stand. We were now in the front row
of the press box.

Henry Blofeld and Tony Lewis had both arrived, just for
this Test match. Tony was somewhat surprised to be greeted
by Don with, 'Oh good, we've evened up the grammar school/
public school balance!'

My proposal was that they could do a rotating shift, each
doing a commentary stint and then summarising for the next
commentator. Don's response was that he was good enough
not to need a summariser. That was a piece of pomposity too
far for me and I told him his fortune, to the huge amusement
and enjoyment of the newspapermen looking on. This is what
is known as a 'PBI' – a press box incident.

My brief without Don in Australia in 1982, during a short period when we had no appointed cricket correspondent, was to raise a commentary team out of those who were already there. Henry Blofeld in those days had a lot of freelance work there every (Australian) summer, so he was inked in first. Christopher Martin-Jenkins was now editor of the *Cricketer* magazine, but would be in Australia for the first two Tests in that capacity. The pair of them had been ten years in the commentary business even then, both having been involved in *TMS* for the first one-day internationals in England in 1972. Christopher had made his Test Match debut the following year and Henry in 1974, though he had cut his teeth earlier for a commercial station in the Caribbean.

When assembling that 1982 team, I also naturally went to the veteran Australian commentator, Alan McGilvray.

Alan had started his broadcasting career in 1935, with studio reports on matches in which he was captaining New South Wales. He had been part of the 'synthetic' Test commentaries in 1938, which the ABC mounted in a studio in Sydney, based on cables from England, and during which they famously made the sound of bat on ball by tapping a pencil on a block of wood. Then, in 1948, he joined the BBC commentary team covering Bradman's last tour of England. He missed joining the BBC team in 1953 and 1956, when he was working for a commercial station, but thereafter covered every Ashes Test with us until his retirement in 1985. Such was his status that the ABC used his name in their battle with Channel Nine television as they took over the Australian coverage of Test cricket. A ditty was used: 'The game is not the same without McGilvray.'

When he retired from broadcasting, the ABC put together as good a trio of commentators as I have come across in Jim

Maxwell, Neville Oliver and Tim Lane – all very different in voice and approach, making an ideal contrast with each other.

Jim, a sharp observer with some of his native Sydney's brashness, has noticeably mellowed over the years. Neville, from Tasmania, was originally considered more of a rowing expert, but as regional Australian sports broadcasters have to be versatile, he found himself doing cricket and the editorial staff liked his style and sent him to England in 1989. There he went down well and, probably it did no harm back home that he was bringing news of an Australian victory. He then became head of sport at ABC radio.

Tim is also originally from Tasmania, but settled in the environs of Melbourne. He was dividing his time on the ABC between cricket and Australian rules football and eventually left the radio to concentrate on the latter for commercial television. In 2011 he took me to my first live AFL game and was patient enough to explain the otherwise totally incomprehensible goings-on. Despite the apparent aggression of that sport, Tim is the gentlest of souls and I was delighted to get him back on *TMS* for two Tests on the 2006–07 tour of Australia.

In 1982, the ABC generally seemed a bit disappointed that we were not taking their commentary, as we had done in the past. A few individuals quietly asked if there was any sinister reason. I was at pains to make it clear that it was our need to control our own programme, rather than any criticism of them. Alan was happy enough with the arrangement, because he had been irritated on recent tours by having to build the commentary rota round Christopher Martin-Jenkins' need to make regular reports for Radio 2 on the phone.

The series started in Perth.

Friday 12 November 1982

In the commentary box – an open fronted affair with a
high fixed desk across the front for three people to sit
side by side – I had recruited the former Surrey and
England fast bowler, Peter Loader, as an expert summariser.
The general consensus was that he was excellent. Another
TMS debutant was Mike Carey. He sounded understandably
a little nervous to start with, but had some good touches
and seemed to fit in well. Otherwise the faces and voices
were familiar – Henry Blofeld; Christopher Martin-Jenkins,
who had flown in at midnight the night before and yet
seemed to be defying jet-lag; Alan McGilvray, who had to
walk round from the luxury of the ABC box at the far end
from our perch; Fred Trueman, who was there for Channel
Nine television in the air conditioned box above us; and Bill
Frindall, setting out his bits and pieces as usual at one end
of the desk.

At the end of the day I had a great feeling of satisfaction at a
good job done.

So, Michael Carey, forbidden by his paper from joining us the
previous winter, was now part of the team. His efforts drew
comment from one wife, arriving mid-way through the series,
who informed him in a very strong Brummie accent, 'Yow're
very popular in the machine room at Dunlop.' It was a compliment
to cherish.

He was to continue in our team for the 1983 World Cup and
on our next visit to India in 1984–85, where he became my
regular partner in the games of Scrabble which whiled away
waits for delayed flights and overdue phone calls. Being highly
intelligent he was a fearsome opponent. This intelligence also

fed a very sharp wit. He regarded each of his reports for the *Telegraph* as an opportunity to get a joke or a pun past the sub-editors intact.

For instance, a match against India's East Zone in Gauhati at the end of 1984, featured an Indian player called Das and our own Vic Marks. Carey succeeded in slipping in '... stout resistance by Das. Capital bowling by Marks...' He was triumphant when it got into the paper un-subbed.

Jack Bannister and Tony Lewis also took part in the commentary team on that 1982 Australian tour. Jack had had a 19-year career with Warwickshire as a fast-medium bowler, passing a hundred wickets for the season four times. He once told me that after he retired it took two years before everything stopped hurting. He was another who accomplished both roles as commentator and summariser and also alternated between radio and television for a time.

At the end of that tour, when I had left, he joined the ABC commentary team for the one-day internationals and in Sydney found himself – uncharacteristically – getting the giggles. The summariser with him, describing David Gower's dismissal, had ventured the opinion that he would have done better to get his leg over more. As Jack put it to me later, 'I was like a rabbit in the headlights.' 'Wouldn't we all?' he said. Years before the Johnston/Agnew debacle, it was heard on Australian radio. Subsequently, after his time on BBC television, Jack was at the heart of the Talk Sport commentary team.

Before that 1982 Australian tour I had heard the former Australian Test batsman, Paul Sheahan, doing commentary on television. It seemed to be a one-off and as a television commentary it was not quite right. I knew why – it was a perfect radio commentary. Paul was then a housemaster at

Geelong Grammar School not far from Melbourne. When I got in touch with him he was only available for the Boxing Day Test at the MCG, but that was where he qualified to wear the *TMS* tie.

It became my practice to take a couple of the ties with the crossed bats and lightning flash motif with me on tour in case of debut appearances. It had been created in the 1950s as the Test match broadcasters' tie, worn by television and radio commentators on the first day of a Test match. It fell into disuse among our TV colleagues and just became known as the *TMS* tie.

There was a touching little ceremony in the rather gloomy bar of the Park Hotel, Calcutta in 1987, when Tim Rice, after two commentaries on World Cup matches, was presented with his. It might not have meant as much to him as his Oscars, but he seemed quite pleased.

The demands from all BBC outlets from a Test match are extensive these days. Explaining this to foreign cricket authorities is usually difficult. They tend to think one radio organisation means one commentary box. On my early tours, I would get away with a commentary position and a telephone for reports for Radio 2 and Radio 4. In India and Pakistan, where no amount of trying to pre-book a telephone seemed to work, it was always a case of finding the telegraph office or the secretary's office. In Australia it was refreshing to find that if you booked a phone, there was a man waiting to see where you wanted it installed.

With England having won back the Ashes in 2005, I knew that the demands of all BBC networks from Australia in 2006–07 would be prodigious. I also knew that, for all the size of Australian grounds, the press and broadcasting facilities are limited. I was despatched for a whirlwind tour round the five Test venues, which was a worthwhile exercise, if only to explain the size of our operation these days.

Perth had long since been improved to a set of roomy commentary boxes high in the Lillee/Marsh Stand. Even then, while that meant that all other reports could be accommodated at the back of that box, Radio 5 Live had to be on a floor below in a cordoned-off section of a hospitality suite.

The boxes in Adelaide, since we moved from our 1982 elevated Portakabin, have been small and shut in behind thick, tinted glass, a long way from the action. So small was our usual one, that the summariser would sit on the step behind the commentator and scorer.

It was while commentating in here in 1998 that I was handed by Jonathan Agnew, after a phone call from London, a list of the leaders in some golf tournament that was going on. Apparently some misguided editor was keen that we should give this news. No sooner did I have it in my hand than Aggers snatched it back, to scribble another name on the list. Thus, when it returned to me, I discovered that Hugh Jarce was one under par – an old commentary box joke.

I thought to myself, 'Silly boy, if he thinks I'm going to read that out.' But the thought was now in my mind and the chuckles rising in my throat. Trying to suppress the laughter and keep commentating, my glasses steamed up and I looked for help to my expert summariser, David Gower. He just smiled beatifically back at me and left me well alone.

In Sydney, when I first went there, there was only one radio commentary box and that was obviously the ABC's. We had to go outside at a desk tied to a row of seats in the members' stand. The engineer provided by the ABC was an American, who proclaimed himself to be converted to cricket by the end of the Test.

Subsequently the large Brewongle Stand was built on an arc of fine to square leg. Having heard that the South African Broadcasting Corporation commentary team had been put in that, I managed, just in time, to have a requirement for our commentary position to be as nearly as possible on a wicket-to-wicket line written into our contract. The boxes provided for *TMS* since then have been fairly disgraceful for such a famous old ground – the most recent being behind the official scorers, so that the view is not only from the back of the stand, but through two separate panes of glass. Somehow, though, Australians have a way of letting you know that you are the one that is being awkward, not them.

Melbourne is better, though there does sometimes remain the problem of putting in Radio 5's substantial coverage. I can remember trying to sort that out on one very hot, sticky Christmas Eve.

Thursday 24 December 1998

I got a bit of a shock on arrival at the MCG, when I found Sky setting up in the box I had been promised for Radio 5. It took a while to locate the Victorian Cricket Association's media man who had made that promise. His only response was an aggressive and officious, 'That facility is not available'. He seemed unwilling to help any further.

His response to my explanation of our needs was to give me the number of a woman in the VCA office. Her suggestion was the top deck of the Members' Stand, which turned out to be the position we had occupied in 1982.

The telecom man, when I found him, would do nothing for us on Christmas Eve, so I set about working out how to connect that position to our ISDN point in the commentary box. The cable I was carrying would make about two-thirds of the distance, so I went to find an electronics shop in the city.

Flying the cable across the void between the two stands was an interesting exercise. At one point I was using the hooked handle of a long ladle, borrowed from the caterers to lean over a balcony and haul the cable in, in order to secure the necessary join in it.

Amazingly on the day, it worked and Radio 5's reporter, Pat Murphy, got on the air, though I don't think he knew the effort that had gone into saving his bacon.

The requirement to be behind the wicket-to-wicket line took us very high under the roof of the new stand at the Gabba in Brisbane. The boxes there had been designed for match officials and police control at football matches. Hermetically sealed as they were, I had to run a microphone for some sort of outside effect through the door at the back and then sling it as far as I could over girders under the roof. Thus, when the storm hit to save England at the end of the 1998 Test, the sound was impressive. Henry Blofeld and Vic Marks had such a memorable session describing the rain and lightning that it made an item on Radio 4's *Pick of the Week*. At one stage Vic suggested, 'We've seen lots of lightning, but I haven't heard any …'

At which point he was interrupted by an enormous crash of thunder, right overhead.

'… thunder,' he finished, weakly.

Another under-the-eaves commentary box where the weather is a factor is Wellington, New Zealand. In 2002, the authorities there conned me into paying for a commentary hut to be built for us. It was small, but otherwise ideal, until the southerly change came and the wind blew straight at us, seemingly direct from the Antarctic. After that we certainly knew why they call it 'Windy Wellington'.

Radio Sport, New Zealand, have their own box in the middle of the same gantry, which I shared with them during the 1992 World Cup. On that day when New Zealand played England, Jeremy Coney, the former New Zealand captain, was also in the box. He is generally an excellent and amusing summariser, but on this occasion had been to a wedding the day before. He had not slept much and so he closed his eyes at the back of the box. I was all for rousing him when his turn came, but the Radio Sport commentary team was made of more irreverent stuff. They determined to see how much of the match they could get through without him waking up. The answer was – the whole thing. John Parker did sterling work throughout the day in his place, buoyed, no doubt, by a New Zealand victory.

The 1992 World Cup semi-final in Auckland marked the retirement from commentary of two New Zealand stalwarts, Alan Richards and Iain Gallaway. Richards' commentary spells at home were always interspersed by the need to check on how his horses were running. I had known him from several tours of England. He had played first-class cricket for Auckland and a good level of soccer. He did once suggest to me at the end of a New Zealand tour of England that I ought to have a word with Brian Johnston about treating cricket with too much levity.

While by that 1992 World Cup Alan did perhaps seem ready for retirement, Iain Gallaway, I felt, was going too early. He still had so much to offer. Known as 'Father' to the rest of the team, particularly Bryan Waddle, he used to be assiduous in his homework on the opposition in the nets the day before a game. He showed me his notes to aid recognition and I saw against one player, 'arse sticks out'.

Richards and his successor, Waddle, could get quite morose if New Zealand were not doing well and both had a tendency to join in the general New Zealand disdain for all things Australian.

Early in 1997, in Auckland, New Zealand found themselves staring down the barrel of certain defeat. England had taken a first innings lead of 131 and just before lunch on the final day, New Zealand lost their eighth second innings wicket at 105. The lunch interval followed soon after, with an innings defeat still the most likely outcome. I was sitting in the London studio, waiting to take *Test Match Special* through the lunch interval, as Bryan Waddle finished his summing up with, 'That's it, the wheels are off. Not just one – the whole bloody lot. Back to the studio.'

In the event, the wheels were firmly secured again in a famous last wicket stand between Nathan Astle and Danny Morrison, which saved the match. Morrison went on to do his bit on *Test Match Special* and then television commentaries all over the world, particularly relishing the mayhem of the Indian Premier League.

It's a close contest, but I have no doubt that the best of the overseas commentators I have shared the box with over the years has been Tony Cozier. The Barbadian worked with *Test Match Special* first in the 1960s and has been a 'must have' for any *TMS* involving the West Indies ever since. Generally round the world now he is regarded as a television commentator, even in an era in which his colleagues are almost entirely former Test players. But he is very much part of the *Test Match Special* family.

The new media centre at the Kensington Oval in Barbados bears his name, though, as his father and his son have both graced the journalistic business, we like to tease him that it may be named for one of the other Coziers.

When we first mounted our own commentaries throughout the Caribbean, in 1994, we were allocated a delightful hut on the roof of the Pickwick Pavilion at Kensington. When we arrived on the island four years later, however, it was to find a new stand just being finished off. The top deck would be the press box, we were told, with the broadcasting boxes behind the four rows of writers. Despite the height of this top floor, there was only a shallow rake to the seating, which had the effect that from the second row back, there was an increasingly limited view of the field of play. By the time you reached the proposed commentary boxes, you would not be able to see the middle of the ground, even in the unlikely event that the press all stayed seated and nobody used the gangway in front of the boxes. I have dealt with architects of media facilities in many different places and have found them amazingly clueless about the needs of those covering the game, but this was on a different scale.

I pointed the problem out to the television producer, whose commentators would be in the same boat. Together we addressed the ground authorities, who eventually, reluctantly, acknowledged the problem. We sketched a possible solution, which was constructed in the week leading up to the Test. After some trial and error, it became a gantry over the heads of the press, housing three boxes.

Wednesday 11 March 1998

A small meeting formed on the outfield to discuss the allocation of commentary positions. I was asking the TV people, 'Which is you and which is us?' so that the telecom men could install the lines.

At that point Calvin, from the Barbados Cricket Association's marketing department piped up, 'No, it's TWI television, Voice of Barbados and Caribbean Broadcasting Corporation. No foreign broadcaster there.'

'So where are we going?' I asked.

'I don't know,' he shrugged. 'We have not made provision for you. You probably haven't even got a contract.' Even the television people rolled their eyes at that. Fortunately, experience has taught me to carry a copy of the contract with me in these parts.

A very smart man in a suit and tie joined in. 'Where do you want to go?' he asked.

I pointed back at our old familiar green hut on the roof of the Pickwick Pavilion.

'That's where you go, then,' he said.

As he moved away, I asked Calvin if there was any danger of this, too, being countermanded.

'No,' he said sullenly, 'He's a government minister.'

It took most of the rest of the day to find the key for it, but we were eventually restored to our hut. During the Test match, Henry Blofeld, realising that being so far from the press we would not be fed, arranged for giant pizzas to be delivered daily in the lunch interval.

The only real drawback to that box was the series of five very heavy wooden shutters that had to be manhandled out of the front every morning and back in again in the evening, in the right order every time. It rained during the course of the match and the shutters warped in the wet, making their installation all the more difficult and requiring plenty of 'impact technology' – or bashing them hard, as it is otherwise known. It was interesting how many pressing engagements elsewhere the rest of the commentary team discovered during these operations.

By the time of our next tour of the Caribbean, when we had lost the commentary rights to Talk Sport, we had a far grander perch on the gantry I had helped to design over the heads of the press.

In 1994 I decided that our commentary team for the West Indies tour should include, as an expert summariser, someone from the island we were on in each case. Michael Holding joined us in Jamaica, Ian Bishop in Trinidad and Colin Croft in Guyana. By this time Vic Marks, who was performing as a ball-by-ball commentator on that tour, said to me, 'We're working with all these big fast bowlers who I spent most of my career being terrified of – but it turns out they're all very nice!'

For the last two Tests, I broke the mould of using fast bowlers. In Barbados it was Sir Everton Weekes. Having him – the last and some would argue the greatest of the three 'Ws' – on the team was particularly exciting for me. I remembered my first bat at the age of eight being an Everton Weekes autograph. And who else could it be in Antigua, but the uncrowned king of the island, Viv Richards.

On the first day of the Test, he asked me if I had a pass for him. 'Sorry,' I said, 'I assumed you wouldn't need one here. After all, the stand over there is named after you.'

'They forget,' said the great man, sadly.

So I dug out the only spare pass I had, which had previously been used by Trevor Bailey and still bore his photograph. For the rest of the Test that was what he used, despite the very obvious discrepancy.

I particularly relished the sessions when Viv and Victor, the two old Somerset colleagues were on together. After a couple of days, Vic said to me, 'I thought you were mad signing Viv, but he's really rather good.' He was also the most punctual member of the team, contrary to the usual view of Caribbean attitudes.

Four years later, when I was laying on an end of tour *Test Match Special* dinner in Antigua, I naturally invited him. 'He won't come,' was the general view. 'He's far too well known here.' But he came – and of course the whole restaurant stopped when he strolled genially in.

Heat is another thing that you often have to contend with on tour. I have known some very sticky days at Test matches in Trinidad and I can think of days in Adelaide when opening the door of the air-conditioned media centre was like opening an oven door. But I have no hesitation in declaring the 1993 Test match in Colombo as the hottest I have ever been at. A sparse crowd was confined to the pools of shade afforded by the trees on the grassy banks and my stop watch, carelessly left in the sun, became far too hot to handle.

To make matters worse, after a tour of India, our resources were somewhat depleted. Christopher Martin-Jenkins and I were the two ball-by-ball men, joined by the former Sussex and England fast bowler, John Snow, who was also our travel agent, and Gamini Goonesena, whose first-class cricket career pre-dated Sri Lanka's Test status.

We had a fair-sized, open-sided area for our commentary point, so I could site the desk in a central position to avoid the ferocious sun shining on it at any time of day. In the circumstances, I rotated CMJ's and my stints in half-hours, rather than the usual twenty minutes. Christopher does have a little reputation for forgetting the time and overrunning. In this heat he was consistently handing over early. When John Snow was asked by the England management for some bowling advice in the nets, Gamini found himself doing an uncomfortably long time at the sweat-drenched microphone.

The Military Attaché at the British High Commission, obviously knowing about *TMS* traditions, kindly brought us a cake. Unfortunately, he must have been expecting an air-conditioned box and the chocolate confection quickly became little more than a brown puddle.

I had also conducted a reconnaissance of the small ground to be used for the second one-day international at Moratuwa that followed this Test. This was one of those occasions when the time spent was totally wasted.

Saturday 20 March 1993

All the decisions which had been made at my recce eleven days ago had gone by the board. Nothing had happened. The canopy on the roof I had been promised for a commentary position had not been erected and we had to commentate from a tiny and inadequate press box, made worse by a number of non-working locals, armed with press passes they had obtained from somewhere and the telephone and fax operators, who were crammed in just behind our seats.

In all the circumstances, it was only appropriate that England also had one of their worst days on the field.

By the time of the 2005 tour of Pakistan I was beginning to feel the winds of change in the radio sports department blowing quite fiercely. It was also apparent that it was the intention of the BBC hierarchy that I should. There had been an aggressive edge to a meeting I had been to at the end of the English season, which was ostensibly to review the season's *Test Match Special*. I had felt quite good about the way we had covered the series in which England had recovered the Ashes, but the meeting had been packed with the upper echelons of Radio 5 Live, who were clearly bent on changing the status quo.

Monday 7 November 2005

I managed to get into my e-mails and found one from the head of sport delivering rather terse orders about how *Test Match Special* would be done on the tour and what I should and shouldn't have in the intervals. It contained the chilling line that, since 5 Live Sports Extra was now to be the driving network (which was news to me), we had to 'change the style and tone' of the programme.

There could be no doubting it – I was being ordered to take *TMS* down market. I felt quite sick.

It took some time after that before I realised that it was only because we had been quite successful that they wanted *TMS* to be a leader in pushing the uptake of digital radio. Putting it like that might have made me feel good about it, but then man management has never been a great BBC skill.

Arlo White had been sent out to join the commentary team at the insistence of the management and this was obviously a move in the direction towards 'the Radio 5 sound'. I commented to him that I had noticed that he introduced himself to people in Pakistan as, 'Arlo White, 5 Live', while I would always have said, 'BBC Radio', or just 'BBC'. It was something I had noticed about the culture of the new station – it seemed to view itself as not quite part of the BBC.

I had worked with Arlo in South Africa during the 2003 World Cup, where he had been a reporter, rather than a ball-by-ball commentator. Indeed, he had brilliantly saved my skin with a lengthy contribution from Soweto to help me fill a lunch interval, when every other item had failed to materialise.

In his radio commentary he adopts the 5 Live trait of running something more akin to an interview with their summariser, rather than a description of the action. He is good company and a very fine operator from a studio, preferring to write himself a script than to deliver an ad lib account of what he is seeing in front of him. An incident during the Faisalabad Test match on the 2005 tour highlighted that, when a gas canister exploded in the crowd. In the heightened state of alert at the time, first reactions were that it must be a bomb. I was surprised at his reluctance to switch to the role of live eye-witness reporter, describing what was going on.

(The incident became more notorious for the actions of Shahid Afridi, who took the chance of everyone being distracted to try to rough up the pitch – an action which was spotted by the television cameras.)

I fear that some adverse press coverage of his introduction to the team may have scarred the normally ebullient and cheerful Arlo and I can't help feeling that a more sensitive and less aggressive approach to their plans by the BBC management might have been kinder to him as well as the programme.

One of the scheduling problems that famously hits *Test Match Special* is the Shipping Forecast. With all other Test playing countries except the West Indies lying to the east of the UK, there are other hurdles to be jumped by a Radio 4 long wave audience on a Test Match morning. *Yesterday in Parliament* and the *Daily Service* are both confined to long wave and therefore take over from *TMS* when it is their time.

While resenting the interruption, Aggers was not slow to see the opportunity of a leg-pull in South Africa in 1995. We were sharing the English language commentary with the SABC, who would depart from it for some of the time to carry the commentary on in Afrikaans. It was the days before the digital alternative of Sports Extra existed, so Aggers spotted a period when Radio 4 were at *Yesterday in Parliament* and SABC were taking the Afrikaans description, so his commentary was only being used to record any possible highlights for posterity.

He was on with Geoffrey Boycott when his chance came. After describing a ball bowled and no run scored, he said, 'Mind you, you were a pretty boring batsman.'

Geoffrey was surprised, but silent as the next delivery was described. After a few more allusions to turgid play, he tried to mount a half-hearted defence and if possible to make a joke of it, but Aggers pursued the point, ending with, 'God, you were boring.'

At long last, a shell-shocked Boycott was let into the secret that we had not been on the air to anyone for twenty minutes.

That commentary was mounted in a large glassed-in enclosure at the top of the stand at the Wanderers in Johannesburg. Afrikaans, English, Xhosa, Zulu and other commentaries all came from the same resonant room, which I christened the Tower of Babel. In recent years – and certainly since the World Cup – better facilities have been installed in most of the South African Test grounds.

South African commentators and writers do tend to have a

patriotic slant to their outpourings. I recall one commentator turning up for the first match of the 2003 World Cup actually wearing his team's replica shirt. A New Zealand rugby commentator once said to me that commentary should be biased, but that, I hope, has never been the *TMS* way. The word 'we' is banned from the box in reference to England. If you are the one representative of the BBC in a foreign commentary team on tour, your hosts do treat you as being your team's man, but that should not come over in the way you describe the action.

In South Africa's case, Gerald de Kock was a model of that art, but sadly, when we were in his country he was usually more tied up, first with television duties and eventually as the media liaison man for the South African team. South Africa's political changes have inevitably affected what the SABC does and the cricket commentary has borne part of that change.

As mentioned earlier in the book, political change would be an understatement when it comes to their northern neighbour, Zimbabwe. On my first visit in 1996, I had no idea what to expect.

In the days leading up to the first one-day international, to be followed by the Test, I went to Bulawayo's Queen's Club every afternoon to see what progress was being made, while England were playing a match against Matabeleland on another ground nearby. After two visits, I found that a low platform had been constructed for radio, which would have its view obstructed by Sky's large satellite dish. So I got that moved. Then a canvas screen was hung down one side, to conceal the scoreboard from us. That I found I could roll back. I was not to know that on the morning of the match a large model of an elephant's head would be placed in the same line of sight, as an advertisement for a local taxidermist.

The day before the one-day international a pile of wide, flat boards was left on the platform. I established that there was no further plan to do anything with them, so armed with some wire and a large amount of gaffer tape, I constructed three commentary booths – for *Test Match Special*, Radio 5 and the Zimbabwe Broadcasting Corporation, who I was told, would 'probably' be doing commentary.

Telecom engineers appeared late in the day and left me with eight bare wires and, by trial and error, using an open telephone line to the local exchange and the helpful operator in Harare, I established a broadcast connection with London for both our positions.

The following year I played a part in the outside broadcast production for the funeral of Princess Diana and received more than one effusive and undeserved letter of thanks for my efforts. For getting *Test Match Special* on the air from Bulawayo, which I regarded as a crowning achievement, I heard nothing. That is the way of the world.

We had a very jolly commentary team for that inaugural Test match. Henry Blofeld and Simon Mann arrived just before the one-day match.

Saturday 14 December 1996

Blowers and Simon arrived at the hotel in the evening to a scene of chaos, as a great many of the delegates to the ZANU PF party conference, which has been going on here, had omitted to check out before they went off to the conference hall in the morning. The hotel staff were reluctant to sling politicians out of their rooms, so there was nothing available for the influx of England supporters – including our two.

While it was being sorted out, I offered to buy Blowers a glass of 'Bollinger' in the bar. I was treated to a delighted

'My dear old thing!' before he discovered that Bohlinger is the local beer.

Trevor Bailey and Chris Cowdrey arrived with groups of supporters in tow and we had Jo King to do the scoring.

For Simon Mann it was a *Test Match Special* debut. He had been in the radio sports room for a time and had gone on two or three England 'A' tours, so fitted in immediately. His is a sound commentary method, flavoured with knowledge of the game from a good level of club cricket and a pleasantly light touch of humour. Most of his commentary opportunities have come overseas and I have found him a really good touring companion.

He was back in Zimbabwe with us four years later for a series of one-day internationals, for which we also took Jonny Saunders, who was reporting for Radio 5. And the year after that, the three of us had the perfect trip to Sri Lanka for the Champions' Trophy. There was no travelling involved because all the games were played on two grounds in Colombo and the whole exercise lasted little more than a fortnight. Saunders, who went on to be Chris Evans' sports man on Radio 2, was called on the hotel tannoy as, 'Mr Surrenders', not something he was going to be allowed to forget.

In 2003 the Chittagong Test match in Bangladesh ended on Simon's fortieth birthday. Amazingly, opposite the otherwise fairly awful Harbour View Hotel, a fancy cake shop and a Hallmark card shop stood side by side. Both were as incongruous as an umbrella store in the middle of the Sahara, but at least I was able to surprise him with a cake ablaze with candles to mark the great day.

In front of our commentary position at the Queen's Club in Bulawayo in 1996, a few yards onto the outfield itself, Sky television set up their morning presentation, not handing up to the commentary until the players were on the field. On the first day this meant that both the start and the resumption after lunch were delayed while their equipment was cleared off the ground. After the second occasion, the umpires had a stern word with the production team.

On the second morning, they had cleared the field by the time play was due to start. That would have been fine, but they had stacked the equipment against the end of the sightscreen, which, with Alan Mullally bowling the first over left arm over the wicket, meant that the screen needed to be moved immediately. So play was again delayed while the kit was removed.

On the final evening of the Test, with England striving for a win and Zimbabwe employing an ever slower over rate, Blowers decided that he was the man for the big finish and chose to ignore rotas, signals and the eventual amusement of his colleagues. He embarked on a stint of commentary which, far from the standard twenty minutes, occupied an hour and a quarter. It was a tour de force, but now when anyone – particularly Blowers – over-runs his time in the commentary box, the cry goes up, 'Bulawayo!'

Such is the nature of cricket and of cricket tours, that we spend a great deal of time in each other's company. Generally we are pretty lucky in that company.

The Cricket Highlights (vii)
Bulawayo 1996

There was an edge to the inaugural England/Zimbabwe Test provided by the knowledge that England had opposed Zimbabwe's elevation to the top table of world cricket. When they arrived in southern Africa at the end of 1996, they found many who were keen to twist the lion's tail. It was a series in which England did not cover themselves with glory, but the first Test in Bulawayo made history.

The match followed a one-day international in which England's batsmen had been humiliated on the same Queen's Club ground. At least, after being bowled out for 152, they made Zimbabwe work hard for their two-wicket win.

England's bowling on each of the first two mornings of the first Test was wayward, though better in the afternoons of those two days, thanks to the spin of Robert Croft and Phil Tufnell. There were at that time a couple of class acts in the Zimbabwean side, Heath Streak to open the bowling and Andy Flower, who made 112 of Zimbabwe's first innings 376.

England saved their faces with the bat, replying with 406 and centuries from Nasser Hussain and John Crawley. By the end of the fourth day, England had asserted some control by reducing Zimbabwe to 107 for five. They were only 77 ahead. Was there enough time for England to win it?

Sunday 22 December 1996

It turned into an exciting last day, with Zimbabwe resisting and then eventually all out for 234, leaving England 205 to win in 37 overs.

I was commentating with Chris Cowdrey when the change of innings came and we speculated whether they would go for them. Chris reckoned that if Stewart, rather than Atherton, came out to open with Knight, they were going for it. If Atherton came out, they weren't.

I thought that Atherton would open – and that they would go for the win. And I turned out to be right.

It was a tremendous chase. Even with the field set deep and

negative bowling, runs came quickly. Stewart and Knight set up the chance of victory with 137 for the second wicket. The odds were with them when Stewart was out with 51 needed and eight overs to go. At that point Alistair Campbell seemed to be having to turn to the guidance of David Houghton more and more in the field.

After Stewart's departure, a clatter of three wickets gave Zimbabwe the brake they needed on England's scoring rate. But Nick Knight was still there. Off the final over, bowled by Heath Streak, England needed 11 to win. Knight hit the second ball for six over square leg, prompting Streak to test the tolerance of the Zimbabwean umpire, Ian Robinson, to wide bowling. To the amazement of all of us, he proved very tolerant.

It came down to Knight being run out off the last ball, trying, hopelessly, to scamper the winning run. The scores were level, but as the match had run out of time, it was a draw. Back then this was a unique result in Test cricket, but in November 2011 India and the West Indies achieved a tie-draw in Bombay.

Streak told the British press that he was surprised to have got away with bowling so wide and so he was fined for criticising the umpire – a fine which the newspapers happily paid. Meanwhile the England coach, David Lloyd, was telling all and sundry, 'We flippin' murdered 'em. And they know it!'

That night in the hotel bar the Barmy Army were in full voice. Late in proceedings they were joined by members of the Zimbabwe team, who were in a mood to celebrate their escape. To welcome them, the Barmies changed their song, to, 'You bowl wides, you know you do,' and the players, led by Campbell, their captain, joined in, signalling the wides along with the rest.

Then it was back to Harare for a rather low-key Christmas and the second Test, starting on Boxing Day.

Thursday 26 December 1996

After heavy overnight rain, play started on time. England were put in to bat and started confidently on a slow pitch, but then lost regular wickets rather carelessly, to be 147 for nine at the end of the day.

Friday 27 December 1996

England's last wicket hung on for 40 minutes before Tufnell fell, leaving Crawley top scorer with 47 not out. All out for 156 – something of a debacle.

From that point, it was probably just as well for England that the match was disrupted by rain. After Zimbabwe had taken a first innings lead of 59, Alec Stewart responded with an undefeated century. England were only 140 ahead at the end of the fourth day, with three wickets down. They were probably safe, but in the event the weather took out the whole of the last day.

Not that all embarrassment was ended by that. Zimbabweans celebrated the New Year holiday with two one-day international wins over England, the second by a colossal 113 runs, for a three-nil whitewash.

Friday 3 January 1997

England ran into Eddo Brandes in top form, swinging the ball and starting an irreversible slide to 118 all out with a hat trick and finishing with five wickets, bowling his ten overs straight through.

The Zimbabweans and the crowd were ecstatic and the Barmy Army largely silent. Atherton, though, handled the press conference afterwards brilliantly, facing up to the inevitable assertion that his side had been humiliated by cricketing minnows, with great candour.

8. The Teams

John Arlott always used to say of cricketers that to have known only two bad ones in his years close to the game spoke very well of them as a breed. (Of course he would never let us know who the two were.)

Relationships with the players on my early tours, particularly in India and Pakistan, were much more casual and friendly than they have become later. I would reckon to count all those who toured with England on my first two trips to India as friends.

In between those two tours, I found that it was slightly different in Australia, because it was so much easier for them to go out and socialise or find other leisure occupations in a country where they quite often had friends. On the subcontinent, especially 30 years ago, press and players were more thrown together in a totally foreign environment. We almost always shared hotels, which happens less nowadays. The first few down to breakfast in the morning would join each other at a table, regardless of which side of the divide they came from. That would not happen now.

On my first tour, there were two or three occasions when I was given a lift on the team bus, because the press transport was going to be too late for my needs. And it was a given that any sightseeing expedition – such as they were – would be a joint venture, as on the eve of the first one-day international in Ahmedabad.

Tuesday 24 November 1981

The afternoon featured an excursion to a local mosque, which boasted 'shaking towers'. The drive through the crowded, dusty streets of the city gave me my first real view of Indian life, with all manner of people, beasts and vehicles on the move and activity in every open-fronted business premises along the way.

The 'shaking towers' had been the twin minarets of a small mosque. They had been reduced to one tower, though, with the other little more than a roof-high stump. The first players to rush up the remaining minaret revealed with disappointment that it didn't shake. This was a challenge to Ian Botham. 'I'll make the bastard shake,' he declared, advancing on it.

Looking at the truncated stump of its twin, I wondered if our Beefy had been this way before.

Of course, both parties were much smaller in those days. A manager, a coach, a physiotherapist and maybe a scorer formed the back-up for the team, while, for instance, there were only two photographers among the press on my first tour. And the few separate Sunday newspapermen (and we were all men) who appeared, did so only fleetingly for the most accessible locations.

It was quite normal for me to be invited into the dressing room at the close of play to record an interview. That applied to both sides. Apart from anything else, in India it was often the only place that was quiet enough and no player wanted to be mobbed outside the door.

The press were probably trusted more in small numbers and in more isolated locations, when they seemed keen only to report the cricket rather than rake up a scandal. But, on later tours, dressing rooms became generally a no-go area. Thereafter I did interview Graeme Hick on the massage table in St Vincent in 1994, after the tour manager, Mike Smith, had prepared the way with: 'Hicky, you don't want to talk to the BBC, do you?' Fortunately Graeme Hick is a thoroughly nice man.

In India in the eighties, the press were usually included in the invitations to official functions, sometimes even going to them on the team bus. One such was in Hyderabad.

Saturday 5 December 1981

The Chief Minister of Andhra Pradesh held a reception in the evening for the two teams and the visiting press, though our host did not appear until the two lots of players had been sitting in semi-circles, facing each other for half an hour. They were presented to the great man, each received a large brass plaque and then we repaired to a buffet dinner in the beautiful courtyard of the hall – one of the Nizam of Hyderabad's former palaces.

During the course of the meal, Bob Taylor and Bernard Thomas, the physiotherapist, encouraged me to try paan – betel nuts wrapped in a leaf.

'Keep chewing, it gets better,' was Bob's mischievous advice. It doesn't. It gets considerably worse and at last I saw the amusement on their faces, showing that they knew this.

Keith Fletcher, the captain on that tour, would usually have to introduce his team publicly to whatever VIP was hosting the reception. Being someone who can never remember a name, this was something of a torture for him, but it gave his team a great deal of fun, as they waited to see if he would forget who they were.

It is inevitable that you get to know the captain best, as you are going to interview him more than the rest of his team. Fletcher was brought back to captain this touring side, having not played a Test for four and a half years. He followed Mike Brearley, who had returned to replace Botham in the previous English summer but had made it clear that he was not available for the winter tour.

I always found Keith a very good man, though I am not sure that the way in which he was able to bind together an Essex side to win its first County Championship was quite so successful at international level, and he must surely have found it difficult to come into the side that had just won the Ashes, when he had been out of Test cricket for a period. I went on to renew dealings with him when he later became England coach and I can remember interviewing him in various hotel rooms as he indulged his hobby of tying elaborate fishing flies.

Five of Fletcher's next six successors as England captain were on that 1981 tour and at the time it was being suggested that Geoff Cook, then captain of Northamptonshire, who did not get a Test match until the seventh of the tour, the one-off Test in Colombo, might be the next candidate for the job. The role he played in elevating Durham to a Championship-winning side might suggest that he would have been a good England captain, if only he had the runs to back him up. He was on standby to make his Test debut in Madras, where Ian Botham was due to have a fitness test on the morning of the match. He was fairly late in the bar the night before, when his concerned room-mate, Derek Underwood, appeared to remind him that he might be playing next day. Geoff pointed out – accurately as it turned out – that there was no chance that Botham would not play.

As it was, it was the vice captain on the tour, Bob Willis, who took over the captaincy at the start of the next English summer and took the team to Australia for the next tour. His occasional interventions in India were telling. Doing an interview with me when he was leading the side in the up-country match at Jammu, he expressed his exasperation with David Gower, whose rapid scampering down the pitch had led to a spate of run-outs. 'That's not a dismissal I have very much time for,' said Bob. Then, in Sri Lanka, his dressing room lecture was reckoned to have triggered England's only Test win of the tour. By the next England Test, having turned down the rebel trip to South Africa, he was captain.

Geoff Boycott, it subsequently transpired, had been at the heart of the planning of that rebel tour, though the players who went on it were to elect Graham Gooch as their captain. Fletcher cannot have found the presence of Boycott easy in India, and he also had the man who had started the year as captain, Ian Botham, there. Certainly a couple of members of the team suggested to me that, rather than a united team, they were fifteen players plus Boycott. His hundred in Delhi gave him what was at that stage the highest Test aggregate in the world and it also drew him level with Wally Hammond and Colin Cowdrey in the number of centuries scored for England. But he was to play no further part after the following Test in Calcutta.

The 24-year-old Mike Gatting, with his pudding-basin mop

of hair, was increasingly frustrated at the fragility of his position as an all-rounder in the side, though he did play in five of the seven Tests.

Graham Gooch and John Emburey and their wives were a constant foursome. Most of the wives who came on the tour saved their appearance for the more relaxed end of it in Sri Lanka.

Those who did not make it into the Test side were frequent visitors to the commentary box as expert summarisers, along with the manager. That was a practice that I only used regularly on that 1981 Indian tour, with the notable exception of the emergency recruitment of Vic Marks in Delhi in 1984.

After the experience of being cheek by jowl with the players in India, there was a different feel about the tour of Australia in 1982, though I did find myself being mistaken for one of them in Melbourne. The previous winter, young Indians had tugged my sleeve, apparently thinking I was Mike Brearley. Now, on my way to the MCG, I was asked to sign an autograph book as Bob Taylor. A week after that, in Adelaide, I was pursued by another autograph hunter.

'Look,' I said, 'I'm not Mike Brearley and I'm not Bob Taylor.'

'No, I know that,' said the slightly bemused man. 'You're Vladimir Ashkenazy, aren't you?'

The old practice of the Christmas Day drinks party given by the press for the team was part of an Australian tour until 1994. The manager on that tour, M.J.K. Smith, seemed very reluctant to have his team enjoying our hospitality and by the next visit to Australia the tradition had rather sadly ended.

It was simple enough in 1982. We all gathered round the hotel pool. The *Daily Mirror* correspondent, Chris Lander, and the photographer, Graham Morris, dressed up in tail coats to act as waiters – and Messrs Botham and Lamb duly threw them in the water.

Allan Lamb was a great integrator with the press, just taking everyone as he found them, even when there was a management warning out to be wary of too much contact. (I can remember giving a young player a cheery 'Good morning' in a hotel lift in Australia and being given a terrified look in return, as if I was about to swallow his soul.) 'Lamb's Tours' became something of a feature on tour, as his entrepreneurial spirit would find an expedition worth doing in the most unpromising of places.

In India on the 1984–85 tour he was sent on one occasion down to the boundary to replace Phil Edmonds, who had been having problems fielding there. Lamb was able to entertain an unruly crowd who had been beginning to get under the Edmonds' skin.

Lamb was the vice captain on the 1990 West Indies tour. In the hotel pool in Guyana, when another day's play had been called off for the waterlogged outfield, he was letting out his usual high spirits in loud and extrovert fashion. I was with David Gower, who was broadcasting with us and writing for *The Times*. We watched Lamb's antics and I saw a smile on David's face.

'It would only take a broken finger and we're looking at the England captain,' he said. And we both laughed heartily. Within a fortnight it had happened and Allan Lamb replaced Gooch as captain for the last two Tests of the series.

The 1984 India tour was my favourite to a large extent because of the players who were on it. It was in David Gower's character to tolerate independent thought in his team. He had held out for the inclusion of two who probably would not have been there on the selectors' say-so alone – Phil Edmonds and

Mike Gatting. He made the latter his vice captain. Both were to have considerable influence on the success of the tour.

For all the laid-back appearance, Gower can have a short fuse when he thinks he is being messed around. An informal rest day press conference in Madras turned sour when he was pushed about the decision to employ two nightwatch-men before he came in himself at seven. From my point of view, interviewing him was never a problem. In later years interviews with the captain were rather rationed to before and after a Test unless he himself performed spectacularly. David was always prepared to talk if there was no other obvi-ous candidate.

Left out of the touring team to the West Indies in 1990, Gower was there anyway, doing a column for *The Times* and summarising on *Test Match Special*. After the injury that Gooch suffered in the Trinidad Test, David was summoned to the colours for the game against Barbados, which preceded the fourth Test there. Although the management played down the possibility, it was clear that, if he made runs, he would be likely to play in the Test. As it was, he only got one innings and made four. But I did present him with his *TMS* tie in the nets.

At the end of that same year, included in the England team again, but clearly disaffected with the new ethos, he approached me about the then vacant job of BBC cricket correspondent. We walked round the boundary of a practice game in which he was playing to talk it through, but I could not see him – as I told him – waiting in dressing room corri-dors for prima donna cricketers to give him an interview.

The majority of the players on his 1984–85 tour of India had had the benefit of either public school or university edu-cation and I remember speculating about whether the advan-tages gained from those better sporting facilities might make that the norm for future England teams. That has not really proved the case until quite recently.

It is probably no coincidence that several members of that touring team went on to join *Test Match Special*. Most notable, of course, was Jonathan Agnew, who actually arrived at Christmas in Calcutta as the replacement for the injured Paul Allott. Allott himself, having cut his teeth with us in India in 1981, did a tour of the West Indies working in the *TMS* box in 1994. Mike Atherton was captain by then and I recall sign language between them, which was translated by Allott to give us an insight into the captain's thinking in the field.

Vic Marks' debut in Delhi was, as I told him a few days later when we were having a Christmas Eve beer in Calcutta, always going to be the start of a new post-playing career. His wife, I am afraid, was not keen on that idea then, so my belated apologies to Anna Marks, but Victor has been a jewel in the crowns of both *The Observer* and *Test Match Special*.

He and Aggers formed part of a *TMS* teatime feature I started soon after that trip, called 'County Talk'. The third member was also on the tour – Graeme Fowler. 'Foxy's' ebullient and irreverent personality made a good contrast – as did the Accrington humour. I remember him making a point of travelling on the press bus on one sight-seeing excursion in India, in order to talk to the photographers in our party about the techniques of using his new camera. And he has contributed a quotation which appears in most anthologies of cricketers' sayings: 'It's Friday night. What the hell am I doing in Ahmedabad?'

Another team member who would go on to join *TMS* was Chris Cowdrey. I was obviously very disappointed when he decided to throw in his hat with Talk Sport, but I know that he had the ambition to move his radio career from expert summarising, at which he was excellent, with a nice, light touch and quick wit, into the job of the ball-by-ball commentator.

In commentaries on county knockout matches subsequently, I also used the likes of Paul Downton, Richard Ellison and Pat Pocock, who were all vital parts of David Gower's team.

Gower himself, as captain, had a successful Ashes series at home in 1985, followed by suffering a whitewash in the West Indies. When that happens, critics are hard on a laid-back style. His replacement by Mike Gatting would not be long delayed.

Mike and Micky Stewart were a very close-knit captain/coach combination and it is possible that that closeness allowed an understandable outrage at some of the things that went on in Pakistan at the end of 1987 to overcome what might have been a more cautious path of diplomacy. Still, I could not help but admire the straightforwardness of 'Gatt'.

The tales of his capacity to eat are legion and he does not deny them. So I don't think I am breaking any confidence by saying that, when I went to his room for an interview during the height of the Faisalabad confrontation with Shakoor Rana, I saw on the desk the largest jar of Branston Pickle I have ever seen anywhere. He did not object to my laughing at it.

Gatting's openness could get him into trouble, always saying a little bit more than would be wise in the face of a voracious press. When Graham Gooch took over he had learned that lesson. When I joined the 1990 tour of the West Indies in Trinidad it had been going for a couple of weeks already. I went to one of the captain's press briefings on my first day and found that he was certainly not going to give anything away.

As we left the room, one of the journalists moaned: 'That's what it's been like. He doesn't give us anything.' I could not help feeling that, while it might not help our job, it was only wise for Gooch.

Graham was utterly dedicated to driving himself to physical fitness. I came across him bursting out of the door from the fire stairs on the twelfth floor of our hotel in Jamaica, having run up them several times and on his way down to do it yet again. Still I got a breathless 'Good morning'. Not all his team quite embraced his work ethic all the time. Most notably there was never a meeting of minds on this with David Gower.

And he probably would not have been unique among captains to have torn his hair out over Phil Tufnell. In Visakapatnam, on India's east coast, in 1993, I came across Vic Marks at breakfast on a Saturday morning. I asked if he was fully geared up to fill the space he commanded in the next day's *Observer*. 'I've got the feature done,' he said, 'and I'll be all right, provided Tufnell doesn't take none for a hundred and get fined for bad behaviour.'

Prophetic words. Tufnell had a bad day with the ball and did indeed pick up a £500 fine, so that the next morning's *Observer* had articles on facing pages expressing the reasons why he must and must not play in the next Test. As it turned out, that day Tufnell bowled beautifully and picked up four wickets.

Subsequently – and since my retirement – Phil has been one of the recent successes of *Test Match Special*, closely guarding the secret that he is not the fool he likes to pretend he is.

Gooch's successor, Mike Atherton, took the policy of never volunteering any information even further, frustrating journalists at press conferences, though I always found him easy enough in the one-to-one situation of a radio interview. A practice grew up at this time, treated warily by the press, of having the radio interview lead the press conference. In some circumstances, as far as we were concerned, it was the only way we were going to get our interview and I could see that, for a harassed media manager, it made sense in his attempt to get the captain or selected player in and out of the press conference as quickly as possible.

It was not ideal for us, but better than having a grumpy captain feeling he should not have to answer the same questions over again. I found on occasions that the writers would have few questions for Atherton when I had finished. He would appear to be quite amused by the notion that he might have intimidated them. And yet he was one of the most delightfully honest captains I have dealt with. I came across him having a quiet beer in the bar of our hotel in East London, South Africa in 1996. England had just lost yet another one-day international and instead of taking the short journey back in the team coach, Mike had opted to walk the direct route through the cemetery. I saw he had taken the precaution of turning his shirt inside out. 'It would be too good a photo opportunity,' he said with a wry grin. 'The Atherton shirt walking through the graveyard.'

When Mike started on Sky and writing for the *Telegraph* and then *The Times*, there were still some in the press box who seemed to have been scarred by their time trying to get a word out of him. But if anyone is his own man, it is Mike Atherton.

Alec Stewart had probably seen enough of his predecessors in action to appreciate the potential pitfalls. He had a very friendly relationship with the press, while not actually giving away too much, and he is another who has gone on to be part of a few radio teams on both Five Live and *Test Match Special*.

Nasser Hussain's approach was intriguing. I would not

have thought it was in his nature to embrace the media, but, as Atherton's vice captain in the West Indies in 1998, I found him encouragingly open and interesting to interview, often apparently volunteering to appear when there was no other obvious candidate. Soon after arriving in Pakistan in 2000, when he had become captain, I attended one of his press briefings. The comment of one of the journalists this time was that he must be the best at a press conference since Tony Greig. Unlike the writer in question, I had often interviewed Greig when he was England captain, so I could make the comparison, which was probably fair enough, though in an entirely different style. I am sure that Hussain was more pragmatic about the need to do it and more controlled in what he gave away.

He and Atherton have, I believe, been excellent on Sky, avoiding the blandness that has become a problem in, for instance, Australia's Channel Nine commentary team. As Atherton must have found it strange – and certainly his first victim, Stephen Fleming, did – to be on the other side of the interview microphone, I found it interesting to be waiting with Nasser Hussain most evenings for the close of play interview in South Africa in 2004–05. The pair of us would often have to negotiate with the team's media manager for the player we wanted. If Nasser found the position ironic, he did not show it.

Nasser Hussain's tenure as captain coincided with the appointment of Duncan Fletcher as coach. In Fletcher there was a very entertaining and friendly man in private, who put up an impenetrable public façade to deter those who might want to see inside the team 'bubble'.

Fletcher had the job of handling the fall-out from Marcus Trescothick's withdrawal from two consecutive tours. Now the team management would be likely to acknowledge that the player was suffering from depression at an early stage, as happened in the case of Mike Yardy in 2011. Then, the fog of disinformation led to far too much unwarranted speculation.

On the first occasion, in India, it had seemed odd when every gruesome detail of every other player's internal health problems was being given to us, that this one was not. In Sydney in 2006, when we knew what the problem was, it was not revealed that he had gone until he had already left. A call very late at night had Jonathan Agnew broadcasting from the roof of our hotel on the eve of a very early departure for Adelaide.

The loss of Trescothick from those two tours was worse than just his runs. There was a presence about him that Somerset have benefited from and I believe England did too. I remember him taking part in one of our *TMS Report* programmes from my hotel room in Colombo and being fascinated by everything that went into putting a live radio programme on the air via a small satellite dish in an ordinary hotel room. He does well in the Sky studio, so when the time comes, which I hope is much delayed by his playing career, my successors in *TMS* might look to him to join the team.

Other players were more inclined to take such miracle technology for granted. The team management have encouraged a bit of coverage of some of their charitable doings and so I put Andrew Flintoff live on the air from a playing field in Bombay, where he was visiting the Magic Bus charity in 2006, and Kevin Pietersen had broadcast from an orphanage playground in Multan in Pakistan a few months before.

Both those broadcasts were for Radio 5 Live and the thrust of the arrival of that rolling news and sport network called for more personal contributions from players. John Crawley recorded regular newsletters from the 1998 tour of Australia. I had no editorial input to those at all, but was just required to send what were fairly lengthy epistles down the line to London.

It was perhaps more sensible in 2006 in India when they decided that Steve Harmison's newsletters should be recorded with me prompting him. They would be edited in London anyway. It did mean that he could be guided in what people might be interested in. Inevitably we had to have the team's media man sitting in most of the time to monitor what he might say.

Those media managers have assumed a great importance between the team and the accompanying press. They appeared in the nineties, treading the awkward line of trying to be trusted by both sides. Unfortunately, the size of the press party nowadays makes them more necessary, but their need to control things has driven a wedge between dressing room and press box. A journalist with an imaginative idea cannot decide on his interview and get it to himself. The daily interview is agreed between the two sides and carefully monitored by the media manager.

Thus, when England are on tour, you know that the player quoted in the *Telegraph* will be the same one whose words appear in *The Times*, the *Mail* and the *Sun*, even if the angle put on his remarks may vary a little.

At one time, journalists could make friends with a player and get him to talk, having just cleared permission with the manager or the captain. That was probably an age of greater trust, though. I always looked forward to the chance to interview players who were friends, but funnily that could often be far more difficult than recording those I barely knew. It does, I suppose, sharpen you up to the task that bit more.

I had never really spoken to Angus Fraser until I had to interview him following a magnificent spell of bowling in Jamaica in 1990. I told him that in the press box he was being likened to Alec Bedser at his best and was impressed by the way he seemed genuinely touched by the comparison. He became a stalwart of the *TMS* summariser's chair and a good friend, though I wonder if he found the move to the writing side of the media a little harder than he had expected.

One little on-the-field exchange came back to us in the press box during that 1990 tour. At Pointe-à-Pierre in Trinidad, England seemed to be facing defeat on the final day of their match against the West Indies Board President's XI. What held up the opposition bowlers was Robin Smith. He was 76 when the ninth wicket in England's second innings fell, with England just past a lead of 200. His last partner was Devon Malcolm, whose batting was not his greatest attribute.

Robin manoeuvred the strike well enough to make 23 of a last-wicket stand of 29 and take himself to 99. Eventually, Malcolm had to face the last two balls of an over from Patrick Patterson. He took a huge swipe and lost all three stumps. Smith's reaction was to throw back his head and laugh.

At the end of the game, which England won comfortably enough in the end, thanks to the bowling of DeFreitas and Malcolm, I interviewed Robin as the players were leaving the field. He told me that Devon had said to him, as he approached his hundred: 'Don't worry, Judge. I'll play for you.' Hence the laughter at the ambitious Malcolm air shot.

It was a typical reaction from an always-cheerful character. He seems an ideal person to have organised supporters' tours on subsequent trips.

Playing in that match among the oil tanks at Guaracara Park was a twenty-year-old who Trinidadians reckoned should be getting into the West Indies Test side. He made 134 in the first innings to underline his case. His name was Brian Lara.

The relationship with the opposition Test captain is

variable. I suppose the closest I had was with Sunil Gavaskar, who, despite having god-like status in India, was always very accommodating. Perhaps that was because no one there treated him as a normal human being.

Lara, when he became captain, was one of those who believed that radio should just take their chances with press conferences and not be granted any special favours. He could look furiously at his media manager when I ambushed him as he was leaving such a press briefing, but he always gave a good interview, even if we had to do it while on the rapid walk back towards the dressing room. He also had the grace to pop into my farewell dinner at Lord's and say a few kind words.

Just occasionally an overseas player might seem to be remarkably flattered just to be interviewed by the BBC, as was the case with the Bangladesh captain, Khaled Mahmud. But generally outside England an undue (in my view) preference is given to television, probably not helped by the proliferation of small radio stations in some places. Captains need to be reminded that radio rights holders have also paid substantial sums into their boards' coffers.

The managers on tour and their attitude can make a big difference. Raman Subba Row and Doug Insole, who were on my first two tours, were always charming and helpful. Tony Brown, who managed the 1984–85 tour of India that started with Mrs Gandhi's assassination, was probably surprised to find that in that sort of situation, the press can be quite helpful.

Peter Lush, who had the unenviable job of handling the fall-out from the Gatting/Shakoor Rana row in Pakistan in 1987, was someone I had dealt with in his role at the Test and County Cricket Board, which involved media matters in the days before there was any liaison person specifically appointed. He was an old friend, but in the circumstances of that tour a heavyweight ex-player or administrator might just have made a difference then and there.

In later years it became the coach, rather than the manager, who was the principal figure in leading the team. Ray Illingworth probably started that trend in South Africa in 1995. I think he had come to the job a decade too late for him, but he had the enthusiastic John Barclay as his minder there, with the title of assistant manager. By the next winter Barclay was the manager, with David Lloyd – our old friend Bumble – as the coach. Those were two very different but very interesting situations for Johnny Barclay to handle, but then he had had some interesting characters under his command at Sussex. He tackled it all with cheerfulness, enthusiasm and his trademark encouragement, 'On, on'.

There seemed no doubt who was in charge when Duncan Fletcher was the England coach, even if he seemed to try to blend into the background. To a certain extent, that seems to have continued under the auspices of Andy Flower.

Both men captained Zimbabwe and both would know the importance of getting the right man as captain, not just for the obvious on-the-field decisions, but for the whole presentation of the team.

When Andrew Flintoff took over in the crisis in India in 2006, he was probably the right man for the moment – the talisman of the team. But the following English summer, it was Andrew Strauss, the stand-in for the stand-in, who secured a three-nil victory over Pakistan. To my mind, he was the man to take the side to Australia to defend the Ashes.

I thought that at the time and not as a result of subsequent events and revelations. I do not think he would have been able to retain the Ashes, but he might have moderated the disaster. Of course, we would not have known the outcome of the alternative course, so it might be just as well for him that he was not appointed for that series.

Like Michael Vaughan before him, Andrew Strauss conducts himself in a way that makes those of us who care about the way our team is perceived abroad – on and off the field – feel confident. And if they're winning as well, that is wonderful.

The Cricket Highlights (viii)

Barbados 2004

There was about the England side that went to Bangladesh and Sri Lanka at the end of 2003 the feeling of a new regimen. Fitness was a priority embraced by all and ice baths appeared for the first time. The new captain, Michael Vaughan, had taken over during the previous summer and his predecessor, Nasser Hussain, was now to be found under the helmet at short leg.

The win in Bangladesh was expected, but they lost one-nil in Sri Lanka. In the new year they would be off to the Caribbean.

There was no hint over the first three days of the first Test in Jamaica of the way things would eventually go. Devon Smith made a hundred for West Indies, but England, with no one making more than 58 (though there were 60 extras), managed a slender lead of 28 on first innings.

Saturday 13 March 2004

My close of play interview with Nasser Hussain, who, like Mark Butcher, had made 58, was about what a close battle it is.

Then on the fourth morning Steve Harmison just swept the

home side away. Starting the day at eight for no wicket, they were dismissed for 47 in an hour and 50 minutes. Harmison took seven for twelve, to leave Trescothick and Vaughan only twenty runs to knock off for a ten-wicket win.

Six days later Harmison was at the West Indies again, this time in Trinidad, where on the first morning he changed ends after a bit of a pasting from Chris Gayle and from being 100 for no wicket, bowled them out for 208 and figures of six for 61. England took a lead of 111 and then it was Simon Jones' turn to get at the opposition. His five for 57 left England needing 99 and they got them with three wickets down.

After two Tests of the four-match series, the Wisden Trophy was retained, but there was still the series to win. Next came Barbados.

I have a newspaper cutting from the Barbados paper, *The Nation*, on 2 April 2004 in my notebook. Under the headline 'What home advantage?', it first bemoans the domination of English supporters and then the West Indian batting: 'Home advantage isn't home advantage these days. And March Madness is now April Foolery.'

On 1 April, the first day of the Test, Andrew Flintoff had bowled them out for 224, taking five for 58, with Harmison taking another three. In fact, *The Nation* should have been happy with the second day. Only 119 from Graham Thorpe stood between the West Indies taking a big lead and England's eventual advantage of a paltry two runs.

Again, it was the second innings that was decisive. So far in the series, Harmison, Jones and Flintoff had each had a moment in the spotlight. On the third day, bowling the 21st over of the innings, Matthew Hoggard gave the match its decisive push towards England. In three consecutive balls he had Sarwan caught at gully, Chanderpaul lbw and Ryan

Hinds, obviously caught completely on the hop by the clatter of wickets, as he had to finish dressing at the crease, caught at second slip. Hoggard had become the tenth England bowler to take a Test hat-trick.

There was no comeback from 45 for five and we looked down on the ironically unfamiliar sight of England fast bowlers setting umbrella fields behind the West Indies batsmen. The world order was turned on its head. The West Indies were all out for 94 and England won by eight wickets on the third day.

There was one more Test to come and in that Brian Lara was to take it on himself to restore the region's pride with his unbeaten 400. It is possible that an earlier declaration in Antigua might have embarrassed England, but much succour was taken from his innings.

Back in Barbados, as the England players celebrated their series win on the outfield, I watched a liner putting out to sea from the deep water harbour just beyond the stands of Kensington, sailing towards the setting sun. It seemed almost symbolic of the end of an era.

For England, the building blocks had been laid for the side that would recapture the Ashes in England the following year.

9. The Talk Sport Years

In the spring of 1999, I was working hard on preparations for the Cricket World Cup to be held in England that year. But, as always, I was keeping an eye on the planning to be done further ahead and so, early one morning in the office, when I ran into the man who dealt with all our rights issues, I asked if the deal was concluded with South Africa for the coming winter's tour there.

The broadcasting rights have to be negotiated for each tour separately with that country's cricket board and, until this point, it had only ever been a question of bargaining over how much we would have to pay.

I was told that the South African board seemed to be dragging their feet in responding in an extraordinary way. I agreed to ring Ali Bacher, the managing director of the board, immediately. He sounded evasive, but, when I pushed him, eventually admitted that they had sold the UK radio rights to a commercial station called Talk Radio. He further admitted that they had not sought to find out if we would better Talk's bid and I discovered later that keeping the deal quiet from the BBC was a crucial part of the offer.

BBC Television had just lost the rights to broadcast Test cricket in England and this seemed like a moment of crisis.

I felt that we must be in South Africa to make our presence felt as the brand name for cricket coverage on the radio and so I proposed a round-up on each day, to be called *Test Match Special Report*. I established that we could use the recorded commentaries of SABC, who would be happy to include one of our commentators in their team. And we would still be able to get interviews – particularly with an England management who were sympathetic to our cause. Our live updates during play itself were restricted to a total of two minutes in each hour.

The first-ever *TMS Report* was done at the end of the first day of the series on a day at the Wanderers in Johannesburg when England, after being two for four, had been bowled out for 122.

We were aware that that frantic start to the Test had caused some chaos with the Talk team, for whom Geoff Boycott (loudly), Chris Cowdrey and Mark Nicholas were operating. I did feel some sympathy for their producer, Claire, who, when I met her the day before, had told me that she had never pro-duced any outside broadcast before.

Jonathan Agnew, after reporting all day for Radio 5, hosted the programme. Pat Murphy, while somewhat miffed to have had to surrender his usual reporting duties, provided crucial interviews with Allan Donald and Chris Adams, just in time for me to tidy them up for broadcast. To make it sound as much like *Test Match Special* as possible, I got our regulars, Mike Selvey and Vic Marks, in for the discussion of the day and with a hastily prepared script for the commentary high-lights, we were in business. I had decided we needed a signa-ture tune and had selected the opening bars of Toto's 'Africa', which seemed appropriate.

Thursday 25 November 1999

I think it's going to be all right. There were calls from London after the programme from several management

people, including the controller of Radio 4, Andrew Boyle.
They must all have been as anxious about it as I was!

It's been a knackering day.

We had certainly had drama to report on. In the third over
England lost their fourth wicket with only two runs on the
board. That was the moment when Michael Vaughan had
walked in for his first Test innings. There was something
about the way he handled the crisis, although he only made
33, that gave onlookers the feeling that he belonged at this
level.

Unlike the dramatic escape led by Mike Atherton four
years before, there was to be none this time. South Africa won
by an innings and Atherton, returning to the scene of his finest hour, bagged a pair.

As time went on, of course, our operation became slicker. It
was always quite tense, putting together a programme within
an hour of the close of play, so bad light ending play early was
a popular occurrence.

Test Match Special had previously been something of a
pariah with Radio 4, but, as I suppose that congratulatory
phone call from James Boyle indicated, in the face of a threat
from a usurper, we now had all the political support we could
want. That never overcame the frustration of not being able
to do a proper commentary – a frustration that was probably
most keenly felt by Aggers, who became quite grumpy on
occasions.

We had varying degrees of co-operation in our endeavours.
The England and Wales Cricket Board and the South African
Broadcasting Corporation were organisations with which
we had close ties, but the press officer of the United Cricket

Board of South Africa, Chris Day, seemed on a mission to make our lives as difficult as possible, usually allocating us seats in thoroughly inappropriate places. Happily, the local ground authorities were almost always more helpful.

I had come across Mr Day on the previous tour, when he had been similarly difficult with us. It may have been that he was just one of those old-style journalists who resents radio. And I've come across plenty of those.

Press boxes were not generally ideal locations for our live *Test Match Special Report* programmes anyway, though we were given no other choice in Cape Town or at Centurion Park. In Durban, we set up a table on an untenanted seating area in the stand and on one evening had to broadcast by torchlight, when the stand lights were turned off just before we went on the air.

That Millennium tour ended with a unique event in the final Test at Centurion Park. Like all the Tests I have seen at that ground on the southern side of Pretoria, it was dogged by rain.

After that South African win in Johannesburg, England had hung on for a draw in Port Elizabeth and South Africa had had to do the same in Durban. Cape Town, though, had given South Africa a second win by an innings. The series was theirs.

The weather at Centurion was not promising from the outset and Hussain put South Africa in. On a truncated day they made 155 for six. For the next two days it rained and on the fourth the ground was too wet for any play to be possible. With one day left, there seemed hardly any point in turning up. Discussions were even rumoured about putting on a one-day game.

But the fifth day went ahead, with South Africa still continuing their first innings. During the morning we saw Nasser

Hussain running off the ground to have talks in the dressing room. Then, after nearly two hours' play, South Africa declared at 248 for eight. To our amazement it was announced that England had forfeited their first innings (pedantically it was 0 for no wicket declared, but no one took the field for it) and South Africa their second innings. England had been set 249 to win in 76 overs.

The story gradually filled in. Hansie Cronje had made the offer to Hussain before the start of play, but Hussain wanted to see how the pitch was behaving after three days under cover before he committed himself. When he had done so, he ran off to strike the deal with his opposite number.

Subsequently we know of the involvement of Cronje with match-fixing for bookmakers, but then most of us were innocents. *Test Match Special Report* even awarded the 'Champagne Moment' to both captains for their initiative. Only Michael Atherton in the England dressing room, who knows the betting world, was uneasy. Cronje's job for the bookies was to make sure that, even after so much play had been lost, there was a positive result either way.

I believe that he was not fixing the match to the extent of handing it to England. I think that he reckoned South Africa could win. What he had to avoid for his bookmaking masters, though, was England shutting up shop to secure a draw if things started going badly for them. That meant a few risky ploys had to be tried.

South Africa had gone into the match without an injured Allan Donald and they lost the services of Paul Adams' left-arm spin before it had been used. Nonetheless at 102 for four, a draw looked like England's best option. Michael Vaughan joined Alec Stewart and their fluent stand of 126 put England in sight of victory. There was a nervy little clatter of wickets as the last twenty runs were gathered, but with five balls to spare, Darren Gough despatched Nantie Hayward for four and the match was won by England by two wickets.

In the post-match euphoria, Hussain paid tribute to Cronje. Not many months were to go by before he was to feel that the win was severely tainted, as the depth of the match-fixing corruption began to emerge.

Naturally, we hoped that that tour would be a one-off as far as commentary rights were concerned, but it later transpired that the deal that Talk – now known as Talk Sport – had done with South Africa was for two tours and also that they had concluded similar agreements with Pakistan and Sri Lanka for England's tours there the following winter.

To compound the problem of covering a tour without commentary rights, the day before my scheduled departure for Karachi in the autumn of 2000, I got a call from my office to say that my Pakistan visa had been refused. It seemed in the end to be just someone in the Pakistan High Commission objecting to a travel agent's courier bringing in a stack of passports for rubber stamping and preferring to vet applicants – particularly journalists – face-to-face, but it meant postponing my flight to Karachi for 24 hours.

This trip, setting off in October 2000, was the first time we had taken the Nera 'World Communicator' satellite dish, which was to change our touring lives. While not being our main route for covering matches, because it is expensive to use, it provides us with the ability to deliver unscheduled pieces from places not otherwise equipped for broadcasting.

A couple of years before, I had asked our engineers to tell me how news correspondents could report in perfect quality from refugee camps in Africa and they had explained the satellite system, but had said that the equipment was the size of a fridge and frequently not permitted to be used. Evidently it had been refined, because I was issued with something the size of a heavy laptop. I was a little apprehensive of getting it through Pakistan customs, but they didn't turn a hair.

As in South Africa, the first problem at any ground was trying to establish the best place from which we could broadcast our reports and the *TMS Report* at the close of play. Before the arrival of Aggers on the tour, I would be doing those programmes solo for the one-day internationals, as presenter and producer, with interviews supplied by Pat Murphy.

The first floodlit game in Karachi was certainly a harsh test, with a late finish and difficult working conditions in an open stand. The noise was deafening and, when I came to pack up all the equipment, I discovered that someone – even in the area where we were sitting, which I was told was occupied by police officers' families – had cut through the cable to steal the effects microphone.

Happily, after that, the match referee for the series, Barry Jarman, decided that the dew was having too much of an adverse effect on these floodlit games and that therefore there would be earlier starts for the rest of the series. That obviously made my deadline a great deal easier.

Relations with Talk Sport on these tours were never antagonistic. These were, after all, in many cases old colleagues. I see one note from my diary on the day of the second one-day international in Lahore.

Friday 27 October 2000

As I was setting up our position on the balcony, Chris Cowdrey sportingly pointed out that an advertising banner hung across the railings in front of us would mask the outfield to a large extent. So, when I was deploying the effects mic., I also re-hung the banner for them.

The Talk Sport engineer was very helpful too. Though I had often called on the host broadcaster's engineering assistance at the matches themselves – at least in the early days – I had never at that stage been granted the luxury of travelling abroad with an engineer, a situation that had always tested my rudimentary grasp of the technical side of things. But, when it came, for instance, to replacing the connection on the end of the cable that had been cut in Karachi, Talk's man, Nick, came up trumps. He was, as he pointed out, a freelance anyway.

His production team, however, did almost gloat over one problem that we had in the early stages of the tour, when the satellite equipment developed a fault.

The three one-day internationals done – and won three-nil by Pakistan – England were playing their first first-class match of the tour, a four-day game in Rawalpindi. As the game was starting, a report into the currently hot topic of match-fixing was released in India. In the report an Indian bookmaker claimed to have paid Alec Stewart for information. After 48 hours of speculation and rumour and the England press officer's statement of denial, Stewart called a press conference.

It was to be held back at the hotel after the day's play and inevitably Radio 5 Live were keen to broadcast it live. Unable to rely on the faulty satellite dish, I was put on the spot when the request from London came.

Thursday 2 November 2000

I took a snap decision that, provided I could get hold of a phone, I could do it. Back at the hotel I asked the staff if there was a phone in the conference room. 'No,' I was told.

So I had to gauge whether I could reach the reception desk with the leads I had. However, while I was trying to work that out, they found a cordless phone for me to use. I was a bit nervous of it, but a test with London seemed to sound all right. So I was able to run a microphone from the desk at the front, another for Pat Murphy to put his questions and a third to catch any other questions I could reach in the body of the room. Then I patched the mixer into the cordless phone.

It was all a bit Heath Robinson, but, remarkably, it worked and the quality was evidently good enough for Five Live to stay with it for twenty minutes. Just after I'd had a very pleased editor on the line from London, one of the Talk Sport people commiserated with me, thinking that we had not been able to broadcast it. It turned out that we had carried a good deal more of it than they had.

One other moment I remember rather poignantly about that match in Rawalpindi was getting a call through to my father on his 80th birthday. It was to be the last time that I spoke to him. A couple of weeks later, just as I returned to the hotel in Lahore at the end of a day's play in the first Test Match, I received a call from my mother to say that he had died in his sleep. She had – typically not wanting to be a nuisance – waited until the end of the day's play to tell me.

Naturally, I flew home, finding the local Pakistani travel agents with whom we were dealing immensely kind and understanding, as they helped me to rearrange plans.

The BBC team had a council of war before I left, to decide who we might best request as a replacement for the different roles I had to perform. The technical side threatened to cause the most problems, so we asked for our regular senior engineer on *Test Match Special* in England, Andy Leslie.

Fortunately, all the teething troubles we had been having with the satellite dish seemed to have been sorted out and our usual mode of operation for the *TMS Report* programme was now to set up a little group in some open area of the hotel premises where we could get power and light. A digital editing machine carried the commentary highlights and interviews.

Thus I was at home in England a fortnight later when I received a call from Christopher Martin-Jenkins in Karachi. 'There's a scene in front of me you would be very familiar with,' he said. 'Andy Leslie is surrounded by about ten Pakistani telecom engineers trying to sort out the problem with the line.'

'So where's Aggers reporting from?' I asked.

'Oh, he's had to go and sit by the boundary rope so he can get a line on the satellite.'

And, while I could have a little chuckle at missing that performance, I was sorry only to be able to watch on television England's dramatic win in the dark in that Test Match. Though I gather I would not have been able to see it so well, had I been there in the flesh.

Rather like the South African board, the Sri Lankans, who were England's hosts for the second tour of that winter, had simply refused to discuss rights with us, for fear that Talk Sport would, as they threatened, withdraw their offer.

This time the Sri Lankan customs were a bit more sticky about the satellite dish, but their original demand for a bond of £5,000 in cash came gradually down to just needing my business card, which I found much more reasonable. I had to promise to come and see them when I left at the end of March, to prove that I was taking the equipment home.

After a couple of games in Colombo, we headed down the west coast to Galle, where the first Test was to be played, through a coastal area that would be devastated a little less than four years later by the tsunami of Boxing Day 2004.

There was another warm-up game at Matara, a little further along the road that curves round Sri Lanka's south coast. For this a number of us in the press party were staying at a quirky hotel on a promontory overlooking a magnificent beach at Weligama. It had a terrace, which was to prove very valuable as a broadcasting point when a tropical downpour washed out play at Matara one day.

Aggers had a room overlooking what looked like a tempting swimming pool. From his window he watched CMJ take his regular morning swim and then, as soon as he had left the water, he was replaced by a troupe of monkeys, who preferred to use the pool as a lavatory.

It was at Matara that the Talk Sport team turned up in order to have a full dress rehearsal before the first Test. It also provided the only instance I have ever seen of a large monitor lizard holding up play when it wandered across the ground and the players decided to give it a fairly wide berth.

Sunday 18 February

During the course of the day, the hitherto much admired Vrai, one of the media managers of the Sri Lankan board, came to tell me that during the Test Matches we would be allowed to do reports totalling no more than two minutes an hour.

I told her that our reciprocal agreement with Talk allowed for eight minutes an hour. She said that she would need a letter from Talk to that effect. Fortunately the Talk Sport

producer, Jim Brown, was happy to oblige, but the board
seem to be getting a little bullish about our presence.

At an official reception before the Test, in talking to various
officials, including the president of the Sri Lankan board,
Thilanka Sumathipala, I was left in no doubt that they felt they
might have missed a trick by not demanding rights money
from us as well as Talk Sport. Media managers who had previously been friendly were now being a little stand-offish.

As in Pakistan, to put together our highlights for each day
we had to record a commentary on every ball, known in the
business as 'stop/start' commentary. If nothing happens, you
can delete the recording on the digital machine immediately.
If a wicket falls, or significant runs are scored, you have to
make sure you catalogue it so that you can find it later.

For the Test Match, we moved our hotel to a
resort – Hikkaduwa – where we had the sort of problems
we encounter in the Caribbean of working out of a holiday
hotel. At least the time difference did give me the chance to
get back there and set up the equipment in the grounds –
in the case of Hikkaduwa this meant some pleasant gardens
by the sea. The west coast of Sri Lanka is very conveniently
situated to lock onto the appropriate satellite for a broadcast
signal.

After a little bit of reluctance to co-operate from the board
officials, we were allocated a rooftop position at Galle's
International Stadium from which we could report and record
our snippets of commentary.

On the first morning of the Test there was a muttered
remark from one of the media managers about agreeing an
'access fee' for the BBC. I started to get the impression that
they were spoiling for a fight.

Thursday 22 February 2001

'We need to talk about this,' I said to Vrai, but she carried on sorting through tickets, ignoring me. After five minutes of that, her boss, Shaan, appeared and I tried him. But he, too, looked through me as if I wasn't there.

After a minute or two of that I said, 'Well, I've got a job to do. You know where I am.'

And, apart from Vrai stalking past our point a couple of times, that was the last I saw of them for the day. Maybe sanity has prevailed.

Friday 23 February

We arrived at the ground in the morning at 8.30 and unloaded the kit from the car under the gaze of four security guards, one of whom showed us that he had a letter, which apparently told him not to allow any BBC personnel through the gates.

There followed some unseemly scenes, in which Shaan and Vrai informed us that we had done more than two minutes an hour the previous day (which we hadn't) and that we had not paid an access fee (which they had refused to discuss the previous morning). They refused to listen to any counter argument.

So we were left in the dust outside the gates.

Tim Lamb [then chief executive of the ECB] had offered a few days earlier to provide any help if we needed it, so I rang him, but his mobile was switched off. It seemed to be an impasse.

I despatched Aggers, Pat Murphy and Radio Wales' Edward
Bevan to the walls of the Dutch-built Fort, which overlooks
the far end of the ground. We loaded the kit into the boot of
the car and our driver, 'Simmons', took them round there.

I told Aggers to be meticulous about keeping it to two
minutes an hour, even though he would now be outside the
ground. He could set up a position on the battlements from
where he could see the middle and the scoreboard, and I just
hoped he would have enough battery in the mixer and the
satellite dish. Of course, I told him, he could go to town on
describing the scene outside the ground.

I settled down outside the gates to await developments
and to try to talk to someone. The England media manager,
Andrew Walpole, brought me drinks and a chocolate bar
from the dressing room and I made friends with the security
guards who were keeping us out. They – unlike their masters
– were courtesy and charm personified and one even shared
a sandwich that he said his wife had made, filled with
vegetable curry. Another found me a stool to sit on.

Press photographers took pictures of my predicament and
then went off to snap Aggers in operation on the fort walls.

The crucial point was the arrival of Tim Lamb, shortly before
the lunch interval, after a morning spent negotiating a
change of hotels. He suggested to the Sri Lankan board that
this spectacle did not reflect well on cricket and got them to
let me in.

Tim then pulled together a meeting, which involved the Sri
Lankan officials and the television rights holders for the
series, Nimbus. They spoke to their boss in India and it

was decided that we could carry on for this Test Match and discuss it further before the next. Faces have been saved all round, I suppose.

Tim was rightly pleased with his intervention. 'The ECB gets something right – for once!' he declared.

The Sri Lankan Board then offered me lunch in the VIP box, which, with a reporting position to set up, I had to decline, but Tim's wife, Denise, handed me her binoculars. 'Look,' she said, 'you can see Aggers up there on the battlements.'

I reported to Five Live from our position and heard Aggers do his last piece from the ramparts, before we were reunited.

We had to decide for the evening how to handle *TMS Report*, particularly having managed to collect only one recorded highlight. So I opted for a tabloid man – Mike Walters of the *Mirror* – and Patrick Eagar, as a senior snapper and former chairman of the Cricket Writers' Club, to set our row in context and Vic Marks to deal with the cricket.

For the rest of the Test Match the board officials ignored us completely, though my friends the security guards gave us a huge smiling welcome every morning and even helped with the unloading of the kit.

Monday 26 February

As I was going in to breakfast, I got a call to say that Don Bradman had died during the night. I got onto the sportsroom in London immediately to tell them where to find all the pre-prepared obituary material.

Despite England losing the Test that day by an innings, a large part of our evening programme was naturally devoted to the passing of the great man.

In the days before the next Test Match in Kandy, our rights man in London did his stuff with WSG, the firm holding the broadcast rights on behalf of the Sri Lankan board, and all was confirmed as being in order, a state of affairs that was still not accepted by the board's own media people.

Late on the afternoon before the Test they seemed to have been told that they had no option but to accept us and their final throw was to get me to re-do our accreditation forms, which had originally been submitted from London months before.

One plus was that, as we were staying in the team hotel and broadcasting our *TMS Report* programme from a terrace of the rambling hillside buildings, we had the chance to get players live on the programme occasionally.

Thursday 8 March

During the day a man came to our reporting position above the press box and introduced himself as the marketing manager of the Sri Lankan Cricket Board. He was almost apologetic about what had happened to us. Could there be a change of strategy and a realisation that their public relations had been appalling?

For the evening's programme we had Duncan Fletcher on. He was very good with Aggers and possibly even better, because, as we were starting, so did the world's worst bagpiper on a terrace below us. Duncan, normally famous for being so taciturn, got the giggles.

With England winning the Test in Kandy to square the three-match series, we wanted to get the captain, Nasser Hussain, on *TMS Report* in the evening live. However, with a fairly early finish, the team decided to set off for the drive down to Colombo immediately. So Aggers recorded him as if it was live, leaving spaces for other interviews and highlights to be played in. I took everything back to the hotel to edit it all together, with the sound of the birds round the gardens there mixed in and was quite pleased with the relaxed sound it made.

Ever since the visit from the marketing manager, everyone from the Sri Lankan board had been surprisingly friendly again. And so it continued for the final Test in Colombo, which England won, to take the series.

On the day before the match I ran into one of the media managers.

Wednesday 14 March

I was anxious and so I asked Vrai, 'Are we going to have any problems this time?'

'Only,' she said, 'in the matter of ...', and my heart started to sink, '... location.' It seemed the spot she had selected was not the one the club had earmarked for us.

We have ended up on a precarious platform above a stairwell, which allows little space, but I have certainly worked in worse.

The three one-day internationals followed the Test series. The first of these was at a ground which had taken six months to build from virgin jungle. This was at Dambulla, in the centre of the island and was very much the brainchild of the board president. It seemed the day before the game that, with builders still busy, it could not possibly be ready.

I was allocated a broadcasting booth which was completely sealed in, so, to avoid it sounding like a basement bathroom, I had to find a way to worm a cable through the air conditioning duct to deploy an effects microphone.

A great deal of effort went into making the ground look good for television. Extra spectators were bussed in and an elephant was spotted casually grazing in the jungle beyond the boundary. The fact that it was in the same spot several hours later suggested that it just might be tethered.

Unfortunately, when a difficult day came to an end with Sri Lanka winning the day-night game, the power for the stadium was turned off shortly afterwards. Completing the *TMS Report* in total darkness was an interesting exercise, but luckily experience had taught me always to have a torch in my kit bag.

England lost the next game, too, at the Premadasa Stadium in Colombo, where I spotted a large rat symbolically scuttling out of the commentary box, just as the last wicket went down. At the SSC ground Sri Lanka made the one-day series a whitewash.

The following British winter would take England to Australia in an attempt to recapture the Ashes. The Australian Cricket Board, by contrast with those of South Africa, Pakistan and Sri Lanka, kept the negotiations for the UK radio rights above board, but eventually the depth of the BBC purse was simply not enough, particularly for a series that is, after all, played through the night in UK time.

The story came to us from inside Talk Sport that their boss, Kelvin McKenzie, the former editor of the *Sun*, had failed to realise that the Australians had the bad sense to play cricket in the middle of the night. When he did find out, we were told, he was quite keen to unload the coverage of a series for which it was difficult to sell enough advertising to cover the huge rights fee he had agreed.

Whatever the details, we did manage to take on that coverage after all.

During the summer of 2003, the secretary of the West Indies Cricket Board of Control visited the *Test Match Special* box at Edgbaston. He assured us that all was well with our rights for the broadcasting of the England tour of the Caribbean in the early months of the following year.

Thus it was a considerable surprise to find nearer the time that his marketing manager had apparently done a different deal behind his back and that Talk Sport would be doing the commentary to the UK. Our protests at sharp practice fell on deaf – if slightly embarrassed – ears.

The irony of this was that Geoff Boycott had now rejoined the BBC team from Talk for the coverage of this tour. So now he would be part of another series of the *TMS Report* programme.

In the run-up to the first Test, the *Sun* correspondent told us that he had been ordered to write a piece on how we were to be forced to cover the Tests from outside the ground. It seemed an aggressive as well as inaccurate start, particularly as the same day we had our confirmation from the West Indies board that our limit was three minutes an hour – reporting from inside the ground.

Three days before the Test, to preview the series, we put on a live programme for Radio 5 Live at a golf club in Jamaica, where the team sponsors, Vodafone, were staging a 'players vs. press' golf tournament. I set Aggers and Geoffrey up on the clubhouse veranda and procured players and journalists for them to talk to as they came off the course.

That worked well, but, with the time difference in the West Indies – and particularly Jamaica – it was going to be a very tight deadline for the evening programmes during the Tests.

Five Live also asked for a daily live chat with Geoff Boycott during their *Drive* programme. As this would exceed our three minutes an hour on its own, I had to find a position to broadcast outside the ground. A primary school yard just outside the gates of Sabina Park looked the best bet for the first Test and the head teacher was pleased to help.

Thursday 11 March 2004

At lunch I set up the satellite dish in the street for *Drive* to do a two-way with Geoffrey. We performed under the stern gaze of an enormous woman selling patties with rice and peas and jerk chicken. Fortunately we were not asked to repeat this exercise at tea.

Eventually, it was decided that, if these updates were confined to intervals, they did not count in our hourly allocation, so thereafter we were able to do the contributions from our box.

One problem we have in the Caribbean in the brave new world of digital communications is that generally they operate on an American system, which is not compatible with that in Europe. In the days before the series started, I worked closely with the Talk Sport freelance engineer, to get hold of the necessary box to make the conversion. Then he had to teach me how to use it.

In South Africa, Pakistan and Sri Lanka I had started *TMS Report* with a signature tune that had something to do with where we were. Here in the West Indies I decided to do something that Aggers had suggested to me five years earlier, when BBC Television lost the rights to broadcast Test cricket. Their signature tune had for years been the familiar 'Soul Limbo', by Booker T and the MGs. Aggers reckoned that we should have taken it over straight away.

My view was that we should leave a little space and not seem to be hanging on television's coat-tails. But now, I felt, was the right time. Apart from anything else, it has a Caribbean sound to it. It also had a sort of 'BBC brand' sound about it, which was important in our current situation. So, 'Soul Limbo' was first used by *Test Match Special* for its highlights programme on 11 March 2004 and it has been used ever since.

After having to do our own 'stop/start' recorded commentaries to compile highlights in Pakistan and Sri Lanka, for this tour I reached agreements with the local stations around the islands, who were employing Vic Marks and Christopher Martin-Jenkins to supplement their teams. Aggers was too tied up with his reporting duties for Radio 5 Live to be available for this, a situation that did not improve his humour at the loss of commentary rights. So, on each ground, I would run a cable from the local station's commentary position to record and edit my highlights for the evening.

There were still the interviews to gather for the programme, which, with only the two of us, fell to me. On every West Indian Test ground the dressing rooms are at the far end from the media, a factor that added to the pressure of time. I ran the highlights together in a package for each session, to keep it simple in case I was not back in time for the programme, and Aggers could press each carefully labelled button if necessary.

In the middle of the second Test in Trinidad, however, we

ran into the perfect storm. A late finish was followed by problems with the satellite – no ISDN in Trinidad – and then a power failure. *TMS Report* did not go out that evening.

Monday 22 March 2004

Aggers went on at the scheduled end of *TMS Report* to do a short piece, give the scores and apologise for a technical failure. I was appalled to hear that the announcer had not said anything about the problem at the start, but had just introduced the next programme on Radio 4 FM.

I felt utterly suicidal about the whole business. Back at the hotel, Aggers and I just sat, having a beer. Almost the worst thing was that none of the useless hierarchy of the BBC have rung to enquire what went wrong.

Eventually, after some prompting, the management verdict was that had I not had to be off at the other end of the ground gathering an interview with the day's hero, Simon Jones, I might have been able to sort out the technical problem.

That was, I suppose, flattering, even if it was not accurate. The solution was to despatch Simon Mann, who was due to be with us in a fortnight anyway for the one-day internationals, to be our close-of-play interviewer. It was an extravagance, perhaps, but once he joined us in Barbados I found a great deal more for him to do.

Happily, the day after this debacle, the Test Match finished in a very early win for England and we were able to do the programme from the hotel – recorded well in advance, for safety.

One of the features of any Caribbean tour has been the beach party at Tony Cozier's holiday shack on the rugged east coast of Barbados. In the days leading up to it he seems to invite just about everyone he bumps into. Fortunately, perhaps, finding the place after a drive across the island through the narrow lanes that separate the cane fields is usually so tricky that the numbers actually attending are whittled down.

On this occasion, following the successful programme from the golf club in Jamaica before the first Test, Five Live decided they would like another one from the Cozier party. With England two-up in the Caribbean, with two to play, it seemed a good time. And so, in the unlikely surroundings of the scrub round Tony and Gillian's wooden chalet, we mounted a Five Live programme.

Monday 29 March

It was surely a first for Cozier's garden. When we had done, we could enjoy the party – Banks beer, flying fish sandwiches and all – before Victor's slightly less successful navigating of the return journey in the dark.

For the Barbados Test we were allocated a splendidly situated, spacious commentary box, which was, in fact, rather better than the one that Talk Sport had. We only had three days of Test cricket, which was hurried towards its end by a Matthew Hoggard hat-trick. It meant that next day Aggers could meet all his Sunday morning broadcasting requirements from the relative comfort of my hotel balcony – on his birthday.

The Recreation Ground in Antigua was less accommodating, providing only a seat in the press box for Aggers to operate from, and from there we had to do our programme. My perch on a camera gantry to record and edit the commentary for highlights was even less comfortable, roasted by a fierce Caribbean sun. So it was perhaps a test on the nerves that the match went to five days.

It had been a huge disappointment to us when we discovered that Talk Sport's deal with South Africa was for two tours. Since they first started to mount their commentaries, we had only had the overseas rights for India and New Zealand in 2001–02 and, when Talk had backed out, Australia in 2002–03. We had also covered the World Cup in South Africa, because our contract for that was with the ICC, rather than the South African board. But I had heard the remark that the BBC didn't cover overseas cricket tours and had to handle angry correspondence demanding to know why we had decided to stop doing so, and that sort of thing really hurt.

At least by the 2004–05 South African tour there was something of a formula to *Test Match Special Report*, which involved a bit of Agnew/Boycott banter – a forerunner of their close-of-play podcasts. We still took our commentary for highlights from the SABC, though some of their recent recruits were given to the sort of flights of fancy that made editing of the clips an interesting exercise.

Not much had changed for the first Test venue, Port Elizabeth, or the second at Durban. At Cape Town we found ourselves at the back of the large, but hermetically sealed, press box built for the 2003 World Cup. This posed a difficult problem for the sound of a broadcast, but with every piece of cable I could lay my hands on I found a fire escape door out of which I could run an effects microphone.

The series was a crucial part of England's progress towards the dramatic summer of 2005.

They had come to South Africa at the end of a very good year. They had started it by beating the West Indies three-nil in the Caribbean. Then they won all seven Tests at home, against New Zealand and the West Indies. So they set off for South Africa with ten Test wins and one draw already under their belts for the year. At the beginning of December they made it eleven, thanks to their new recruit, Andrew Strauss, who made 126 and 94 not out in a seven-wicket win at Port Elizabeth.

In Durban they got themselves out of a mess, to see South Africa hanging on for the draw at the end. They were soundly beaten in Cape Town a few days later in the New Year Test.

So they came to the Wanderers in Johannesburg one-all, with the momentum thought to have swung to the hosts. Here we were allocated a splendid vacant hospitality box, though I spent the time there thinking that someone would find they had made a mistake and evict us. But what a Test Match we witnessed from our lofty perch.

On the first day, Strauss made his third hundred of the series – 147. On a second day curtailed by the weather, a rollicking unbroken ninth-wicket stand of 82, of which Harmison had made an unlikely 30, took England past 400. In my close-of-play interview with him, Michael Vaughan, himself 82 not out, said: 'Don't rule out an overnight declaration.' And that's what he did – at 411 for eight.

A big hundred from Herschelle Gibbs made sure that South Africa took a lead, but only one of eight runs, with the England attack being carried by Matthew Hoggard, who took five wickets in his 34 overs.

England were batting again before lunch on the fourth day and were 189 ahead with five wickets in hand at the end of it, with Marcus Trescothick 101 not out. When he was out for 180, shortly before lunch on the last day, Vaughan declared again at 332 for nine, setting South Africa 325 to win in 68 overs, though bad light had set in every evening of the match and so was likely to curtail that.

Through the afternoon Hoggard, swinging the ball

prodigiously, was magnificent. In his second over after lunch he had de Villiers lbw. Two overs later he bowled Rudolph and had Kallis caught at slip. It was eighteen for three and now there were jitters in the South African camp. They also had the handicap of having their captain, Graeme Smith, laid up, having been concussed by a ball in the morning's fielding practice.

At last Boeta Dippenaar stayed with Gibbs for a little over an hour, as they added 62. But then Hoggard was back to claim two more wickets in successive overs. Dippenaar was caught at gully for fourteen and Mark Boucher, just back in the side, was caught behind for a duck. It was 86 for five and Hoggard had all five of them.

Straight after tea, he claimed his sixth, by catching Boje off his own bowling. At that point the South African captain had seen enough and, despite doctor's orders, he came in to bat at 118 for six. There were theoretically 35 overs still to be bowled, but the fickle High Veldt weather was a factor not to be ignored, so England's race against time was all the more urgent and South Africa had something to bat for.

Gibbs and Smith more than hung on for another ten overs, before Giles had Gibbs lbw for 98. Three overs later Flintoff had Shaun Pollock dropped and then caught at the wicket next ball. With England in all-out attack, the runs flowed, but Smith now had the tail with him. In the 53rd over, Ntini was lbw to Flintoff and at ten to six, with eight and a half overs left in the match, Hoggard returned to have Steyn caught behind. Smith was left with a valiant 67 not out to his name.

England had won by 77 runs and with twelve wickets in the match it was an easy choice to make Matthew Hoggard man of the match.

A week later, an hour up the motorway at Centurion,

England clinched the series with a draw in the rain-affected final Test. Since South Africa's re-admittance to world cricket, it was the first series victory on their turf for England. It was a moment to be savoured by the tourists.

For *Test Match Special* it was a relief that Talk Sport's interest in covering cricket rather waned from that point. Football had always been their preferred sport, anyway. The England and Wales Cricket Board played a few canny games to try to convince us that they were a viable option for domestic rights and certainly they did us the service of reinforcing our standing within the BBC.

The Cricket Highlights (ix)

Kandy 2001

Three days before the first Test of the 2001 series in Sri Lanka, Jonathan Agnew and I called in to have a quick look at the International Stadium in Galle, on the south coast of the island. We found the groundsman, Jayananda Warnaweera, who I remembered having one of the most suspect looking bowling actions I had ever seen. That may have been one of the reasons that he only ever played a couple of Test Matches outside Sri Lanka.

Monday 19 February 2001

Aggers had played against him on an England 'B' tour.

'You bounced me,' said Warnaweera.

'Surely not,' said Aggers.

As we were leaving, Aggers muttered to me: 'Actually, we all bounced him, because we knew he was a chucker.' It seemed that England had forced him out of the game. I wondered if

we should be worried that he was now preparing a pitch for
them to play a Test Match on against Muralitharan.

In the event, Sanath Jayasuriya out-bowled Murali by eight
wickets to seven. Atapattu made a double hundred and,
though Trescothick made his first Test hundred, Sri Lanka
won by an innings and 28 runs. It made what happened in the
other two Tests of the series all the more remarkable.

That Galle Test Match was a bad-tempered affair, probably
not helped by some poor umpiring. Neither aspect was any
better in Kandy for the second Test, but this time the breaks
seemed more inclined to go England's way.

Gough, Caddick and White had removed the top four Sri
Lankan batsmen by lunch on the first day, though there was
to be no further wicket till after tea, by which time Mahela
Jayawardene had made a lively 101 and added 141 for the fifth
wicket with Russel Arnold. Thereafter, Gough and Caddick
with the second new ball finished the innings off that evening.

After losing Atherton and Trescothick early on the second
day, Hussain and Thorpe put on 167 for the third wicket, with
Hussain enjoying a certain amount of good fortune over decisions in getting to 109, before he was bowled by Muralitharan.

The eventual England lead was 90 and the start they
made on the Sri Lankan second innings seemed to put them
in complete control. In the third over Gough and Caddick
had reduced them to three for three, though one of those
did involve an umpiring howler. Jayasuriya stood his ground
when a bump ball went to third slip. The third umpire was
asked only whether the catch was clean and was not permitted to point out that it had hit the ground as it left the bat. So,
by the end of the third day, Sri Lanka seemed to be in disarray, only eight runs on and six wickets down.

Friday 9 March 2001

The Test has been played amidst a good deal of rancour between the players. There were more incidents today and Jayasuriya has already been given a suspended ban and a large fine. So we decided to have the match referee, Hanumant Singh, on *TMS Report* tonight.

If England had hopes of finishing the match on the fourth day, they reckoned without Sangakkara. He took the fight to them, adding 93 with Dharmasena for the seventh wicket, before becoming Robert Croft's third victim, just before lunch, for 95.

Even then, Sri Lanka kept their innings going until the tea interval, with a potentially difficult target for England growing all the time. In the end it was to be 161 in four sessions. At 25 for two, with both Atherton and Trescothick out to Vaas, that looked some way off. And it was by no means certain at the end of the fourth day, with England 91 for four. Alec Stewart was in with the nightwatchman, Croft, and Graeme Hick to come.

Sunday 11 March

The day started with the match intriguingly poised. Stewart was out to Vaas, with the score 97. At 122, Hick was bowled by Jayasuriya. 39 needed – four wickets in hand. It was agonising stuff, with the spinners now in control. Croft went just before lunch, which came with nine runs still needed.

It took twenty minutes after the interval to get those nine, but Craig White and Ashley Giles held their nerve and you could see it was a very big moment for the team when the win came.

In all the circumstances, there was euphoria in the England camp at having levelled the series.

As in the previous two Tests, Sri Lanka won the toss at the Sinhalese Sports Club in Colombo for the final match of the series and batted. England were pleased enough to bowl them out on the second morning for 241, with Croft taking four, including the crucial wickets of Jayawardene for 71 and Jayasuriya for 45.

It took an undefeated 113 from Graham Thorpe to give England a first innings lead of only eight. Chaminda Vaas had been the main destroyer, taking six wickets.

There was no hint of what was to come when Sri Lanka started their second innings just after lunch on the third day. It began with Gough making sure that Atapattu bagged a pair and finished with Giles and Croft in control and Sri Lanka all out for 81.

England needed only 74 to win and, while all the rest of the specialist batting fell – largely to Jayasuriya's left-arm spin – Graham Thorpe kept cool and saw them home by four wickets in the gathering dusk that same evening.

Remarkably, England had come from behind to take the series 2-1. That does not happen much – particularly on the sub-continent.

10. The World Cups

The first three cricket World Cups were held in England in 1975, 1979 and 1983. While the West Indies, who won the first two tournaments, had no real ambition at that time to try to stage anything like that in the Caribbean, when India were the surprise winners in 1983, it was different.

The fourth World Cup would be shared between India and Pakistan.

Tuesday 29 September 1987

Even arriving in the early morning, Delhi had the promise of a hot day ahead. As soon as the advance guard of the press checked into our hotel we were bidden to a reception at which the Reliance Cup was dramatically unveiled.

Then it was a gentle stroll to the hotel where all the teams – 112 cricketers – were being put up, for the purpose of accreditation. This inevitably was peppered with interminable delays, particularly when the police photographer disappeared. But we filled in plenty of forms and I had the opportunity to clarify some points in our broadcast rights contract.

We were back at the same hotel in the evening for a banquet to launch the tournament. It was a glittering affair, impressing particularly those of us who had experienced functions in India before.

The eight countries involved mixed happily with each other, though I for one found the lack of sleep on the overnight flight from London catching up with me and was not sorry when the end of the fifth speech meant that we could slip away.

Opening ceremonies thus far had really been confined to photo calls, but this time it was a little more ambitious, though mainly centred on a game between the two host nations, not part of the competition and played under lights at an athletics venue – Delhi's Nehru Stadium.

Wednesday 30 September

As the Prime Minister, Rajiv Gandhi, was to meet the teams, security was very tight. I was searched twice and one Indian TV commentator was refused entry because, although he had the right pass, he was carrying binoculars and throat lozenges.

The opening ceremony was pretty low-key. The players lined up in files in front of the Prime Minister's box and then, led by Pakistan and India and followed by the rest in alphabetical order, they trooped up the steps to shake Mr Gandhi by the hand.

As India and Pakistan took the field for their match, hundreds of balloons were released. Only a few went up and the first big bunch, carrying the sponsor's banner, caught in a floodlight pylon, but most just bounced round the playing area until a bunch of pyjama-clad Keystone Cops rounded them up. By that time the start of the game had been delayed by ten minutes.

The next day I went to Pakistan for the first time.

Thursday 1 October

At the airport we were told we weren't on the flight to Lahore. The problem was eventually solved when we realised that the travel agent had listed the names, for instance, as 'Mr Baxter'. But when local officials who check it see 'Peter Baxter', they look for 'Mr Peter'. And so we are greeted with, 'You are not on flight.'

With a flight to Pakistan from India, there were even more security checks than usual, including a final one at the door of the PIA aircraft by a smiling Pakistani sky marshal.

On our arrival in Lahore, we were all – players from both England and the West Indies and the British press party together – crammed into a small, but plush VIP waiting room. There was a considerable hold-up while the West Indian team discovered to their surprise that you need a visa for Pakistan, even during a World Cup.

Eventually the England part of the crowd was allowed to catch our onward flight to Islamabad. When we checked into our hotel I saw that the journey had taken over eight hours – for a distance of perhaps a couple of hundred miles.

By that time I knew all too well that travel days on the sub-continent are usually a bit like that.

England warmed up for that tournament in Rawalpindi, a

fifteen-mile drive from our rather more sedate surroundings in the modern capital of Islamabad.

Sunday 4 October

There was a strenuous practice session for the England players in the morning – the hottest day since we left Delhi. Our journey back in the minibus consisted mainly of getting stuck in spectacular Rawalpindi traffic jams, including some time alongside a small ambulance, whose number plate read 'R.I.P.' Considering he had been stationary for ten minutes, with his red light flashing, it may have been all too appropriate.

A couple of days later we moved south to Lahore, our base for England's opening match.

Thursday 8 October

My morning task was to check on our facilities at Gujranwala, where England are due to play their first game tomorrow. It is 40 miles from Lahore, but Micky Stewart, the coach, was also planning to go and make an inspection, so we agreed to go together.

Our chauffeur was the local MP for Gujranwala, Sheikh Masood, who told us proudly that he had unseated a cabinet minister to win his seat in Parliament.

The road there was an impressive dual carriageway without much traffic, except at one stage a tractor and overloaded trailer, which was coming towards us in the fast lane. Some local farmers had evidently not quite got the hang of modern road regulations.

Sheikh Masood was inordinately proud of his city and the stadium, which was impressive. I was invited to choose a commentary box and Micky was astonished by the size of the dressing rooms.

After seeing what we needed, we were asked to the home of the match organiser for a cup of tea. With the tea came a huge array of finger food, from toasted sandwiches to cakes. Micky, not being a huge fan of the local food, declined, but, when we were told that our host's wife had spent all day preparing this, we felt we had to have a toasted sandwich at least.

As Micky was just taking his first bite, our host said, 'I hope you are liking green chillies.' Micky, with his eyes out on stalks, was just discovering how hot his sandwich was. But he ploughed on manfully.

We went back up that same road next morning well before dawn in a convoy of six minibuses – two for each team, England and the West Indies – and two for the press – with a truckload of armed police fore and aft.

And a very exciting game we had for the start of England's campaign. The West Indies rather broke the shackles towards the end of their innings on an exceptionally sticky day, to get to 243 for seven and, after a slow-ish start, England seemed to be in trouble at 131 for six in the 39th over. At that point, needing over ten an over, Allan Lamb was joined by first John Emburey and then Phil DeFreitas, who helped him keep the challenge up.

With both those partners gone, an exhausted Lamb had to be cajoled by the number 10, Neil Foster, with 35 needed from the last three overs. That came down to thirteen needed off the last over from Courtney Walsh. And it was Walsh who found the pressure too much. After giving away six runs from his first two balls, he bowled four wides and a no ball and Foster hit the third legitimate ball for four to win the match by two wickets.

Friday 9 October

Lamb almost had to be carried off, so I was flattered that he agreed to see me for an interview afterwards – 'As long as it's only you' – and I found him slumped in a wicker armchair in the dressing room.

As we followed England round, Christopher Martin-Jenkins and I did our best to cover other matches in the tournament from hotel room televisions, whenever travel plans allowed. With half the commentary in Urdu, this was not always straightforward.

Meanwhile, in India, Henry Blofeld, sometimes accompanied by Trevor Bailey, was providing reports from various selected matches.

England were beaten by Pakistan in their second game, back in Rawalpindi.

Tuesday 13 October

There was one unsavoury incident, when Javed Miandad was given out lbw by the Australian umpire, Tony Crafter. It was the first time, apparently, that he had ever been out lbw in Pakistan and it was followed by a bit of a shoving match with Mike Gatting before he would leave.

Our next journey involved a three-hour bus trip from Islamabad to Peshawar, on the North-West Frontier.

Thursday 15 October

I decided to go for a walk after we arrived, to see more of this fascinating place and maybe find the cricket ground.

Some poor information from a policeman sent me on a circuitous route. When I came past him again, he looked most concerned.

'There is a problem?' he asked.

'I don't think the cricket ground's up there,' I said.

'You want bus ticket or train ticket?'

I explained, with appropriate gestures and we both laughed at the misunderstanding and shook hands, before he showed me the right way.

It led me past a row of barbers, each one operating on a plank over an open drain on which he and his customer squatted. I managed to cross a very busy junction only when it became sufficiently clogged with tonga-carts, auto-rickshaws, lorries and buses. Just by it was a roadside stable, mostly for donkeys, with a farrier's hut attached. And there, just behind this mayhem, was a beautifully peaceful park, with the cricket ground at the end.

In those days in the World Cup group matches, each team played the other three in their group twice. Here in Peshawar, it was to be England's first encounter with Sri Lanka.

Friday 16 October 1987

I went down to the ground in the morning and met the PBC
engineers who were rigging our box for tomorrow's game.
It was split by a half-glazed partition, which made it rather
impractical. I asked why.

'One half for Sri Lanka Radio,' I was told.

'But they're not covering it,' I said.

'No, they are taking your commentary.'

I tried to work out the logic that had produced one
microphone in each box for this purpose and proposed
that the partition be removed and that we might use both
microphones and let the feed to Sri Lanka be split by the
engineers at their equipment.

This revolutionary thinking seemed to satisfy everyone.

This tournament was, I think, the only time that BBC television staged their own commentary on an overseas cricket
series. Although members of their commentary team, like
Tony Lewis, Ray Illingworth and Jack Bannister, fitted in with
the usual press party, the production team never quite managed to.

We had agreed, before leaving England, that we would
share the services of Messrs. Lewis and Bannister. I would fit
our commentary rota round the television one. The television
producer was not accustomed to co-operating with anyone
else and matters came to a head in Karachi during England's
second game against Pakistan.

Tuesday 20 October

Tony Lewis had been more and more in demand in the
television box – so much so that he told me he would only
be available during one hour in the first half of the day. I
allocated him two twenty-minute spells in that hour, but
he had just begun the first of them when the TV producer,
Keith McKenzie, burst in, pushed between CMJ and me and,
ignoring the fact that Tony was in full flow, tugged his sleeve
and said, 'You're wanted.' Then, still ignoring the rest of us,
he stalked out.

Tony handed over to CMJ in mid-over and was back later to
apologise and explain that the demand had come from the
Breakfast Time programme in London. But there was never
a word from McKenzie.

After a later discussion with Tony, it was clear that it was not
going to be possible to continue the arrangement of sharing
resources with what was nominally another branch of the
same organisation.

Pakistan had won again in Karachi, leaving England needing to win both their remaining group matches to progress.
That was their task. Mine was to find another commentator to
replace Lewis and Bannister.

Tim Rice was travelling with us as what he called a 'cricket
groupie' and so I asked him if he'd like to try his hand at commentary for England's next game in Jaipur. I had woken him
with my phone call, so when I saw him as we were setting off
to return to India, he asked, 'Was that a dream, Backers, or
did you ask me to join the commentary team?'

At that point in the tournament, all roads seemed to cross
in Delhi.

Friday 23 October

I met Henry Blofeld and Trevor Bailey in the hotel and we were able to exchange tales and discuss their future plans.

It has been a pleasant crossroads, with the same hotel housing for 24 hours England, the West Indies, India, Australia and Sri Lanka, before we all separate again. I also came across the two English umpires, David Shepherd and Dickie Bird, who have been operating in the other group. Shep reports that Dickie's really happy now he's feeling properly ill!

And so to Jaipur and the first of England's must-win games – against the West Indies. We had found ourselves at the opposite end of the ground from the television boxes, so the shared commentary arrangement would have been doomed anyway.

Monday 26 October

It was a big day for Tim Rice and, if he wasn't perhaps quite as nervous as for a big first night, there can't have been much in it. He need not have worried. He did splendidly and had a good match to start on.

England survived a torrid opening hour on a lively pitch to make 269 for five, but we were a little afraid that that wasn't enough.

When Richards and Richardson were in full cry, it certainly didn't look enough, but, not for the first time in this competition, scoreboard pressure told and they were all out 34 runs short.

In Pune four days later, England made sure of their semi-final place by beating Sri Lanka comfortably and Tim Rice made the acquaintance of some long Sri Lankan names. He eventually decided that Vinothen John, 'the burly John', was going to be credited with a lot of the fielding, whether he did it or not.

The semi-finals had been resolved as Pakistan vs. Australia in Lahore and India vs. England in Bombay. The locals in both countries and the organisers now knew for certain that the cup had resolved itself as intended to provide an India–Pakistan final in Calcutta.

There was, therefore, stunned reaction first when Australia won in Lahore and then when England did the same the following day in Bombay. In fact, so disappointed were the organisers with the final line-up, that a play-off match between India and Pakistan was discussed, but eventually rejected. And the day after the second semi-final we were off to Calcutta, a thousand miles to the east.

Friday 6 November

'Interview anything that moves,' was our instruction from London, as the home audience was apparently becoming enthused by England's success. So, CMJ recorded Micky Stewart, John Emburey and Phil DeFreitas, while I talked to Dickie Bird, who was distraught that he was now going to miss umpiring in a fourth World Cup Final, because England were in it.

England may well have gone into the match as slight favourites, too, but the pressure of requiring the largest second innings total to win for that tournament proved too much. That Calcutta final of 1987 is remembered mainly for Mike

Gatting's reverse sweep, which cost him his wicket and checked England's progress just when the match seemed to be in hand. It was the turning point that led to an Australian win.

Four and a half years later Australia were defending their title on their own soil, sharing the tournament with New Zealand. They had just tacked the tournament onto the end of their normal season, which did not do them any favours.

A number of other things were different. The matches up to the semi-finals, instead of being divided into two groups, would be played as a round-robin, each team playing all the others. There were nine countries involved, because South Africa had just re-entered the international fold. For the first time, coloured clothing would be used. And then there was the rain rule, which, with the tournament being played so late in the Australasian season, could become very important.

Until that time, the system for re-calculating targets in rain-affected one-day matches had always just been a simple run-rate equation. That could obviously favour a side batting second that had not lost too many wickets. A revised sprint was usually a lot easier. Australia had suffered defeat in such circumstances not long before and therefore set about creating a new system.

Richie Benaud is credited with coming up with the plan, which set the overs available only against the highest scoring overs of their opposition. Therefore, if you had bowled five maiden overs and your reply was docked five overs by the weather, your target did not change. Until we saw it in practice, we did not really notice any possible iniquity in this.

For listeners in the UK, there were thirteen different sets of playing times, with the different time zones in Australia and New Zealand, the fact that for the first time there would be floodlit games, and with New Zealand and some of the Australian states changing their clocks to winter time during the course of the four and a half weeks of the competition. A further problem they would face during the tournament would be the switching off of Radio 3's AM frequency, our old home network.

After touching base with Jonathan Agnew, who had come on from New Zealand – his first tour as BBC correspondent – in Sydney, I headed east to Auckland for the opening match between the host countries, while he went west to Perth for England's opening game against India. The matches were on the same day, but with the Auckland game in daylight and the Perth one under lights, coupled with the vast distance between them, they barely overlapped.

Saturday 22 February 1992

I was at Eden Park in good time for the start of the opening ceremony. After seeing yesterday's chaotic rehearsal, I didn't want to miss it. There was a fly-past of vintage aircraft and then a procession of army lorries came on, each decked out as a float representing one of the countries.

It seemed that they had wanted to have an ex-player from each country on the float, but they appeared only to have approached whoever they could get hold of on the day. So India and Pakistan led off with no representatives, other than two girls on each float in the relevant cricket uniforms.

For England, ironically, it was Tony Greig, for Australia (who were given a loud boo) Richie Benaud and for South Africa (who received a rousing cheer) Clive Rice. All three men, by chance, were part of the Channel Nine television

commentary team. They were also using Richard Hadlee,
who followed the whole parade in a vintage Rolls-Royce,
holding the trophy – a large glass ball on a stalk.

From that point, doing regular phone reports, I watched quite
an upset as New Zealand won against all predictions, and from
commentating on the end of that I handed on to Aggers in
Perth, where England went on to beat India.

South Africa's first-ever World Cup match was clearly
going to be a big event. Australia had saved that plum for
themselves – at the Sydney Cricket Ground. I was part of the
ABC's commentary team, describing a nine-wicket win for the
newcomers. The next day I was in Melbourne for England's
win over the West Indies and the day after that in Brisbane,
ready for two back-to-back games.

The second of those was Australia vs. India, which was
being played at the same time as England were meeting
Pakistan in Adelaide. For the telephone reports at this time
we were using a piece of kit called a Reportophone, which
plugged into an ordinary phone line.

Sunday 1 March

At the Gabba I rigged up my telephone line to the scaffolding
platform on the roof, which we had used for *Test Match
Special* ten years ago. We were to make good use of it.

I did the occasional update into the commentary on
England's game in Adelaide. They seemed to be going well,
with Pakistan bowled out for 74, but then it rained there and
so, with help from Tony Lewis, I had to start commentary on
our game.

After an hour, when India were preparing to chase 238, it rained on us, too. When our game resumed, so did our commentary, but it soon became clear that water had got into the Reportophone, which gave out increasingly loud and frequent crackles and then went to mush. Happily, soon after that, they resumed in Adelaide.

One of the television engineers operating near me said that his mate was an expert on bits of equipment like this. So I showed the man the Reportophone.

'Water in it?' he said.

'I think so.'

'Then it's buggered.'

In fact that night I restored it to working order with the hotel hair dryer.

Both the matches that day provided examples of the vagaries of the new rain rule. In Adelaide, after dismissing Pakistan in 41 overs for 74, England's target was revised to 64 from sixteen overs, while that rain in Brisbane cost India three fewer overs to get two fewer runs. They lost by one run, while the England chase was eventually washed out by more rain.

During the course of that tournament I made four separate trips from Australia to New Zealand and back, dispelling any notion that the Tasman Sea is just a narrow channel between the two. The next one of these journeys was to see an historic occasion, the first time South Africa and the West Indies had ever met on a cricket field. Both sides tried naturally to play down the political significance of the moment.

Thursday 5 March

There were a lot of fairly tense-looking South Africans at breakfast in the hotel and outside the ground there were no more than a handful of quiet protesters. But inside all was happy at the thought that these two were able to play against each other.

Billed as a clash of the fast bowlers, it was South Africa's Meyrick Pringle who came out on top.

I was reunited with England, who were top of the table along with New Zealand at this stage, in Ballarat in Victoria for the game against Sri Lanka.

Monday 9 March

On a hot, sunny morning, Aggers and I set off early for the ground to establish our commentary position in what looked like an old railway signal box. In its confined space were the official scorers, the public address man and a reporter from Associated Press. That didn't make it any cooler in a stifling box.

I had recruited the ABC's Peter Booth to join our team. He is originally from Ballarat and so provided some very interesting background stuff.

The ground was packed with 13,000, many of whom had made the journey from Melbourne in the early morning on the train, and most of those were Sri Lankan. It was a noisy, enthusiastic, banner-waving crowd – partisan for the most part, but seeded with a few curious Australians. It was entirely good-humoured.

England won by a huge margin, but the bad news came from a hamstring injury to Graham Gooch. So the scrum-like press conference after the game centred on that news.

That injury to Gooch meant that Alec Stewart captained England in their next two matches. Against South Africa in a tense game on a hot night in Melbourne, the task was not made any easier by the rain docking them nine overs but the new rule taking only eleven runs off their target. I watched that from the comfort of the New Zealand commentator Iain Gallaway's house in Dunedin, after an exceptionally cold day watching New Zealand beat India at Carisbrook.

I was on England watch for their next game in Wellington, though. Having just enjoyed a successful tour of New Zealand, England found their hosts very keen indeed to redress the balance.

Sunday 15 March

I was part of the Radio New Zealand commentary team, with my telephone for reports conveniently situated right outside the box.

Unfortunately, injuries were obviously taking their toll on England and dictated the selection of a team in which by no means everybody was fit. The total they put together of 200 was mercilessly overhauled by New Zealand, thanks to Jones and Crowe. And, although the result meant little in the context of the World Cup, as the two sides would finish first and second anyway, there was a tremendous feeling of revenge in the air – not least in the commentary box.

The final day of the round-robin stage was important

principally to determine the fourth semi-finalist, but it turned out to be quite dramatic.

England had a game against Zimbabwe, who had lost all seven previous matches, at Albury-Wodonga, on the Victoria/ New South Wales border. Pakistan had improved a little on a poor start to the tournament and now could sneak into the semi-finals in the unlikely event that they beat the previously unbeaten New Zealanders in Christchurch and that Australia, who had had a wretched time, could beat the West Indies, the other contenders for a place. Australia had a chance if they and New Zealand both won.

The Australia–West Indies match was under the lights in Melbourne, where I was. Aggers and CMJ were doing commentary on the England game, while our day's reporting was started by Henry Blofeld in Christchurch.

First Pakistan did indeed sweep New Zealand aside and, while my game at the MCG was starting, England collapsed against Zimbabwe, thanks to the medium pace of Eddo Brandes. Although Australia were now out of it, I found myself busy with reports as they beat the West Indies and thereby put Pakistan – remarkably – into the semi-finals.

For the first of these I was back in Auckland.

Saturday 21 March

The Radio New Zealand commentary team, which I was part of, for most of the day had no doubts that New Zealand would easily dispose of Pakistan. And, with a total of 262, it did look likely. I was lucky enough to be commentating for quite a bit of Inzamam's innings of 60 from 37 balls, but the rest of the commentary box had gone very quiet. He had pulled the innings round and put Pakistan into a winning position. It was difficult after Pakistan's victory to do objective reports on the day with Bryan Waddle and Alan Richards looking stunned and suicidal.

The final stages of the second semi-final are what most people remember about the 1992 World Cup.

I started the day heading for Auckland airport at 5.30 in the morning and finished it late at night, on my knees, trying to record a chaotic press conference in the Sydney Cricket Ground pavilion.

Plenty of sympathy has always gone to South Africa about this game, but their tactic in the field had been to slow the over-rate, after they had put England in on a day with a poor forecast for the evening and England only received 45 overs in the allotted time, from which they made 252 for six.

Sunday 22 March

Sadly the day finished in utter farce. South Africa, with six wickets down, needed 22 off thirteen balls when the rain came down and the players went off. They were back within a quarter of an hour, but the crazy rain rule here meant that, to finish within the statutory playing times, there could only be one more ball bowled. England had lost their two most unproductive overs and South Africa had one ball to score 21 runs.

At the press conference in the Members' Dining Room, I scrabbled round on hands and knees putting out microphones in what I hoped would be the right places for Graham Halbish, the chairman of the organising committee, Graham Gooch and Kepler Wessels.

> The conference was packed and the bar next to it was open
> to the room, so that the noise from it became impossible and
> the curious drinkers kept wandering in and adding their
> opinions.

My abiding memories of the final, which, after Pakistan had enjoyed most of the luck in setting England 250 to win, became rather one-sided, are of the newly opened Great Southern Stand at the MCG, packed and towering into the night sky and then of interviewing a victorious Imran Khan, resplendent in his tiger T-shirt.

I was also grateful that, when I was commentating as the final catch went up off Richard Illingworth's bat, it was the easily identifiable Ramiz Raja who was under it. England's best chance of winning the World Cup had gone.

Probably no World Cup since has been as good, partly because they now all take too long to play.

I was in Calcutta in 1993, when news came through of a particularly acrimonious ICC meeting at Lord's at which the Asian countries exercised their muscle to insist on staging the next World Cup in 1996, previously agreed to be in England, in India, Pakistan and Sri Lanka instead. More politics was to attend the start of that competition. On the cricketing side a new strategy was to prove very successful and this was an expanded World Cup – twelve teams – and the first involving quarter-finals.

Perhaps mundanely, but crucially, for me it was the first time I had had a mobile phone in the sub-continent, which made a huge difference.

England had not been to Pakistan since the antagonistic events of the Gatting–Shakoor Rana confrontation eight years before. This time they did their acclimatisation in Lahore, where they were extremely hospitably looked after. The diplomatic trouble that was waiting in Calcutta in the run-up to the opening ceremony did not really involve them.

On the last day of January that year – six weeks before the start of the tournament – a bomb had gone off in Colombo, killing 100 people. Australia and the West Indies were both due to play in Sri Lanka and both refused to go.

Enormous efforts were made to persuade particularly the Australians to change their minds. (The England delegation reported something like annoyance that recriminations could not be laid at the door of the old colonial power, as they were not scheduled to go to Sri Lanka.) Conversations I had with members of the Australian board revealed extraordinary lengths being gone to get them to change their minds. At lunchtime on the day of the opening ceremony, I went to a press conference at the Taj Bengal hotel, where I was told I would only need to put out one microphone for the ICC Chairman, Clyde Walcott.

In the event, most of the talking was done by the chairman of the organising committee, Jagmohan Dalmiya, the volume of whose rant was sufficient that it did not matter that he was nowhere near a microphone. But the announcement was that neither Australia nor the West Indies would fulfil their fixtures in Sri Lanka.

It would take something for the opening ceremony to be memorable after that, but it was.

Sunday 11 February 1996

It was an extravagant event, featuring a laser show, which didn't quite work, because the curtains on which it was projected billowed in the wind. But the twelve teams were led out – and mis-identified by Saeed Jaffrey – and when it was all over they did the whole show again, this time with boy scouts holding down the curtains.

Monday 12 February

We left for the airport at 5.00 a.m., where our press party and five cricket teams were boarding the flight to Delhi – England, South Africa, UAE, New Zealand and Pakistan. It made one wonder why it had been necessary for us all to make the journey to Calcutta at all.

The UAE team baggage got itself tagged for Amsterdam, but luckily someone spotted it as it was disappearing towards the international terminal.

England and New Zealand were bound for Ahmedabad to play the first match of the Cup.

Our broadcast circuits for commentary were to use the system we had tried in the Caribbean two years before, running a cable to the television control point to use a leg of their satellite transmission to London. While that still left the back-up circuitry sometimes unreliable, it should at least give us one clear and reliable line.

Our New Zealand colleagues had decided that their best policy was to take our commentary from London and we included Bryan Waddle and Richard Hadlee in our team. They were delighted with the outcome of that – and of the match, because England fell eleven runs short, after seeming to have things in hand.

So pleased were his masters back home, that Bryan Waddle found himself asked to do full commentary on the rest of New Zealand's matches. Their next was in Baroda, where he could get no broadcast line and spent the whole day on the telephone at the back of the pavilion.

Often on tour, to get a clean interview without holding the press conference up, it was our practice, supported by the team management, to sit beside the captain, manager or whichever player was selected, and start off the questioning. This was the case after the defeat in Ahmedabad.

Wednesday 14 February

All was chaos in front of the dressing room, but I saw Mike Atherton being escorted towards the stairs. I asked him what he was going to do and he said, 'I've no idea, Bartex!' So he was in quite good form when I led off the press conference in an office upstairs.

Apparently, though, this was not the thing to do, as an Indian official approached me afterwards to say, 'You are very naughty man.'

England – and we camp followers – had a tortuous journey now to Peshawar, via Delhi and Karachi.

Friday 16 February

We arrived long after dark and I was reminded of the wild west feel of the place, with guns everywhere, including a truck-mounted machine gun trained on us as we walked across the tarmac.

The baggage hall was a shambles. Turbaned tribesmen surrounded the small, dilapidated conveyor belt four deep and after a bit it became clear that nothing was going to happen, because the team's cricket coffins were going round and round with no room for any more luggage to be added.

So some of us nudged through the tribesmen, to break the stalemate by unloading the coffins and stacking them in a pile.

Next came the tribesmen's bundles, each one more enormous than the last. We managed to strike up some banter with these fearsome characters despite the language problem, as we applauded the most outrageous bundles off the belt.

At last, after an hour, came our own luggage.

England were in Peshawar for a week, to play the United Arab Emirates and Holland, the only two games they were to win. In between the two matches, while Aggers stayed on England watch, I went to Faisalabad to report on South Africa vs. New Zealand.

We joined forces with the SABC commentary team in Rawalpindi for England's game against South Africa, who still had the edge acquired in their home series ended barely a month before.

Next day I was off to Lahore to see Pakistan play Holland. In something of a hurry to get to the ground, I was waiting with the other passengers for the luggage to emerge in Lahore's then fairly ramshackle airport. As my frustration increased at the delay, I was muttering, 'This lot couldn't organise a piss-up in a brewery.'

A helpful porter, overhearing me, offered, 'You want toilet?'

Next day a terrifying drive through thick fog took me back to Faisalabad for New Zealand against the UAE. Poking my head round Radio New Zealand's door at the ground, I found a desperate Bryan Waddle, who had been commentating solo for a couple of hours. With, 'Now it's time to hand over to Peter Baxter,' he threw the microphone at me and disappeared for a breather.

Sub-continental travel has its own mystique and this tournament's planning required a sit down with the travel agent to work out a plan as soon as we knew who was going to which quarter-final. Happily for us, England's poor form in only being able to beat Holland and the UAE, meant that we got relatively early notice that they would be in Faisalabad as the bottom qualifier in their group. That affected the semi-final schedule, too. The winner in Faisalabad would go to Calcutta.

We were committed to full commentaries on both semi-finals and, of course, the final in Lahore, so I had to have a hard look at the practicalities. The timing made it all but impossible for anyone other than VIPs with private planes to attend both semis, so I decided that Aggers and Simon Mann had better go to Calcutta in case England got through. I had been there for the opening ceremony, so I could give Aggers the lie of the land. I would go to the second match in Chandigarh.

Sri Lanka had taken everyone by surprise with their style of play in the tournament. They had, of course, been gifted two wins by Australia and the West Indies both refusing to play them in Sri Lanka, but their batting assault to beat India in Delhi had made everyone sit up and take notice. Now, after topping their group, they were England's quarter-final opponents.

England were by now an unsettled team. The captain, Mike Atherton, and the manager, Ray Illingworth, did not seem to be on the same wavelength at all.

They might not have had the best of the luck, either. Our rooftop commentary position was separated from the third umpire by a sheet of canvas, but we could see the red and green buttons for indicating the ruling on line decisions perched on the wall in front of him. When he reviewed Robin Smith's run out, the television replay showed that there was ample doubt and the decision should be not out. So we watched in fascination as the tentative hand crept forward – hesitated – and then hit the red button to fire Smith out.

England's 235 was made to look very slender anyway, when Sanath Jayasuriya got to work, blasting sixes into the pavilion below us. On the drive back to Lahore, after the comfortable Sri Lankan victory, we listened to commentary – sometimes having to get the driver to translate from Urdu – on India vs. Pakistan in Bangalore. The streets of Lahore were empty when we got there, as every man, woman and child was glued to the floodlit match. But Pakistan were going down.

The next morning I was off to Karachi for the West Indies vs. South Africa quarter-final.

Sunday 10 March

As I checked out of the hotel, the manager took the opportunity to tell me how terrible the defeat by India last night had been. It seemed that the whole country was in mourning. I was told that Wasim Akram should have played, despite his injury, and that the team had quite obviously taken bribes. And plenty more.

The West Indies had had a chequered week before the quarter-final, losing to Kenya and then beating Australia, but South Africa were certainly favourites here – and absolutely stunned when they lost. My interview with Hansie Cronje at the end confirmed that.

Now I had to get to Chandigarh. That entailed a 4.00 a.m. departure to fly to Bombay. Then, because you could not get an Indian domestic ticket in Pakistan, I had to go to the travel agent's office an hour and a quarter away by car and wait for them to find it. The plan was then for me to fly to Delhi and catch the train from there to Chandigarh.

This was where I had earlier spotted a flaw in the plans. My plane was due into Delhi half an hour before the train left and I knew that it takes a good deal longer than half an hour to get from the airport to the main railway station, even if your luggage is first off the aircraft. At my pointing this out, the travel agent had displayed characteristically unreasonable optimism.

The driver who met me off the flight, which had been only ten minutes overdue, moaned sadly, 'You are late.' I told him that I had not been flying the plane myself.

Tuesday 12 March

He took me to their office in the city, which, for a large organisation, seemed an amazingly scruffy hole.

The agent himself, who I had last seen in Calcutta was, like the driver, astonished that I hadn't caught the train. 'Mr Mark (Nicholas) would not go on it either. Someone had been sick on his seat.' He thought Mark's reluctance extraordinary. 'Do you want car?' he asked.

I said that I thought that was the back-up plan, so he summoned one, which turned up in a mere two hours.

The Grand Trunk Road in the dark was a scary experience, with a lot of traffic, much of it unlit and on the wrong side of the road. It took nearly seven hours to get to Chandigarh

and the Hotel Aroma. There the man at the desk denied all
knowledge of me, but I spotted my name on a list on the wall
behind him.

He was unapologetic. 'You have been moved to the Hotel
Metro 35.'

The Aroma wasn't great. And the Metro 35 is not as good as
that, with a bed harder than the floor.

The semi-final here was to be Australia vs. the West Indies,
which meant that I could join forces with Jim Maxwell of the
ABC, but first, as I was setting up the commentary booth
on the afternoon before our game, I was keeping an eye on
Sri Lankan wickets falling to India in Calcutta. That night at
Jim's rather more comfortable hotel we watched that fortune
change dramatically. Sri Lanka had recovered from a poor
start to make 251 for eight and then none of the Indians had
been able to stay with Tendulkar.

Wednesday 13 March

When they were eight wickets down and certain of defeat,
the crowd started throwing bottles onto the ground and
Clive Lloyd, the match referee, advised the umpires to take
them off. They did come back after a quarter of an hour, but
the trouble started again, so Lloyd awarded the match to
Sri Lanka.

We may have been horrified at a major cricket match having
such an outcome, but much worse horror was in the news
coming from home that day. Sixteen small children and a
teacher had been massacred by a gunman at a place called

Dunblane in Scotland. Sometimes something happens to make our lives covering sport seem very trivial.

We still had a match to cover next day, though, under the lights – low lights because of its proximity to the airport – of a new ground in the Chandigarh suburb of Mohali. Australia slumped to fifteen for four at the start, so that 207 for eight in their 50 overs represented a recovery.

Nonetheless the West Indies seemed in no trouble until panic unaccountably set in in the last ten overs and they were all out with five runs and three balls to go. Australia would play Sri Lanka in the final in Lahore. But first we had to get there.

Friday 15 March

There was a fog of rumour and uncertainty surrounding everyone's travel plans, which in my case were meant to be being handled by my elusive travel agent, Rajesh. The rumours were of a charter flight – or maybe even two – direct to Lahore. But I was apprehensive that the needs of players, officials, ICC guests and even television crew and twenty Australian journalists would come ahead of those of a solitary BBC man in the scramble for seats.

I checked out of the Metro 35 to move to the team hotel, where everyone else was based. As I had had to pay cash for every phone call I had made from the hotel as soon as I had made it, I was low on Indian rupees to pay the bill. The man at the desk was not keen on travellers' cheques or credit cards. 'You must change travellers cheques at bank,' he said.

'OK,' I said.

'Bank is closed,' he told me.

So we were back to his original options. He reluctantly went for the credit card. I signed the slip and he examined the signature against the one on the back of the card. Then he took out a ruler from his drawer and measured the two.

'Is not the same,' he said.

'Have you ever tried to sign in the space on the back of those cards?' I asked him. Eventually he realised that he had no choice.

The Shivalik View Hotel was chaos. There was a desk in the foyer where people seemed to be handing over huge wodges of rupees. People were either setting off for Delhi or looking for air tickets. What was definitely missing was my man, Rajesh. I wasn't sure if I should be paying someone or waiting for him.

Twice I was referred to 'Room 209' where I found members of the Indian cricket board handling large bundles of rupees. I was roundly abused when I asked for guidance there.

The first planeload – largely made up of Indian officials – left in the early afternoon and rumours mounted that there would indeed be a later flight, when the aircraft had been to Lahore and returned.

There was a melee inside the airport, when I eventually decided to go there. All sorts of ICC dignitaries, a few with wives, were milling around, none with any idea of what was going on. The Australian journalists had come along, too.

At last a voice started shouting out names to hand out tickets and I saw that it was Rajesh, who I had been looking for all day. He was standing on a crate to deliver the bounty.

There was a pathetic anxiety amongst everyone to hear their names called. I was certainly grateful and amazed when I heard mine.

As Chandigarh is not an international airport, this was a big day for the staff and it was clear they were going for glory. My passport number was written in ledgers at three different desks and the security and customs checks were more thorough than ever.

There was a long wait in the bleak departure lounge and then a further hold up when the doors were at last opened because, the security guard told me, 'Some important people have to get on plane first.'

I passed that news to the President of the MCC and the chairmen of the Australian and West Indies boards, who were just behind me. On boarding the plane, there, sitting in seat 1A, was Sunil Gavaskar, grinning all over his face.

I had stayed in the Lahore hotel many times over the previous six weeks, observing the progress of building works on a huge new wing, which, I was told, would be full for the final. I never believed that it could be finished in time, which would leave a lot of people without accommodation. Arriving on the second plane seemed a little dangerous.

I had repeatedly underlined with the hotel on my last visit that I would be there and they had confirmed it, getting to know me quite well anyway, after my many visits. What I did not know as I headed westwards from Chandigarh was that Jonathan Agnew had also been warning them all day that I was coming in.

My heart sank as I looked at a noisy crowd of frustrated

people, five deep round the reception desk. But my talks with the staff had worked and from behind the throng I was hailed, 'Mr Peter! Here is your key.' And it was passed to me over the envious crowd.

Such mayhem inevitably led on to a chaotic final, with many of these same dignitaries finding that, when they went off to get some interval refreshment, on their return, their seats had been occupied by people with apparently perfectly genuine tickets.

Despite Sri Lanka's unbeaten run, Australia were made favourites for the Lahore final.

It was to be the first game under lights at the Gadaffi Stadium and I had watched the slow progress of the erection of the floodlight towers on every visit I had made to Lahore, thinking all the while that they would never have them ready in time. It was said on the night that a good section of Lahore had to be blacked out to keep them going.

In the commentary box we were joined by Michael Slater, omitted from the Australian playing eleven and therefore given the chance to continue the early steps in a broadcasting career, which has since blossomed on Channel Nine television. His side – and probably the cricketing world – were taken by surprise by the outcome, as Sri Lanka took that world by storm.

Sunday 17 March

Despite the overnight thunderstorm, the match started on time. We had a commentary team of Aggers, CMJ, Maxwell and me, with summaries from Mike Selvey and Peter Roebuck and contributions during the day from Michael Slater, up from the Australian dressing room, Lucien

Wijesinghe, our old friend from Sri Lanka and the Australian
journalist, Mike Coward.

Sri Lanka caused some surprise by putting Australia in, but
they bowled and fielded well to keep them down to 241 for
seven, with Mark Taylor making 74 and Ponting 45. Bevan
was 36 not out at the end.

The two dangerous openers, Jayasuriya and Kaluwitharana,
again went early, but the partnership of Gurusinha and
Aravinda de Silva just seemed to make the outcome appear a
foregone conclusion, pacing themselves more carefully than
in previous games. When Gurusinha was out, Ranatunga
played himself in without panic, seeing Aravinda to his century and Sri Lanka to the World Cup and a coming of age.

The presentations that followed seemed to involve a competition to see how many people you could cram onto a small
platform. But somewhere in the middle of it the Pakistan
Prime Minister, Benazir Bhutto, handed Arjuna Ranatunga
the Wills World Cup trophy.

Three years later the World Cup – now taken over by
the ICC, rather than commercial sponsorship – was staged
again in England, with games in Scotland, Ireland, Wales and
Holland. But in 2003 South Africa had their first chance to
stage the event.

It was bigger than ever. Now there were fourteen teams
involved, to be resolved from two pools in the first stage to a
'Super Six' league for the second part, before semi-finals and
a final. But again it was politics that dominated the lead-in to
the opening matches.

This time it was England refusing to go to Zimbabwe after
various threats had been received, a crisis that continued to

rumble on after the extravagant opening ceremony and the opening match. It overshadowed New Zealand's refusal to go to Kenya to play a match because of security fears.

Our coverage of the tournament was based on what we had done for the 1999 World Cup at home, bolstered by the fact that we were in the midst of the period when so many rights for overseas tours were being lost to Talk Sport. Thus we had a team of engineers with us and an operations centre at the Wanderers in Johannesburg.

For a few days in Cape Town, following on from the opening game there, our attention was on the diplomatic arguments over the question of Zimbabwe. England's game there was to be their first in the tournament. Aggers and I hung around the team hotel, outside which I found a patch of grass from which we could get a signal via the satellite. We covered two press conferences live for Radio 5 Live, both of which they took for granted, not knowing the short-notice scramble that had to be gone through to set them up.

The second of these was in the centre of the city, where I had to borrow a drum of cable from television news to run down a fire escape and across a street to a ledge from which the satellite dish could be aimed between the skyscrapers. I had to hire a security guard to watch the equipment in the street.

Tuesday 11 February 2003 – Cape Town

The press conference upstairs at the *Cape Sun* announced England's definite withdrawal from the trip to Zimbabwe. We broadcast it live by the skin of our teeth. Then Aggers and I set about re-arranging our plans.

The competition had started with the West Indies beating South Africa in Cape Town, in a match on which we mounted a full commentary, as we did for several selected matches in the group stage. It became our practice for me to handle a newsy interval session whenever we were doing commentary on a match, wherever it was and wherever I was. Thus, for instance, after arriving in East London for England's game against Holland, I was doing the programme from the commentary box there, as Australia were playing India at Centurion.

It meant that we could have all the England news and interviews the day before their game against Holland. And the news on that day was that England had officially been docked the points for refusing to go to Zimbabwe and that Nasser Hussain was contemplating resigning the one-day captaincy.

Sunday 16 February – East London

The security check here turned out to be the silliest yet. Although the ground is not far from the hotel, I had decided to take the car, just to reduce the length of the carry for getting the equipment to the box. So I drove the long way round to the vehicle entry.

There I had to get out of the car and stand in a cage, while a large dog sniffed the vehicle. 'He is trained for sniffing and for attack and he might forget which he's doing,' said the policeman.

Then I had to drive up a very high inspection ramp and open the bonnet and boot.

Then I was directed to the traffic lights back on the road I had just turned off. I went past the hotel and back to the ground. I wondered why. And the security man on the gate also wondered why.

At least after that, England's win over Holland was fairly straightforward. In Port Elizabeth three days later they were given a bit of a scare by one of three Burgers in the Namibian side. This one made 85 and was christened 'the Burger King' by Henry Blofeld.

Back in Cape Town they had a good win against Pakistan, in which the young Jimmy Anderson announced himself with a fine four for 29.

Sadly, this World Cup was partly memorable for me for various thefts. I had a bag of bits and pieces stolen from the Cape Town commentary box during the opening game and my mobile phone lifted in the security check at Durban airport. My laptop was very effectively sabotaged by someone with a can of Coca-Cola. Not much effort was made to make it look like an accident, either.

But the most spectacular theft was the portable satellite dish. Aggers and I were staying in neighbouring hotels in Durban for England's game against India. He needed to do various preview pieces before the match while I was busy with other duties, so he took the kit back to his hotel.

The next morning, after India's comfortable win and with our paths about to separate again, he came round, as I was having breakfast, to return the dish. As he handed me the black case I knew that something was wrong. It was a different case, stuffed with magazines to give it the weight of a laptop. He could not work out where the switch had been done. As we talked to the local police, I tried to imagine the reaction of the criminal opening the case. What would he make of a 'World Communicator' satellite dish?

England's game against Australia in Port Elizabeth was something of a crunch and it turned out to be exciting, too, with Australia only sneaking home in a remarkable ninth-wicket stand, with two balls to spare. Still, England were not quite out of the competition yet.

The next evening, in Johannesburg, Aggers and I were able to watch on a restaurant television as South Africa went out of their own World Cup in the Durban rain, after misunderstanding the requirements of the Duckworth-Lewis system. They had settled for a tie under that method against Sri Lanka, not appreciating that that was not enough.

England's failure to qualify for the next stage of the tournament – the 'Super Six' – was sealed by rain in Bulawayo, where Zimbabwe gained the points from an abandonment against Pakistan that took them through with the same number of wins – three – as England.

It meant that the 'Super Six' had a rather odd look. Kenya were second in the starting table, credited with four wins, two of them against other qualifiers – Sri Lanka, who had contrived to fall to Collins Obuya's leg spin, and New Zealand, who had forfeited the points by refusing to go to Nairobi. New Zealand themselves and Zimbabwe were both there with very few points, as their wins had been against non-qualifiers and were therefore more lightly weighted.

Re-drawing the plans for the extensive coverage we were committed to for this phase, without my irreparably damaged laptop, was an interesting exercise. My own participation seemed to involve all too many of the long drives between Johannesburg and Bloemfontein. It was there that I saw Kenya secure a remarkable semi-final place, which they did by overwhelming Zimbabwe.

At least sanity prevailed in the resolving of the finalists

– Australia and India – but as we came to the 54th and final
match of the 2003 World Cup, at least for neutral observers
the prevailing feeling was just a desire for the threatening
weather in Johannesburg to hold off long enough for the
match to be completed on the scheduled date.

Sunday 23 March – Johannesburg

I woke to wet streets, having apparently slept through a
thunderstorm. But it was fine as we arrived early at the
Wanderers and when India put Australia in, only to see them
run up a massive 359 for five, with Gilchrist and Ponting to
the fore. There was an interruption for rain, but only for half
an hour.

India, though, were slaughtered and in the evening we
toasted Jim Maxwell as the eighth commentator to
commentate on a World Cup win in as many tournaments.

For Aggers, like the rest of us, keen to get home after two
months, the final sting in the tail of the trip came from a dodgy
oyster, which laid him low and forced him to delay departure
for 24 hours.

If we felt that the eighth World Cup had been too long,
the ICC must have had other ideas, because for 2007 they
increased the number of teams to sixteen. They were organised into four groups of four for the first stage, this time to go
into a 'Super Eight'.

Several years before I had been talking to an experienced
West Indian administrator and had expressed the view that a
World Cup in the Caribbean could be great fun. He reckoned
that it could never be done for economic and logistic reasons.
In 2007 it was done.

It was only three weeks after the last game of England's tour of Australia that I arrived in Jamaica in advance of an opening ceremony held at a remote ground – the romantically named 'Trelawny Multi-Purpose Stadium', on the north coast.

Sunday 11 March 2007

Aggers and I went to the hotel where all the teams are staying in the morning, for a conveyor belt of captains' press conferences. We recorded Michael Vaughan's one and also managed to beat the system enough to get a proper interview with him.

His appearance was due to be followed by Inzamam and a charming press man from Pakistan told us with a smile that Inzamam and the rest of the team would only be giving press conferences in Urdu, 'To avoid misunderstanding'.

The opening ceremony was a concert until the entry of the teams. Then there were some speeches and a carnival party on the outfield.

We then had to make the drive back through the mountains to Kingston in the south.

Monday 12 March

When we were through Kingston and heading for the hotel at Port Royal, we were stopped by a random police check. The man saw the World Cup car park sticker.

'You runnin' the ICC team?'

'No, I'm running the BBC.'

'Who you, den?'

I told him.

'Oh, you de big man!'

I said that I had an even bigger man beside me – Jonathan Agnew. This really got them going. The sergeant was summoned and there were handshakes all round.

'Have we done anything wrong?' asked Aggers.

'No, man. We jus' checkin'. Respec', Jonathan man.'

And we were on our way.

The 2007 World Cup has had a bad press, not helped by the shambolic way in which it finished, nor by the way it seemed to go on for ever. After that opening ceremony on 11 March, the final was played on 28 April. Seven weeks – and that does not include the warm-up matches during the fortnight before.

But one thing they did organise quite well was the reduction of travel, which might have been much more arduous.

England's early base was St Lucia, where we covered a match on alternate days and mounted interval programmes for commentaries from games elsewhere on the days in between. A broadcast line had been installed in one of the rooms at our hotel and so for these interval programmes our studio would be a balcony with a stunning view over the Caribbean, belying the usual panic involved in putting the programme together.

Such was the security on match days that I would then drive the equipment back to the ground to set up for the following day. No engineers for us on this trip.

The day after England had been beaten by New Zealand in their opening game, our interval programme included early reports on two possible upsets that might set the tournament alight.

Saturday 17 March

Ireland had dismissed Pakistan cheaply in Jamaica and Bangladesh had done the same to India in Trinidad. So there was plenty to talk about, though the technical preparations were a bit of a scramble.

Again I returned the equipment to the commentary box in the afternoon and when I got back to the hotel, news was starting to filter through that there had been some sort of incident with England players out on the town last night.

Sunday 18 March

As we were setting up for the England vs. Canada game, we heard that the *News of the World* at home was claiming that Flintoff had been one of those involved in the late-night binge and that he had then got into trouble on a pedalo off the beach at the team hotel. Scanning the England warm-ups, it seemed that he was missing. At the toss, Michael Vaughan confirmed that he had been left out 'for disciplinary reasons'. During the day we heard that he had had the vice captaincy removed as well.

But worse news was beginning to break. We were hearing from Jamaica that after Pakistan's defeat by Ireland, Bob Woolmer, their coach, had been found unconscious in his room.

A couple of hours later it was being reported that he was dead. It was stunning news.

Everyone on the *TMS* team had known Bob Woolmer well, some of us since his time as an England player, but all of us as coach of Warwickshire, South Africa and Pakistan. Indeed, on the last tour of Pakistan, little more than a year earlier, I remember setting up a live broadcast with him for the World Service from a hotel garden in Faisalabad. He had been keen to stay on the line to listen to the rugby commentary they were carrying afterwards.

Two days later, the word from Jamaica was that Woolmer's death had been 'suspicious' and all sorts of rumours started flying round of various members of the Pakistan team being told not to leave the country. It was a long time after the World Cup finished that it was ruled just to have been natural causes.

On the morning after England's rather lacklustre win against Canada, we were at the team hotel to see Andrew Flintoff compelled to front up to a press conference. Afterwards he spoke to Aggers, whose interview started with, 'Well, Freddie, what have you been up to?'

England still had to beat Kenya to ensure their progress into the Super Eight and, with Flintoff bowling well on his return, they did just that.

Now my next base was in Antigua, though England had first to fly off to Guyana to play Ireland. When Aggers returned from there, he was to report on a small BBC party billeted in some discomfort. In Antigua, meanwhile, we were getting to grips with a hotel entirely made for all-inclusive package holidays, in which we were very much the exception, being there to work.

The new Sir Vivian Richards Stadium, built in the middle of nowhere to replace the intense, noisy centre-of-town Recreation Ground, made its debut with West Indies vs. Australia, but, to the huge disappointment of the man after whom the ground was named, the home side did not put up much of a show. And, also to his disgust, the ground was not a quarter full, as access from St Johns had not been made easy. Subsequently, of course, that stadium had the embarrassment of having a Test Match abandoned after ten balls in 2009 because of its dangerously loose sand-based turf.

When England arrived from Guyana, they lost very narrowly to Sri Lanka and rather more heavily to Australia, despite a Pietersen century. That meant that when we moved on to Barbados they had to win all their remaining three games.

Bangladesh were comparatively easy prey, but South Africa blew them away, winning by nine wickets with over 30 overs to spare. Barbados is always graced by a large British contingent in the crowd and they made their displeasure known.

So the last game of the Super Eights, West Indies vs. England, involved two teams already eliminated. Nonetheless it was a sell-out and one of the best games of the tournament. After a blazing start, the West Indies ran up 300, but another Pietersen hundred saw England to victory by one wicket, with one ball to spare.

It was a game of farewells. Brian Lara played his last match for the West Indies – and was run out for eighteen. And two days before that we had been summoned to the England team hotel for a press conference, which I rigged up to broadcast live, as Duncan Fletcher announced his resignation from the job of England coach.

The semi-finals, in Jamaica and St Lucia, were both one-sided, leaving Sri Lanka and Australia to return to Barbados for the final.

That match is remembered for the farcical end, when bad light brought the players off in a situation where Sri Lanka were in a hopeless position. The Duckworth-Lewis rules should have given Australia the game anyway, but the players returned in the gloom for some anti-climactic pat-ball. What the game should be remembered for is Adam Gilchrist's onslaught of 149 from 104 balls, which determined that the trophy stayed with Australia.

It was a poignant time for me. Having worked on every cricket World Cup, this was my last. And this was the last time I would produce the programme overseas. In two months' time I would be leaving *Test Match Special* after 34 years of running it.

The Cricket Highlights (x)

Calcutta 1987

That England and Australia made it to the first World Cup final outside England at all was not written into the hosts' plan. Everything had been nicely set up for an India–Pakistan final. But over the course of two days, it all went awry.

Wednesday 4 November 1987

I spent a great deal of time at the Wankhede Stadium, trying to get an interview with Sonny Gavaskar in advance of tomorrow's semi-final here. I eventually succeeded, before returning to watch television coverage of the first semi-final in Lahore. The outcome never seemed in doubt and the reaction from all the Pakistanis, as Australia ran out comfortable winners, was stunned silence. Part one of the script written in advance seems to have gone badly wrong.

Australia had run up a substantial 267 for eight, with David Boon the top scorer, making 65. And, though Javed Miandad made 70, Craig McDermott's five wickets made sure Pakistan finished eighteen runs adrift.

The second part of the plot came, appropriately enough, on 5 November in Bombay and that plot was to sweep the Indian left-arm spinners out of the game, after England were not disappointed to have been put in. That was what Graham Gooch achieved, making 115. Mike Gatting joined in the assault and the pair put on 117 for the third wicket, with Gatting making 56. 254 was not necessarily an impregnable score, though.

Thursday 5 November

The celebratory fireworks were mostly discharged somewhat prematurely, when Kapil Dev looked like taking India to their target comfortably. He perished, though, caught off a skier by Gatting off Hemmings and after that things were always under control for England.

England won by 35 runs and Eddie Hemmings finished with four for 52. England had made it to the World Cup final.

Sunday 8 November

World Cup Final day. I made the rare – for me – decision to go to the ground in the press bus, thinking it might make the journey through the crowds easier. In fact it was quite the reverse. It quickly became obvious that it would be faster to walk, as the bus, which was granted no privileged status, was stuck fast in Chowringhee's traffic.

I abandoned the bus and struck off across the Maidan to Eden Gardens, arriving a good 30 minutes ahead of the rest of our party, which included a rather unwell CMJ, who was by no means confident of making it through the day. So I scheduled him for shorter spells than the half-hours he had done in Bombay.

Australia got off to a rapid start, but England pegged them back in mid-innings. They still managed to cut loose towards the end to finish with a challenging total of 253.

David Boon had had a good tournament opening the batting and again he had launched the innings with 75. In the latter stages, it was Allan Border and Mike Veletta who secured that score, leaving England needing the highest winning total batting second in the tournament.

Tim Robinson fell in the first over, but Bill Athey and Gooch set up a sound base, which Gatting and Athey built on, to take England to 135 for two after 31 overs. It was looking relatively comfortable.

Allan Border certainly felt the game was getting away from Australia and something different had to be tried. So he brought himself on to bowl his part-time spin. The first ball was drifting down the leg side, but Gatting had committed to a reverse sweep and the ball lobbed up off a top edge and, via his shoulder, was taken by the keeper, Greg Dyer.

If that wasn't the turning point in the match, it certainly checked England's progress, which might have recovered its momentum, had not Athey gone for a third run on a Steve Waugh misfield and been run out. After that England were always just off the pace, mainly through the steady loss of wickets, until a miserly penultimate over from Waugh left the ninth-wicket partnership needing seventeen from McDermott's last over and that proved too much to ask.

Mid-way through that final over, when it became

mathematically impossible for England to win, Henry Blofeld – well aware that Australia, with no commentary of their own there, were taking ours – declared, 'Now you really can start celebrating in Australia. I give you my final, final permission.'

It was a huge disappointment for England, of course, but for Australia, who had not had the greatest of success thus far in the eighties, it was the start of a new era.

Sunday 8 November

After-match interviews and even reports were quickly rendered impossible by the volume of the public address system's music. But the Australians enjoyed their lap of honour with the cup.

11. The Conclusion

In the summer of 2007 I retired from the BBC after 42 years. For 34 of those I had been producing *Test Match Special*. That made it more than just a job. It really had been my life. People ask if I miss it and I say that of course I do, but a call from Aggers from some remote airport departure lounge as he waits for a delayed flight makes me miss it slightly less.

I had a pang of regret as I listened to the commentary from the World Cup final in Bombay in 2011. It was the first one that I had not worked at. But then I thought of the post match scramble for interviews and the clearing up of filthy cables, the packing up of equipment and the logistics of getting it all out of the ground and ready for the flight home. It is not all glamour.

Certainly I still dream frequently that I am in some strange foreign commentary box, trying to make it work against the odds. Usually in my dream there is a very restricted view of the game and always the line to London or a few of the commentators are missing.

Apart from the camaraderie of touring with fellow broadcasters, press and players, it has been an enormous privilege to have seen so many wonderful sights. I have visited the Taj Mahal and the spectacular Amber Palace at Jaipur on more than one occasion each. I have carried on up the Khyber Pass, with its forbidding rocky mountainsides. I have marvelled at the towering Himalayas and celebrated just being in the presence of such tourist icons as Table Mountain and Sydney Harbour's Bridge and Opera House. I have climbed the vertiginous Sigirya Rock in Sri Lanka and admired the Victoria Falls and the mysterious settlement of Great Zimbabwe. All these and more have given me wonderful memories, which I will always cherish.

Funnily enough, I think it was a piece of British engineering that produced the greatest tingle factor of all.

Monday 8 February 1999

Despite last night's late finish, I was up at 6.30 a.m. to go
to the roof of the hotel. It was a grey, drizzly morning, but
I was just in time to see the QE II gliding slowly past the
Opera House. She stopped when her bows were up to the
Bridge and was manoeuvred by tugs back into Circular Quay.

Over the past week we have seen a couple of European
cruise liners in the same berth, but this was a serious ship
and a hugely impressive sight. I felt quite a surge of pride
and a tingle down the spine as I watched her tie up.

The cheeky little ferries carried on buzzing past her, as
if they were not going to allow such a monster to disrupt
their day.

I have also seen quite a bit of memorable cricket, though I never covered a winning Ashes tour of Australia. The one time England did win down under while I was doing the job – under Mike Gatting in 1986–87 – I was manning the London studio through the night.

Now with an Australian wife, Kim, I divide my time

between Buckinghamshire and Brisbane and so, in advance of the 2010–11 Ashes series, the BBC asked me to reprise my reconnaissance tour of four years previously, going round the Test venues to make sure that they would have the right facilities. I had the advantage not only of having a home there, but also of knowing many of the necessary contacts at the Test grounds and almost all those in the Australian Broadcasting Corporation.

I arrived in Perth for my inspection there at about the same time as England and had the chance to catch up with Aggers and members of the team and the press, some of whom were surprised to see me there. Still, it was a strange feeling to go to the Gabba in Brisbane on the first morning of the first Test as a spectator. After having seen the first ball of the series four years before directed by Steve Harmison straight at second slip, I was determined not to miss the start.

That wayward delivery had seemed to set the tone for the series. This time the shock came with the third ball, which Andrew Strauss cut firmly straight into the hands of the gully fielder. All Englishmen's spirits quailed.

The traditional pre-series Australian hype – in which the Poms are rubbished and the only question is which of the Australian supermen are going to complete the final line up to carry out the humiliation – had been slightly muted this time, relying on attacking the England players for failing to attend a function they had not been invited to. But it went into overdrive after the first day, when Peter Siddle, on his 26th birthday, took a hat-trick – Cook, Prior and Broad falling, just when England were rebuilding. Australia took a large first innings lead and all the hopes for a successful defence of the Ashes seemed to have been dashed at the first hurdle.

I was at the Gabba for every day of that match, anxiously

laying claim to a 'lucky seat' as Strauss, Cook and Trott staged the great second innings fight back that set up the chance of the series win. Then I had an engagement that took me to Melbourne conveniently for the retaining of the Ashes there. Maybe as a simple spectator I was able to savour the moment even more than my successors working at the MCG, but in some ways something did seem to be missing. I was no longer part of it.

Over the years the places, the people and the fact of being involved in the unfolding of cricket history have played equal parts in what has been an enduring adventure.

But for all the thrills, the greatest experience of all remained the feel of the aircraft wheels touching down and the disembodied voice announcing, 'Ladies and gentlemen, welcome to London Heathrow. The temperature is five degrees – and it's raining.'

Index

Index

Hassett, Lindsay 50
Hawke, Bob 72
Hayden, Matthew 132–3
Hayward, Nantie 263
Headley, Dean 74–5
Heffer, Simon 65
Hemmings, Eddie 168, 332
Hick, Graeme 74, 114, 116, 160, 239, 286
Hikkaduwa 269
Hill, David 51
Himalayas 93, 336
Hobart 63–4, 73
Hoggard, Matthew 187, 198, 256–7, 280–3
Holding, Michael 64, 223
Holland 311–12, 320–3
Hollioake, Ben 59
Hoogly, River 96, 98
Houghton, David 234
Howrah 174
Hussain, Nasser 58, 74, 129, 131, 135, 233, 249, 255, 261–3, 274, 285, 322
Hutton, Sir Len 134
Hyderabad 14, 99, 239

ICC 55, 139, 141, 182, 281, 307–8, 316–17, 320, 325–6
Illingworth, Ray 151, 153, 254, 295, 312
Illingworth, Richard 307
India 1–15, 22–9, 33–4, 37, 59, 78, 82–91, 96–109, 121, 163, 172–85, 191, 196–207, 213–15, 220, 224, 234, 237–45, 250–4, 265, 271, 281, 288–90, 293, 296–302, 304, 307, 312–15, 322–3, 325, 328, 331–2
India, Cricket Club of 201

India Premier League 220
Indore 15–16, 20
Insole, Doug 253
International Stadium (Galle) 269, 284
Iqbal Stadium 168
Islamabad 164, 188, 290–1, 294

Jackman, Robin 3–4, 116
Jacob, Satish 77
Jacobs, Ridley 132
Jade Stadium 57
Jaffer, Wasim 199
Jaffrey, Saeed 309
Jaipur 82–3, 173, 296–7, 335
Jamaica 114, 116–17, 123, 127, 134, 137, 223, 247, 251, 255, 276–7, 280, 326, 328–30
Jammu 17, 20, 91, 241
Jamshedpur 24–5, 179–80
Jarce, Hugh 216
Jardine, Douglas
Jarman, Barry 129, 264
Jayasuriya, Sanath 285–7, 313, 320
Jayawardene, Mahela 285, 287
Johannesburg 32, 139–44, 150, 157–9, 202, 228, 259, 261, 282, 321, 324–5
Johnston, Brian 42, 178, 214, 219
Jones, Geraint 197–9
Jones, Simon 196, 256, 279
Jullunder 18, 20, 209

Kandy 29–31, 34, 273–4, 284–5
Kanpur, Test in 26–7, 109
Kapil Dev 11, 14, 28, 88, 98–9, 106, 108–9, 332
Karachi 163–4, 171, 188, 263–7, 295–6, 310, 313
Kashmir 188

Index

Index

Index